FAKING NA

This volume addresses the arguments surrounding the processes of environmental destruction and restoration. Environmental restoration is central to companies' environmental policy, particularly the mining industry, and is a crucial practical and ethical concern, in an increasingly urbanized and industrialized world.

Professor Elliot presents a balanced argument, evaluating the discussions for and against restoring nature. He presents the argument as a dialectic; is environmental damage restoring nature or faking nature? He also examines the role that human beings have in the natural world.

Faking Nature offers a provocative and timely insight into the ethical problems of environmental strategy, which will be relevant to anyone interested in the world we live in and our attitudes to it.

Robert Elliot is Professor of Philosophy and Dean of Arts at Sunshine Coast University College, Queensland, Australia. He has published extensively in the area of environmental ethics and in applied ethics generally.

ENVIRONMENTAL PHILOSOPHIES SERIES
Edited by Andrew Brennan

Philosophy, in its broadest sense, is an effort to get clear on the problems which puzzle us. Our responsibility for and attitude to the environment is one such problem which is now the subject of intense debate. Theorists and policy analysts often discuss environmental issues in the context of a more general understanding of what human beings are and how they relate to each other and to the rest of the world. So economists may argue that humans are basically consumers sending signals to each other by means of the market, while deep ecologists maintain that humans and other animals are knots in a larger web of biospheric relations.

This series examines the theories that lie behind different accounts of our environmental problems and their solution. It includes accounts of holism, feminism, green political themes, and other structures of ideas in terms of which people have tried to make sense of our environmental predicaments. The emphasis is on clarity, combined with a critical approach to the material under study.

Most of the authors are professional philosophers, and each has written a jargon-free, non-technical account of their topic. The books will interest readers from a variety of backgrounds, including philosophers, geographers, policy makers, and all who care for our planet.

Also available in this series

ECOLOGY, POLICY AND POLITICS
John O'Neill

THE SPIRIT OF THE SOIL
Agricultural and environmental ethics
Paul B. Thompson

WHY POSTERITY MATTERS
Environmental policies and future generations
Avner de-Shalit

ENVIRONMENTAL PRAGMATISM
Edited by Andrew Light and Eric Katz

ECOLOGICAL FEMINISM
Edited by Karen J. Warren

FAKING NATURE

The ethics of environmental restoration

Robert Elliot

London and New York

First published 1997
by Routledge
11 New Fetter Lane, London EC4P 4EE

Simultaneously published in the USA and Canada
by Routledge
29 West 35th Street, New York, NY 10001

Typeset in Garamond by
M Rules
Printed and bound in Great Britain by
T.J. International Ltd, Padstow, Cornwall

British Library Cataloguing in Publication Data
A catalogue record for this book is available from the British Library

Library of Congress Cataloging in Publication Data
Elliot, Robert
Faking nature : the ethics of environmental restoration / Robert Elliot
p. cm. — (Environmental philosophies)
Includes bibliographical references and index.
1. Environmental ethics. 2. Restoration ecology. 3. Environmental
degradation. 4. Environmental policy
I. Title. II. Series: Environmental philosophies series.
GE42.E45 1997
179'.1—dc21 97–3754

ISBN 0–415–11139–0 (hbk)
0–415–11140–4 (pbk)

CONTENTS

Preface   vii
Acknowledgements   xii

1 THE NATURE OF NATURAL VALUE   1
Intrinsic value   5
The intrinsic property constraint   11
The indexical theory of intrinsic value   15
Subjectivism, relativism and normative debate   23

2 ENVIRONMENTAL OBLIGATION, AESTHETIC VALUE AND THE BASIS OF NATURAL VALUE   42
Environmental obligation and consequentialism   42
Environmental obligation and deontologies   50
Virtue, value and environmental obligation   53
Naturalness and other bases of natural value   58
Aesthetic value and intrinsic value   62

3 FAKING NATURE   74
The replacement thesis and the restoration proposal   74
The anti-replacement thesis defended   76
The normative significance of origin   83
Faking, restoring, preserving and protecting   97
The value of restoration and the obligation to restore   111

4 NATURALNESS, INTRINSIC VALUE AND RESTORATION ECOLOGY

4 NATURALNESS, INTRINSIC VALUE AND RESTORATION ECOLOGY	116
The natural, the non-natural and the artificial	116
Naturalness and value	130
Restoration ecology: concluding thoughts	143
Notes	150
References	161
Index	169

PREFACE

In 1982 I published a paper entitled 'Faking Nature'. Its aim was to defuse a certain style of defence of the environmental despoliation often associated with mining activity, forestry and, sometimes, agriculture. This style of defence, the restoration defence, makes two crucial assumptions. First, it assumes that environments that have been despoiled, degraded or destroyed can in fact be rehabilitated or restored. Second, it assumes that the values associated with the original, natural environment can likewise be restored. My target was, in particular, this second assumption. I argued that wild nature had a value-adding feature that could not be restored. I argued that the property of being the result of natural processes is one of the bases of the value possessed by wild nature. Restored nature or rehabilitated nature could not, I claimed, possess this property. In the same way that authorship of an artefact is relevant to, and partly determines, our aesthetic appraisals of it, so too the origin of some area of the environment is relevant to our evaluation of it. As the title of the paper implies, the main value claim was that faked nature was less valuable than original nature, just as faked art is less valuable than authentic art.

The central idea for the original paper came from some remarks of the Royal Commission into sandmining on Fraser Island, the great, forested sand island off the coast of southern Queensland (Mosley 1980). The Commissioners rejected the restoration defence, which had been deployed in support of the mining interests. The Commissioners remarked that mining, irrespective of later restoration or rehabilitation, would irreversibly compromise the wildness of the areas that were to be mined. Not only did the Commissioners question the likelihood of the disturbed island ecosystems being restored to their original conditions after the minerals had been extracted, they suggested that one very significant basis of the island's natural value could not even in principle be restored. The Commissioners' remarks concerning the wildness of the island ecosystems are plausibly understood as claiming that one source of the value of those ecosystems is the fact that they are naturally evolved, the fact that they exhibit a natural continuity with the past, the fact that they are authentic and not faked. And, of course, the Commissioners' views concerning Fraser Island are generalizable to natural areas everywhere.

My original paper developed this view about the value-adding significance of naturalness and offered some arguments for it. That view, and those arguments, have since been the objects of considerable discussion and criticism. Despite these criticisms, I think that the position taken in 'Faking Nature' is basically correct, and I think that it articulates a thought of some importance in environmental ethics. It is clear, though, that my view as it was originally stated needed to be carefully reformulated; the arguments for it needed to be better developed; and pertinent criticisms had to be rebutted. In a number of subsequent journal articles, acknowledged below, I offered restatements, with some refinements, of the claims and arguments of 'Faking Nature'. These restatements repaired some of the weaknesses of the original paper but more work needed to be done. This was first brought powerfully home to me in the unpublished version of Richard Sylvan's 'Mucking with Nature', which subsequently appeared as Sylvan 1994. This book aims, among other things, to remedy the faults to which Sylvan and others have drawn attention.

The conclusions I had earlier drawn were both too weak and too broad. They were too weak in that they undervalued naturalness of origin as a determinant of value, and they were insensitive to the general impermissibility of destroying or degrading natural value. I was too willing to allow that the natural value lost through degradation, the value that could not even in principle be restored, could be compensated for, by, for example, economic benefits flowing to humans as a consequence of the degradation in question. The conclusions, moreover, were too broad, in that they failed to distinguish between the various ways in which nature might be restored or rehabilitated, suggesting that there was no great value in restorations. As a consequence, they unhelpfully weakened arguments for the general obligation, that I believe humans have, to restore and rehabilitate natural areas that have been despoiled or degraded. Of course the danger in this modification of my earlier views is that it will be seized upon to inflate the value of restoration so as to justify, seemingly, the degradation of nature for human benefit provided there is subsequent restoration. I hope that the modification is developed in a way that closes off this possibility. Certainly I think the possibility deserves to be closed off.

I noted earlier that the Commissioners questioned the first assumption of the restoration defence, namely that an environment sufficiently like that originally there could in fact be re-created. In particular, the Commissioners noted the failure of other exploiters of nature to deliver on promises to restore or rehabilitate wild areas they had despoiled. Provided enough doubt could be cast on the capacity of the mining company to restore the mined areas, the more abstract and controversial argument concerning naturalness as an irreplaceable value-adding property would not so pressingly need to be deployed in defence of natural areas. This is not to say that the abstract argument would be idle in these circumstances. It would not, since it does highlight an additional and very significant component of natural value. Still, it would no doubt be easier to secure the environmentalist position if the abstract argument were not crucial. But to fail to highlight the abstract argument would be to deflect attention from a value claim that seems, to me at least, central to any robust environmental ethic. The claim is, of course, that naturalness itself is a source of value. Moreover, reliance on questioning the capacity of environmental despoilers to restore the sites that they damage becomes increasingly precarious as the technology of environmental restoration becomes more advanced (Katz 1992a: 231–4; Sylvan 1994: 63, 72–5.)

When I wrote 'Faking Nature', I had read little about restoration ecology apart from a short article reporting the relocation and reconstruction of a river bed (Dunk 1979). In fact I regarded the claims of environmental restoration as extremely fanciful. This was naïve. The technology of environmental restoration was rather more robust than I had imagined, its practice more widespread and its enthusiasts more numerous. Thus in 1983, although I was unaware of it until some years later, the journal *Restoration & Management Notes* began publication. This journal provided one venue for reporting the results of various environmental restoration projects and for developing and advocating a restorationist philosophy somewhat in tension with my own views. Indeed the journal published an early, and scathing, review of my original paper, that emphasized the clash between my value position and that of the restoration ecology movement (Losin 1986). It must be said, though, that the journal does publish a range of views on such matters, including some, such as Katz 1991, that are very critical of restorationist philosophy and that echo the views I endorse in this book. Articles appearing in the journal suggest, moreover, that the empirical claims of restorationists are not entirely fanciful, that it is becoming increasingly possible to re-create degraded natural areas, although we should be very careful not to overstate the practical accomplishments of restoration ecology (Duffy and Meier 1992; Gorchov 1994; Loucks 1994). Even committed restoration ecologists acknowledge the great practical difficulties of replicating historic ecosystems on a large scale (Jordan 1994). Judging, though, by the increasing number of advertisements by companies offering environmental restoration services, which appear at the end of each issue of *Restoration & Management Notes*, environmental restoration is on the way to becoming a flourishing industry.

That environmental restoration is flourishing and that its technologies are becoming increasingly adept may be welcome developments, provided the possibility of adequate restoration is not appealed to in justification of the destruction or degradation of natural areas. They are welcome developments only to the extent that they provide some basis for hoping that natural areas that are already degraded, destroyed and drained of natural value, may be restored, eventually to be reclaimed by nature. Such developments should provide no excuse and no justification for those who want to degrade or destroy the earth's shrinking, relatively natural, areas. It is important, therefore, to try better to elaborate and advance the main value claim of 'Faking Nature'. The elaboration that follows might strike some readers as involving me in a form of nature chauvinism or anti-humanism. There would be some truth in such a judgement. While I do not completely feel at ease with the position, perhaps because of my particular species membership, I do tend to the view that humans have not added much to the value there is in the world, and, more importantly, that the value we have added does not come anywhere near equalling, let along compensating for, the value, in particular natural value, that we have degraded and destroyed. Still, I believe I am not alone in endorsing this view: many advocates for the natural environment would, I conjecture, take it seriously, and certainly it is taken seriously by some who have looked at the issue from a philosophical perspective, such as Goodin 1992, McKibben 1989, and Sylvan and Bennett 1994.

This book, then, is a defence of the main value claim of 'Faking Nature' and of its meta-ethical underpinnings. It provides an account of the nature of value that accommodates core claims concerning natural values, and it defends claims concerning the basis of natural values that entail that the value of restored or, loosely speaking, faked nature is less than the value of original or authentic nature. The meta-ethical underpinnings of the normative theory of natural value are naturalist and subjectivist. This is interesting at least to the extent that some advocates of natural values have taken the view that subjective naturalism, indeed naturalism generally, cannot provide a solid meta-ethical framework for a normative theory of natural value capable of accommodating all of the core claims of green environmentalism. I hope to show that a version of subjective naturalism, which I call 'the indexical theory of intrinsic value', does accommodate these core claims. This would make the meta-ethical underpinnings of green environmentalism rather less mysterious than they are on some alternative views.

Finally, I should note here that I typically use the term 'environmentalist' to refer to advocates for nature who believe that there are natural values that are not simply cashed in terms of human satisfaction, or only in terms of the satisfactions of creatures generally. I use the term 'environmentalism' analogously. In adopting this usage, I am aware that there are powerful arguments for respecting nature that do not invoke natural values but that involve, for the most part, human satisfaction and welfare. While I think such arguments are politically crucial, they are not my concern in this book.

ACKNOWLEDGEMENTS

The ideas developed in this book have been evolving over a number of years, and earlier versions of them have appeared in various journal articles. The articles in question are: 'Faking Nature', *Inquiry* 25 (1982), 81–93; 'Meta-ethics and Environmental Ethics', *Metaphilosophy* 16 (1985), 103–17; 'Environmental Degradation, Vandalism and the Aesthetic Object Argument', *Australasian Journal of Philosophy* 67 (1989), 191–204; 'Intrinsic Value, Environmental Obligation and Naturalness', *Monist* 75 (1992), 138–60; 'Ecology and the Ethics of Environmental Restoration', *Philosophy*, Suppl. vol. 36 (1994), 31–43; 'Extinction, Restoration, Naturalness', *Environmental Ethics* 16 (1994), 135–44; 'Facts about Natural Values', *Environmental Values* 5 (1996), 221–34.

I acknowledge a special debt to the late Richard Sylvan. His uncompromising and inspired contributions to environmental philosophy generally, and to the issues raised in 'Faking Nature' in particular, have very much shaped my current views. I also thank Cheryl Burrell for her invaluable assistance in preparing the final manuscript.

1

THE NATURE OF NATURAL VALUE

A central claim of this book is that wild nature has intrinsic value, which gives rise to obligations to preserve it and to restore it. In other words, our obligations towards wild nature derive, in large part, from the intrinsic value that it possesses. Certainly many of our obligations concerning wild nature are only indirect obligations, being, in the first instance, obligations we have to other humans and to non-human animals. Thus the obligations that we have not to harm other humans or other creatures generally, let alone the more positive obligation we have to promote their interests, are likely by themselves to dictate the protection, preservation and restoration of wild nature (Clark 1979; Elliot 1984 and 1996; Singer 1976). Such human-centred and creature-centred considerations, however, nowhere near exhaust the bases of our obligations to wild nature. The intrinsic value wild nature possesses, that is, its value apart from satisfying human interests or even the interests of sentient creatures, is also an important basis of our obligations to preserve and restore wild nature. Much of the book's argument reflects this claim, speaking, for example, of natural values, the value of wild nature generally and the value of particular natural items. The kind of value referred to in these contexts is certainly intrinsic value. As well, the claims made about obligations to preserve and restore wild nature answer back to the claim that wild nature has intrinsic value.

It is pertinent, therefore, to provide a theory of intrinsic value that describes its structure, its basis, evidence for its presence, and its relationship to duty, obligation and certain other so-called deontological concepts. It is appropriate, moreover, to begin with this theory of value in order to circumvent various critical questions that would otherwise arise: questions such as, 'Where do these intrinsic values come from?', 'Are these so-called intrinsic values objective or are they merely

1

your own subjective preferences?', 'What if other people don't share these alleged intrinsic values?' While some readers will certainly not find all aspects of the theory of environmental value and obligation satisfactory, it is best to have that theory out in the open at the outset. The theory of value developed is quite general. It is not specific to natural value, but applies wherever it is coherent to make judgements about intrinsic value. It has application even outside the domain of moral judgements, for example in the domain of aesthetic judgement. Indeed one of the issues to be pursued in a later chapter is the issue of whether natural value is better understood as aesthetic value than as moral value (Godlovitch 1989 and 1994; Lynch 1996).

The development of the theory of intrinsic value is an instance of meta-ethics. Meta-ethics does not itself, at least in the first instance, involve any attempt to establish particular normative judgements, such as judgements about what has value or about what actions should be carried out. Instead, meta-ethics investigates the framework within which the various claims of normative ethics are made. Some philosophers have claimed, though, that normative conclusions are fairly strictly entailed by meta-ethical considerations. For example, R. M. Hare thinks that the correct meta-ethical theory entails a normative theory known as preference utilitarianism. This particular normative theory says that the only intrinsic value is the satisfaction of preferences, and that the right, indeed obligatory, action is that action that maximizes the satisfaction of preferences (as in Hare 1981). Other philosophers might reject such a tight connection between meta-ethics and normative judgements and yet, as we shall see presently, urge that the correct meta-ethical theory interestingly restricts possible normative positions.

What, then, is meta-ethics? The best way of indicating its content is to list some of the questions it pursues. Thus it asks whether normative judgements can take truth values, that is, whether they can be true or false; it asks whether normative judgements are in any sense relative, for example to particular societies or groups, or whether they are universal; it asks whether, and in what sense, normative judgements are objective or open to rational adjudication; it asks whether there are any significant differences between moral beliefs and subjective preferences or desires; it asks whether there are moral facts which make moral judgements true and what the nature of those facts could be; it asks how normative judgements are connected with decisions to act; and it asks how normative judgements might be supported by evidence. Some of these questions are reminiscent, as one would expect, of the questions implicit in the previous paragraph. They reflect puzzlement about the form, as opposed to the content, of value judgements.

In contrast, normative ethics asks, for example, what kinds of things are good or bad, that is to say, what kinds of things have value or disvalue; what kinds of actions are right or wrong, permissible or obligatory; what it is that duty requires of us; what traits of character are virtuous or vicious. In other words, normative ethics is concerned with either making, or establishing the general principles for making, particular substantive ethical judgements. Thus we might make the meta-ethical claim that value judgements are really just expressions of attitudes of approval or disapproval, and we might make the normative judgement that slavery is wrong. The normative judgement offers a moral appraisal of a certain social institution, whereas the meta-ethical judgement offers an account of what is really going on when a value judgement is made. If we accept the meta-ethical theory described above, then we shall construe the judgement that slavery is wrong as the expression of disapproval of slavery in general.

As suggested above, there are differing views about how meta-ethical theories affect theories in normative ethics and vice versa. The theory of value argued for below assumes that the two domains of enquiry are relatively autonomous. In other words, it assumes that they are relatively independent of one another, with particular meta-ethical positions not overly restrictive of normative positions and particular normative positions not too often dependent on particular meta-ethical positions. It will be sufficient for present purposes, though, to show that the meta-ethical theory defended below is capable of supporting certain core normative claims in environmental ethics. As we shall see, one challenge that is sometimes issued to those who claim that wild nature has intrinsic value is that the claim is only interestingly sustainable if a particular kind of meta-ethical theory is assumed. It is then suggested that the meta-ethical theory, a version of what is called 'objectivism', is either false or incoherent. If this is so, then the relevant core claims of environmental ethics are unsustainable (see McCloskey 1980, and 1983: 59–61; Mannison 1980a; Partridge 1986). One response is to attempt to rehabilitate the meta-ethical theory that is said to be false or incoherent (see Attfield 1987 and 1994; Crisp 1994; Rolston 1982, 1988 and 1994).

Another, related, challenge is that wild nature in general, or certain sorts of natural items in particular, are not the kinds of things to which intrinsic value can be coherently attributed. The suggestion is that core claims of environmental ethics, understood as moral claims, involve a category mistake. A variant of this view, already referred to, is the view that these sorts of claims could not involve moral judgements but must involve aesthetic judgements. Such claims would be analogous to the claims that Wednesday is spherical or that the number one is heavier than air or that the sum of two prime numbers is a cow. These claims do not compute, so to speak, because they apply descriptions to items that those descriptions not only do not fit but could not possibly fit. Such arguments as these, against the possibility of a radical environmental ethics, involve what we might call 'the meta-ethical dependency thesis'. We shall come to the details later but suffice it to say that these meta-ethical dependency theses are shown to be false.[1]

It is common for a distinction to be drawn between axiological considerations and deontological considerations. The emphasis in this book is primarily on the axiological, although deontological issues are also addressed. Axiology is the theory of value. It attends to concepts such as 'good', 'bad', 'evil', 'worthwhile', 'valuable', all of which are used to rank objects, events, actions, and the like, on a scale of value ranging from the negative through the neutral, to the positive. Thus it might be claimed that happiness is a positive value or that pain is a negative value. Axiology has both normative and meta-ethical aspects. The meta-ethical aspect strives to provide accounts of the nature of value. It attempts to say what kinds of properties goodness, etc. are; for example, whether they are properties that things can have even if there are no valuers or whether their existence somehow depends on the existence of valuers. The normative aspect strives to provide an account of what kinds of things are good, bad, etc., or of the various properties things might have which justify particular value assessments of them. It should be noted that axiological approaches to assessments of nature and actions towards nature have been extensively criticized (Fox 1984; Naess and Rothenberg 1989; Weston 1985).

Deontology is concerned not with value or value concepts but with concepts such as 'obligation', 'permissibility', 'duty', 'right' and 'wrong'. Deontology also has both a meta-ethical aspect and a normative aspect analogous to those distinct aspects of axiology. Axiological and deontological considerations are not necessarily disconnected from one another. As we shall see, it is sometimes the case that a deontological assessment is grounded in an axiological assessment, as when something's value is the reason for our being obliged to preserve it. This is most clearly the case with so-called maximizing consequentialisms. According to these views, deontological judgements are entirely functions of axiological judgements. For example, utilitarianism says that we have an obligation to perform that action that is most likely to maximize overall happiness. Here the utilitarian's assessment of the good entirely determines her or his assessment of the obligatory. The connection may hold in the other direction as well, since sometimes axiological assessments flow from deontological assessments. Thus a state of affairs might have less value than it otherwise would have because it includes a wrong or impermissible action: here wrongness is bad-making. These connections will be explored and a theory of environmental obligation will be developed in the next chapter. Nor should it be thought that axiological and deontological considerations exhaust the perspectives from which moral judgements are made. One other perspective, virtue theory, will be considered later. Briefly, virtue theory provides evaluations of agents and actions in terms of the degree to which those agents and actions exemplify virtues or vices. First, the axiological theory of intrinsic value is developed.

INTRINSIC VALUE

The theory of environmental value and obligation argued for in this chapter is a special instance of an indexical theory of intrinsic value. The parameters of this indexical theory of intrinsic value may be helpfully introduced against the background of the theory of intrinsic value advanced by the G. E. Moore. One reason for choosing Moore's theory is that it is the kind of theory that the first version of meta-ethical dependency thesis, described above, attempts to foist upon those who endorse strong environmentalist normative claims. Moore's theory has three central components: (i) that to say that something has intrinsic value is to say that 'it ought to exist for its own sake, is good in itself' (Moore 1963: 5); (ii) that to say of something that it has intrinsic value is to attribute to it a simple, unanalysable, non-natural property; (iii) that concerning the claim that something has intrinsic value, he held that 'no relevant evidence whatever can be adduced. . . . We can guard against error only by taking care, that when we try to answer a question of this kind, we have before our minds that question only, and not some other . . .'. (ibid.).

The first of Moore's components provides an account of what is meant by 'intrinsic value'. It tells us that it is the kind of value that is worth securing for its own sake and that it is the kind of value that makes a thing good considered in itself. Perhaps the best contrast is with instrumental value, which is the value that something has in virtue of its usefulness, in virtue of what it leads to or contributes to, rather than the value it has in virtue of its own properties or characteristics. Thus a glass of wine might be said to have instrumental value in virtue of its capacity to bring into existence a sensation of pleasure. Or it might be claimed that a forest has instrumental value in virtue of the recreational and aesthetic pleasure it affords. In each case the instrumental value connects with a judgement about intrinsic value attaching to some other thing. Thus the instrumental value of the wine is based upon the intrinsic value of pleasure. Likewise in the case of the instrumental value of the forest. There is, by the way, no difficulty in the claim that instrumental and intrinsic value can attach to the very same object. Thus Jane's happiness, which is intrinsically valuable, may be a cause of John's happiness, and so be instrumentally valuable too. As we shall later see, accounts of intrinsic value can become quite complicated, and some commentators argue that to try to understand intrinsic value in terms of the contrast with instrumental value is to misunderstand it. This issue is pursued below.

The second component of Moore's theory of intrinsic value establishes it as realist, objectivist and non-naturalist. It is realist because it entails that judgements about intrinsic value take truth values, that is to say it entails that judgements about intrinsic value can be true or false (Sayre-McCord 1988: 5; Schiffer 1990: 602). Moore's theory is objectivist in that it denies that judgements about intrinsic value can be properly recast as judgements about the psychological states or properties of valuers. The contrast here is with subjectivist theories, which claim that judgements about intrinsic value can be recast in terms of judgements involving the psychological states of valuers. For example, a crude subjectivist might recast the claim that wild nature has intrinsic value as the claim that a particular valuer prefers that wild nature continue to exist. On Moore's view, by contrast, the preferences of the valuer would have no bearing on the question of whether wild nature had intrinsic value. It is important to be very careful in framing the second component of Moore's view. In particular, it should not be taken to deny that the existence of particular psychological states is of intrinsic value or, indeed, is the only thing that has intrinsic value. For example, Moore thought that experiencing pleasure had intrinsic value, and he presumably thought this because of the specific quality of such experiences. So the nature of a psychological state has a bearing on what has intrinsic value. However the judgement that the state in question does have intrinsic value does itself get recast in terms of some psychological state which takes the experiencing of the pleasure as its object – as, for example, the judgement that some particular valuer prefers to experience pleasure. The fact of intrinsic value attaching to the experiencing of pleasure is not, according to Moore, itself a fact about the psychological states of valuers. Although the presence of intrinsic value depends upon such facts, as we shall see below, it is a quite distinct property.

Moore's theory is also non-naturalist, which is to say that the property of being intrinsically valuable is not a natural property of those things that have intrinsic value. It is difficult to characterize a natural property in contrast to a non-natural property. A starting point is to think of natural properties as properties detectable by the senses or through scientific investigation. Natural properties are, in other words, empirically detectable. Non-natural properties are difficult to characterize positively. We could simply say that they are the properties other than the natural properties but that is not very illuminating. A starting point is to say that non-natural properties are those that are discoverable only through the understanding, without recourse to sensations or experience, or through some non-sensory faculty. The properties of numbers are, arguably, non-natural properties in that they are discoverable only through the understanding: they are not discovered through the use of the senses or through empirical investigation. In the case of allegedly non-natural moral properties, the idea is that they are comprehended through some purely intellectual act or through the exercise of some special, non-sensory faculty of moral intuition. Some commentators, as a consequence of this difficulty of explaining what is involved in comprehending non-natural moral properties, have taken the view that there is something too mysterious and unacceptably spooky about them (see Mackie 1977). They do not fit with a scientific view of the world.

While Moore thinks that moral properties are non-natural properties, he accepts that we do not come to know them independently, in one sense at least, of our knowledge of natural properties. Moore takes this view because he believes that, for example, the non-natural property of being intrinsically valuable is not free-floating; in other words it is not a property that a thing possesses independently of other particular properties it possesses. Rather he believes that non-natural moral properties are resultants of, supervene upon, are

7

necessarily connected with, or are otherwise systematically dependent on, other of a thing's properties. And clearly most of these other
properties are natural properties. The reason for saying 'most' as
opposed to 'all' is that it is at least conceivable that the property of
being intrinsically valuable is dependent upon some other non-natural property, for example another non-natural moral property such
as rightness or some non-natural property of a number such as the
property of being prime. One of the problems Moore's view faces is
that of explaining the dependency relationship between moral properties and other, mostly natural, properties. This dependency operates
at both the metaphysical and epistemological levels. In other words
the dependency is a condition of the very existence of moral properties: moral properties cannot be instantiated unless other properties
are instantiated. Furthermore, moral properties are only comprehended after we become aware of certain nonmoral properties. In
attempting to establish whether some action is wrong we seem compelled to attend to and to note its various nonmoral properties. For
example we might note that some act is an act of deception, an act of
gratuitous violence, or a self-seeking act, and having grasped some
such fact about it we come to understand that it is wrong.

The third component of Moore's view concerns evidence for intrinsic value. The chief point is that judgements about a thing's intrinsic
value are established through careful reflection on the thing in question, by attempting to understand, grasp or appreciate all of the
thing's characteristics. The idea is that something akin to a raw feel or
affect is involved at the final stage in judgements about a thing's
intrinsic value.[2] Moore, though, would not endorse this way of
putting the point because it gives the situation too naturalistic a
twist. Moore would instead suggest, as implied above, that such
judgements are best understood as some kind of pure intellectual
act, although one carried out after some understanding of the facts
concerning other properties upon which the moral properties depend.
None of this is to say that there must be a complete or even extensive
understanding of the thing's nonmoral properties before any judgement about intrinsic value is made. Value judgements are made very
early on in the piece, and we might find it very difficult to resist
making them. The point is that the value judgement would seem to
have to depend upon at least some other judgements. Certainly value
judgements made early in the piece, and some will be avowedly pro-
visional, may be revised as more is learnt about the nonmoral
properties of the object being judged.

It is important to differentiate Moore's (non-natural) objectivism from a rather less interesting, although quite important, kind of (natural) objectivism that is adopted by some environmental ethicists. Some who hanker after the perceived benefits of objectivism but who seem to baulk at the metaphysical aspects of Moore's theory have found a more plausible alternative in objective naturalism.[3] This view apparently construes talk about value facts as simply talk about natural, and not especially distinctive, non-subjective facts. Holmes Rolston, for example, seems sometimes to reduce value facts to facts about what does or does not contribute to promoting an organism's, or even a system's, biologically determined goals.[4] So the claim, made by some environmental ethicists, that value attaches to an organism's successful struggle to maintain life and to flourish according to its kind might amount to no more than a pleonasm. Having value, on this view, just is living and flourishing (Rolston 1982, 1988 and 1994). If we are tempted to make such a claim, we would seem first to be noting that organisms do sometimes live and flourish and then to be saying, over above this, that it is a good thing that organisms live and flourish. Objective naturalism seems to neglect this latter component. Perhaps objective naturalists can explain this but there seems no neat and convincing way of so doing (Pigden 1991).

How much of Moore's view should we accept? While realism about intrinsic value seems correct, subjectivism and naturalism seem correct rather than objectivism and non-naturalism. So (ii) is in need of some revision. Likewise (i) requires revision, although it is basically moving in the right direction. And (iii), the claim about the epistemology of value, is, when suitably elaborated, true. Moreover, the acceptance or rejection of (ii) is normatively neutral, that is, its acceptance or rejection does not affect which normative judgements are or are not coherent, are or are not admissible. This last claim is disputed both by some opponents and some defenders of environmentalist normative claims. Let us see how the indexical theory of intrinsic value develops and then return to the issue of why it is preferable to Moore's theory.

Among the various kinds of things that could possess intrinsic value are objects, states of affairs, events, processes and actions. And if they do possess intrinsic value then, as indicated above, they possess it in virtue of possessing certain other properties. The phrase 'in virtue of' might be unpacked in a variety of ways. Whatever way it is unpacked, it signals the dependence, ultimately, of moral properties on nonmoral properties; 'ultimately' because sometimes, as earlier remarked, one moral property will be dependent on another, as, for example, when it is claimed that the action of performing a duty possesses intrinsic value in virtue of its being an act required by duty. Here the fact that the act performed is required by duty is itself an additional basis or source of the total intrinsic value deriving from the performance of the act. For present purposes, all that needs to be conceded is the systematic connectedness of moral properties with nonmoral properties. These nonmoral properties are usefully called 'value-adding properties'.[5] The idea is simply that, other things being equal, value-adding properties function to increase the overall value of the thing that has them, and indeed to increase the value of the universe as a whole. It does not follow, however, from the fact that something possesses value-adding properties that it has positive intrinsic value. Things might have value-subtracting properties too, which must be weighed against value-adding properties. So, value-adding properties might not suffice to ensure that, all things considered, the thing in question has positive intrinsic value but they move the thing further towards the point at which it would have positive intrinsic value. The idea is, that from a value point of view, value-adding properties tend to make things better or tend to increase value. Where the impact of value-adding properties outweighs the impact of value-subtracting properties, a thing has intrinsic value; in the converse case a thing has intrinsic disvalue; otherwise, the thing is value-neutral.[6]

This is straightforward enough so far, but matters rapidly become complicated. For example, it is conceivable that the addition of some value-adding property may render the thing to which it is added less valuable than it was initially. An aesthetic analogy illustrates the point. Imagine that a small component is made and added to a metal sculpture. The component itself has great aesthetic value but its addition to the larger sculpture makes the aesthetic value of the latter significantly less than it was initially. It may be that the balance of the metal sculpture is entirely destroyed by the addition of the new component. The component, considered alone and not in relation to the sculpture, certainly adds aesthetic value to the universe, but its incorporation in the sculpture results in a net loss of aesthetic value. One way of accommodating such examples is to say that properties are not value-adding as such, but are only value-adding relative to a context. The basic point, however, is that there are value-adding properties in virtue of which things have varying degrees of intrinsic value. We shall later touch on some of the complicated ways in which value-adding properties might interact with one another and with other properties, which interactions lead to value transformations, inversions and the like.[7]

Let us now connect the idea of a value-adding property with normative environmentalist claims. Imagine that an environmentalist says that some natural ecosystem has intrinsic value. This value is not merely pinned on to, so to speak, the ecosystem but derives from certain value-adding properties the ecosystem possesses. In order to defend the claim about intrinsic value, the environmentalist needs to specify just what these value-adding properties are that underpin the intrinsic value claimed for the ecosystem. For example, in response, the environmentalist might say that it is because of its richness and species diversity that the ecosystem has intrinsic value. Here the property of being richly diverse is the value-adding property. Of course the environmentalist might give other reasons why the ecosystem has value. She or he might say that it is also valuable because of its aesthetic merit or because it is free of the imprint of human culture and technology. Again, value-adding properties are specified. The environmentalist must say exactly why nature has intrinsic value. Unless one can at least begin to say what these properties are it is not clear that the value judgement or attitude could have any meaningful content. Only when the relevant value-adding properties are indicated is rational debate about whether wild nature has intrinsic value possible. Only when these properties are indicated is it possible to begin to persuade dissenters to change their views. While it is perhaps possible to value something without immediately understanding what it is about the thing that makes it valuable, perhaps because one is only subconsciously aware of the relevant value-adding properties, the failure to come up with any plausible candidate value-adding property after some reflection suggests that the initial value judgement was vacuous.

THE INTRINSIC PROPERTY CONSTRAINT

Are there restrictions on the kinds of properties that can be value-adding? If there are, then a way of defeating normative claims about intrinsic value suggests itself. If it can be shown that a normative claim makes reference to the wrong kind of putative value-adding property, then the claim would have to be withdrawn. Must value-adding properties be, for example, essential properties of a thing, that is, properties the loss of which the thing could not survive? It would seem, though, that something could cease to have intrinsic value without ceasing to be. For example, a sculpture might be so damaged that it loses all aesthetic merit, and so all intrinsic value, although it is not completely destroyed. This example suggests that value-adding properties can include properties that are not essential, although, in the case of natural values, many putative value-adding properties would seem to be essential properties or properties that we cannot unambiguously deny are essential. Take the example of ecosystemic richness and diversity. If richness and diversity are sufficiently depleted, then plausibly one ecosystem ceases to exist and is replaced by another. Here the value-adding properties are, arguably, essential. The issue is complicated, however, by the fact that richness and diversity are matters of degree. The loss of a species or two from an ecosystem decreases richness and diversity and so reduces value, although much remains, and the ecosystem continues to exist having endured a loss of value. Or so it seems reasonable to think.[8]

Of all the possible restrictions on value-adding properties that suggest themselves, one in particular poses a threat to the normative thesis argued for in this book. The restriction in question says that value-adding properties must be intrinsic properties and not, in particular, a certain kind of relational property. This is an important issue, since substantive theories of environmental value do in fact attribute intrinsic value on the basis of just such relational properties, including the properties of being rare, being naturally evolved, and being free of the impact of human culture and technology. The intrinsic property restriction implies that the attribution of intrinsic value on the basis of such properties is false, if not incoherent. Why would anyone endorse the intrinsic property constraint? Well, there might be some temptation to think that, since a thing's having intrinsic value is for it to be good in itself, relational properties cannot be value-adding and that intrinsic properties alone can be value-adding (Chisholm 1978; Green 1996: 34–8). This temptation perhaps derives from a failure to appreciate that 'good in itself' can be read as 'good in virtue of the (value-adding) properties it possesses'. Understood thus, relational properties are not ruled out. We noted earlier that intrinsic value is contrasted with instrumental value, where the latter is the value a thing has in virtue of contributing to the production of some other thing that has intrinsic value. The contrast is not between having value in virtue of certain intrinsic properties, understood in a particularly narrow way that will be explained below, and having value in virtue of certain extrinsic properties. These points require elaboration and argument.

12

The intrinsic property constraint needs to be stated more precisely. For one thing, the crucial distinction upon which it is based is not, strictly speaking, that between non-relational properties and relational properties. Rather it is the distinction between properties intrinsic to, or internal to, a thing, and properties that are partly external to it. The former category may include some relational properties, whereas the latter category will include only relational properties. Take the case in which Jane is contemplating some scene of natural beauty. The case is characterized by innumerable relational properties, but let us focus on one in particular. When Jane contemplates the scene before her, she comprehends certain facts of an ecological, biological and geomorphological kind. This understanding may well enhance any raw affective response she has to the scene (Rolston 1995; Routley 1975). As a result, Jane experiences a cognitively mediated aesthetic pleasure. Here is a complex relational property, linking Jane's cognitive and affective states and some piece of wild nature. Taking the case as a whole, we might judge it to have intrinsic value in virtue of exemplifying the relational property just now loosely described. This relational property is intrinsic to, or internal to, the whole state of affairs to which intrinsic value is attributed. We are not saying here that intrinsic value attaches to Jane or to the scene she is contemplating, although we might agree that it does. Rather it is the whole complex state of affairs, involving both Jane and the natural scene, to which we are attributing value. So the property on which we base our value judgement is internal to, or intrinsic to, the thing valued, although the property itself is relational. The grounding of intrinsic value by such intrinsic relational properties seems not to be in any way problematic for those inclined to endorse the intrinsic property constraint (Chisholm 1978; Moore 1922 and 1942: 579; Ross 1930: 75). The thought is that relational properties are problematic, as bases for intrinsic value, if and only if they entail the existence of something beyond, or external to, the thing possessing intrinsic value.

It is doubtful, though, that all of the significant value-adding properties specified by environmentalists can be accommodated as internal relational properties. Consider the property of being naturally evolved. Many would want to say that intrinsic value attaches to an ecosystem at a particular point in time in virtue of it having a certain natural history, in other words, in virtue of it being naturally evolved. Most environmentalists would not want only to say that it is the entirety of natural history, including the present ecosystem now standing in a particular relation to past ecosystems and past action by natural forces, that is valued. Certainly the entirety of natural history does have value as a whole, but so too do many of the parts that constitute it. Moreover these parts, according to some environmental ethics, have intrinsic value because of properties external to them, such as the property of being naturally evolved.

Whether or not we accept the intrinsic property constraint will depend in large part on our understanding of intrinsic value. The kind of understanding of intrinsic value that supports the intrinsic property constraint is expressed in a test for intrinsic value advocated by Moore and David Ross. According to Moore and Ross, a thing has intrinsic value only if we judge that, considered in isolation, abstractly, by itself, and without regard to its consequences, its existence is better than its non-existence (Chisholm 1978; Moore 1922: 260, 267–70; Ross 1930: 75). This test, stressing in various ways a value-in-isolation understanding of intrinsic value, limits value-adding properties to internal properties. Since the candidates for intrinsic value must have value in isolation if they have intrinsic value at all, external properties seem excluded. While the test is indicative of one common way of thinking about intrinsic value, we do require some assurance that it is not question-begging. Some who favour the intrinsic property constraint perhaps think that it reflects a core idea in attributions of intrinsic value, namely the idea that the thing that has intrinsic value is valuable in itself, in virtue of its own properties. They might think initially that only internal or intrinsic properties can be genuinely a thing's own properties. But a thing's external properties are, quite straightforwardly, genuinely its own, they are instantiated by it, manifested by it or possessed by it, and attributions of the properties to it are true. What is correct is that the properties generally will be instantiated, etc., only if other things exist.[9] They are not properties that something can have in isolation but it is difficult to see why that renders them somehow less assuredly properties that belong to the thing itself.[10]

Perhaps others who favour the constraint are swayed either by the view that intrinsic value is itself an internal property of those things that have it, or at least by the view that it is not an external property. Both views assume, however, meta-ethical views that are at the very least controversial. For one thing, many meta-ethical theories construe the property of being intrinsically valuable as an external property, and we would want to be assured that they are false before endorsing the views under discussion. More significantly, the views that intrinsic value is an internal property, or that it is not an external property, are compatible with the view that external properties are value-adding. This is because the views concern intrinsic value itself, and not the value-adding properties which give rise to it. Thus it is not clear why the property of being naturally evolved could not be value-adding even though the intrinsic value that it supports is an internal property of the ecosystem. It is too easy simply to assume that what is true of the property of being intrinsically valuable is true of the value-adding properties as well. Rejection of the intrinsic property constraint does not entail that intrinsic value is an external property. It entails only that things may have intrinsic value in virtue of their external properties. Moreover, rejection of the view that intrinsic value is an intrinsic property of the thing to which it is attributed, does not entail rejection of the intrinsic property constraint. For example, the subjectivist claim that for a thing to have intrinsic value is for it to be positively regarded when contemplated abstractly or as existing in isolation, is consistent with the view that only intrinsic properties can be value-adding.[11] The intrinsic property constraint requires only that those properties upon which intrinsic value supervenes be intrinsic properties. So the intrinsic property constraint would not beg the question against meta-ethics that construe the core moral properties as relational properties.[12] It seems, then, safe enough to assume that views about whether intrinsic value is an intrinsic property of the bearer of value, and views about whether only internal properties can be value-adding, are relatively autonomous.

THE INDEXICAL THEORY OF INTRINSIC VALUE

The chief claims made so far are that a thing's intrinsic value results from its exemplification of value-adding properties and that value-adding properties are not restricted to intrinsic or internal properties but can include external, relational properties. We might now ask what makes a property value-adding? On Moore's theory, the answer must be that a property is value-adding if the comprehension of non-natural value is mediated by the perception of that property or the belief that that property is instantiated by the thing to which value is attributed. This account seems somewhat obscure but the basic idea is just that a property is recognized as value-adding if it is one of those properties that must be taken into account in a careful

15

act of evaluation. What is obscure is the nature of the act of evaluation. The picture is much simpler on the indexical theory, developed
below, which denies the existence of non-natural moral properties.
On the indexical theory, properties or clusters of properties are value-
adding if they exemplify the property of standing in the approval
relation to an attitudinal framework. In fact the property of being
value-adding is identical with the property of standing in the
approval relation to an attitudinal framework. This latter property,
the precise nature of which will become clearer, is a second-order
relational property which includes, necessarily, among its *relata* psychological states, specifically attitudes, of valuers. Consequently the
indexical theory is naturalist and subjectivist.[13] It claims, roughly,
that a thing has intrinsic value if and only if it is approved of (or
would be approved of) by a valuer in virtue of its properties. And
while some will dispute the adequacy of this account of evaluation, it
is difficult to see how it could be objected to on the grounds of
obscurity. The simple claim that it makes is that it is the attitude of
valuers to the exemplification of some property that renders that
property value-adding.

Humans, by and large, will be valuers. There will be exceptions,
such as infants, children, the severely mentally impaired and the
senile. As we shall see, however, it does not follow from this that
whatever a human values has value. All that follows is that it has
value-for-that human. So, a form of relativism will be defended. First,
it is perhaps useful to comment on the possibility that some non-
humans are valuers. My view is that it is doubtful that many
non-humans are valuers in the sense that humans are. The great ape
species may be an exception. I say this not because I doubt that many
non-humans have attitudes, desires and preferences, but because not
all attitudes, desires and preferences are relevant to judgements about
intrinsic moral value, only those that satisfy certain filtering requirements. These arguably include the requirement that the attitudes be
such that they could be formed against a background of justifiable
beliefs, the requirement that they not arise from defective inference,
the requirement that they survive a more than cursory process of
critical reflection and the requirement that they be attitudes one
prefers to have and to persist with. These ideal requirements presuppose considerable cognitive sophistication. There is, however,
certainly a looser understanding of what a valuer is, requiring only
that a thing have preferences. Indeed the preferences required perhaps
need not even be conscious, nor be associated in any way with

conscious experience, amounting instead to biologically determined goals or tendencies (Rolston 1994: 16–19). This loosening highlights some similarity between my preferring, subject to the requirements listed earlier, some state of affairs and a simple organism's tendency to secure nutrients. Both are plausibly instances of some extremely generic valuing but they are strikingly distant in the detail. Maybe a specification of the ways in which other entities value will encourage me to respect, so to speak, their valuings. I might be led to accept that what is valued, in some generic sense, by another, has value in the narrower sense or that the generic valuing of another itself similarly has value. This tends in the direction of a very general preference consequentialism, extending well beyond the set of conscious creatures. The shift is achieved by persuading us to see others (not necessarily only other humans or even other sentient creatures) as relevantly similar to ourselves. Such normative views arguably can be supported by subjectivism. All that is required is that my attitudes be appropriately generous, which they may, of course, turn out not to be.

Let us now flesh out the indexical theory. To begin with, the valuer has been characterized so far in a deliberately general fashion. Thus it has not been made clear whether a thing has intrinsic value if it is approved of by any valuer at all or whether it has value only if it is approved of by some particular valuer.[14] The latter is closer to what I have in mind and provides the basis of the indexical character of my preferred theory. So, when Jane says 'wild nature has intrinsic value', her assertion will be true only if she, Jane, approves of wild nature. Whether or not anyone else approves of wild nature is beside the point. In fact, what is true is that wild nature has intrinsic-value-for-Jane. How the attribution of intrinsic-value-for-Jane relates to attributions of intrinsic value will be made clear soon. Similarly, when Jill says 'species diversity has intrinsic value', her assertion will be true only if she, Jill, approves of species diversity. Whether Jane likewise approves is beside the point. This is because 'intrinsic value' in this judgement is best understood as intrinsic-value-for-Jill.

Whether anyone else approves of X is irrelevant to the meta-ethical question of whether something has the property of being intrinsically-valuable-for-Jill. This does not mean, by the way, that what others approve of is irrelevant to the normative question of what makes something intrinsically-valuable-for-Jill. What might be thought of as an egocentric aspect of the meta-ethical theory does not entail an egocentric normative perspective. If Jill thinks that included among those properties that are value-adding is the property of being approved of by another, then the property of being approved of by Jane or anyone else will be relevant to her normative judgements. But what makes it relevant to her normative judgements is the fact that it matters to Jill, in her evaluations of things, whether or not those things are approved of by others. Unless Jill herself tends to approve of things because they are approved of by others, their being thus approved of is not, for Jill, value-adding and so does not provide any basis for saying that those things have intrinsic-value-for-Jill.

The suggestion, then, is that judgements that something has intrinsic value have an indexical element. These judgements are indexed, or relativized, to the valuer making the judgement. They are indexical in other ways as well. They are indexed to the time at which the judgement is made, and to the possible world in which it is made. Indexing to times is introduced because the attitudes of a particular valuer might alter over time: what has intrinsic value-for-Jane-at-t1 might not have intrinsic value-for-Jane-at-t2. Indeed we could think of the later Jane as a new valuer, especially if other of her attitudes had changed, although she would have many attitudes overlapping with her earlier self. The situation would be analogous to two distinct people with very similar, although not completely overlapping attitudes. Pointing out to Jane that in the past she did think wild nature had intrinsic value might cause her to rethink or reconsider her present position, but it is her present position that determines whether wild nature has intrinsic-value-for-Jane and therefore, in a meaningful sense, intrinsic value.

Indexing to possible worlds is introduced in order to accommodate the possibility that Jane's attitudes might have been other than they are. It is necessary to distinguish what Jane, in this the actual world, values, both in this world and other possible worlds, from what Jane in some other possible world values, in what are, from the point of view of that world, the actual and other possible worlds. This sounds complex but the underlying idea is relatively simple. Begin with the world, the universe if you like, that we inhabit. This is, from our point of view, the actual world. And Jane shares the actual world with us. Now imagine a different world, which is very much like ours but which differs in some small details. Imagine it is a world in which Jane's history is a little different from what it actually is. Maybe she grew up in a large city, not a small town: maybe she developed an interest in the natural sciences, not the humanities. Call Jane in this second world Jane 2. As it happens, Jane 2 has different attitudes from Jane. Jane 2 thinks wild nature has intrinsic value, Jane does not.

Jane 2 is able to consider Jane's views and make a judgement about her refusal to attribute intrinsic value to wild nature. Jane 2 will say that Jane is mistaken in refusing to agree that wild nature has intrinsic value. Jane 2 will say that in the world Jane inhabits wild nature has intrinsic value, just as it does in the world that she, Jane 2, inhabits. The evaluations that Jane 2 makes from her world range across the whole array of possible worlds. Jane 2 judges states of affairs in this and other worlds, including Jane's attitudes, from the perspective of her beliefs and attitudinal framework in her world, that is, Jane 2's world. This is analogous to the situation with time. Jane now judges states of affairs at this and other times, including the attitudes of her earlier and later selves, from the perspective of her beliefs and attitudes of the time at which she makes the judgements. The usefulness of this indexing to times and worlds will emerge later. And while I will often refrain from spelling out the full indexical details when talking about values, they should be taken as implicit.

While the fact of indexing does entail that the indexical theory is relativistic in one sense, there is at least one important sense in which it is not. If relativism is simply the view that the context of an utterance must be taken into account when establishing that utterance's truth value then the indexical theory is relativistic. If, however, relativism is taken to be the very dubious view that two contradictory assertions can have the same truth-value, then the indexical theory is not relativistic. When Jane says, 'Wild nature has intrinsic value', and John says, 'Wild nature does not have intrinsic value', they are not making contradictory assertions, no more so than when Jane says, 'It is snowing here', and John says, 'It is not snowing here'. The reason that the latter pair are not contradictory is, of course, that Jane and John are using 'here' to refer to different places, the places being specified by Jane's and John's different physical locations. The word 'here' is multiply ambiguous, referring to a multiplicity of different places. Like 'intrinsic value', it is an indexical word. Its content is indexed to the locations of those speakers who utter it. There is, however, a single function which binds uses of the term, namely the function of fixing the location of something relative to the speaker's location. Similarly, the indexical theory entails that 'intrinsic value' is multiply ambiguous: in the most extreme case there could be intrinsic-value-for-Jane, intrinsic-value-for-John, intrinsic-value-for-Georgina, and so on for each and every valuer. The term 'intrinsic value' fixes the value of something relative to the attitudinal framework of the speaker.

Reflection will show, however, that 'intrinsic value' will not be as fragmented as the account just given might suggest. Most significantly, some valuers will share all their value-relevant attitudes with others, and for many more there will be large domains of overlap. This was alluded to in the earlier talk of attitudinal frameworks, which may be shared or partially shared by valuers. Attitudinal frameworks are sets of types of psychological states, which are exemplified by valuers at particular times and worlds, and in virtue of which those valuers regard particular properties as value-adding. These frameworks may be shared or partially shared by any number of valuers. When Jane says 'Wild nature has intrinsic value', intrinsic value is, strictly speaking, indexed to Jane; it is intrinsic-value-for-Jane-now-in-this-world that is attributed to wild nature. It is appropriate, though, to abstract from the particular person and to think of the indexing in terms of the attitudinal set exemplified by Jane now and that set may be exemplified by others as well. Alternatively the indexing may be thought of in terms of all who are attitudinally like Jane, or at least like her in those respects relevant to her present judgement.

Certainly there is considerable fragmentation of intrinsic value, but considerable convergence too. The tendency towards some convergence of value judgements is especially helped if the attitudes relevant to value judgements are to some extent restricted or filtered and are not simply our initial, unreflective attitudes. For example, as was earlier suggested, the attitudes generating indexed intrinsic value might be restricted to those that persist through calm reflection, to those that have as much relevant information as possible, or to those that we would want to motivate our actions in the future irrespective of our future attitudes. It should be clear that our attitudes can be refined by our reflecting on them, by imaginatively examining the paths down which they lead us, by thinking about the degree of their consistency with other of our attitudes, and by thinking about why it is that we have the attitudes that we do. These processes take time. Indeed they might be best thought of as components in an ongoing process in which our attitudes are continually subject to review.

Our initial judgements about what has or doesn't have intrinsic value would often not survive the reflective process. Even our considered judgements may sometimes be replaced after more extensive reflection. Certainly our initial judgements are only our first guess of what, evaluatively speaking, we think of things. On reflection we might revise our judgements. Sometimes this will be because we become aware of new facts that are relevant to them. For example, the discovery that some expanse of forest is naturally evolved and not, as we had thought, planted by humans, might alter our attitude to the forest. Here it is not our value-relevant attitude that changes but rather the judgement we initially made on the basis of that attitude. This is a common enough phenomenon. Often when we discover that things are not what they seemed, our evaluations of them change. More interestingly, the discovery of, and reflection on, new facts may change our attitudes. For example, an increasing understanding of ecology may give someone an appreciation of the natural world that she or he had hitherto lacked. Coming to understand how ecosystems develop, how they are maintained and how they change, may bring a valuer to attribute intrinsic value where previously she or he would attribute none. Increased understanding opens up new possibilities for affective responses, for new attitudes, and so for novel evaluations. Or again, we discover something about our initial attitude that causes it to be revised. For example, we might come to see that our initial reaction was prompted by anger, envy or some other distorting emotion. This discovery might mute, or even eliminate, the initial attitude. Likewise we might come to see that our initial attitudinal reaction is somewhat inconsistent with other of our reactions in similar situations. Noticing that it is thus out of kilter might well lead to its revision.

The third filtering consideration that was mentioned is more complicated than the two just discussed. The latter two involve changes to attitudes as a result of reflection. The former attempts instead to partition attitudes into those that are relevant to moral evaluation and those that are not. One way of trying to partition attitudes is in terms of their content, that is, in terms of what they are about or what they concern. Earlier, a possible objection to the view that wild nature has intrinsic moral value was flagged. This objection has it that wild nature falls outside that category of things to which intrinsic moral value may be properly attributed. The idea is that wild nature does not constitute the correct content for moral evaluations. The third filtering consideration does not, however, suggest a partitioning based on content but rather on the structure or form of attitudes. It suggests that it is at least partly on the basis of second-order attitudes, or attitudes we have to our attitudes, that the partitioning is based. Thus it seems true of some of our attitudes that we would prefer them to persist. For example, the committed environmentalist would likely prefer her or his attitude to wild nature to persist come what may. She or he would regard with dismay the prospect of a change in that particular attitude, regarding it as moral corruption. She or he, moreover, would now want such a changed attitude, even if were the attitude of a future self, to be disregarded. Thus if the environmentalist were brought to think that in the future she or he would not regard wild nature as intrinsically valuable, then she or he, now, would want that future evaluation to be disregarded. Contrast this situation with one in which John comes to believe that his present positive attitude towards Thai cuisine will, in the future, change. He will likely regard this prospect with equanimity. And even if he does not so regard it, he will surely agree that if this change eventuated he would not want his new attitude to be discounted or ignored when others choose where to take him for dinner. The general point is that there seems a reasonably deep distinction between the two kinds of attitudes that are distinguished in these examples, and that the one kind of attitude is more appropriately thought of as the basis for moral evaluation than the other.

These considerations do not so much suggest a revision of the account of intrinsic value thus far endorsed, as much as an elaboration of the idea of indexing to an attitudinal framework. First, the attitudinal framework in question is not constituted by all of our attitudes. Second, we index, strictly speaking, not to our actual attitudinal framework but to the one we would have were we to reflect calmly and carefully, in the light of all relevant information, on our actual one. It might not be entirely surprising that the more of our attitudes that are thus filtered, and the more the constitutive attitudes are idealized, the more our moral evaluations converge. This is a plausible suggestion. Even if is not true that filtering increases the degree of convergence, it does provide a way in which evaluations can turn out false. They are false if the attitudinal framework to which they are relativized would not survive calm reflection, etc. That might well mean, by the way, that a good portion of our evaluations are false.

While technically the indexical theory is not relativistic in the very dubious sense outlined above, some critics might say that its impact is the same as that of the dubious view.[15] It might be urged, moreover, that it drains value judgements of any interesting kind of mind-independent objectivity. If objectivity is merely the property of taking truth-values non-relativistically, then technically the indexical theory is consistent with value judgements having objectivity. This, however, might not be a sufficiently robust kind of objectivity, since it ties a thing's intrinsic value to the subjective states of valuers, and does so in a way which removes real cognitive disagreement from many apparent value disagreements. For example, John can agree that wild nature has intrinsic-value-for-Jane, while maintaining that wild nature lacks intrinsic-value-for-John. This relativism objection seeks to emphasize the valuer-relativity of the indexical theory. This is what is presumably thought to erode real, robust objectivity. The same concern is evident in a related objection, the subjectivity objection, which focuses on the indexical theory's claim that intrinsic value does not exist independently of the states of mind of valuers. The suggestion is that the indexical theory, because it embraces a mind-dependent conception of intrinsic value, cannot properly be regarded as anything but a deflated or truncated understanding of intrinsic value.[16] The relativism and subjectivism objections will be discussed in the next section.

SUBJECTIVISM, RELATIVISM AND NORMATIVE DEBATE

The subjectivism objection is likely to be partly motivated by the view, earlier discussed, that intrinsic value has to be an intrinsic property. According to the indexical theory, it is, of course, a relational property. The subjectivism objection might also be partly motivated by the belief, again earlier discussed, that value-adding properties must themselves be intrinsic properties and that this is guaranteed only if intrinsic value is an intrinsic property. These concerns were dealt with earlier in our discussion, and rejection, of the intrinsic property requirement. There is, though, another concern, perhaps best thought of as a special instance of the first, namely that intrinsic value cannot be somehow constituted by the attitudes of valuers, that it must be independent of what valuers feel or desire or prefer. The force of the subjectivism objection must somehow derive from the fact that the indexical theory construes intrinsic value as a relational property in which, necessarily, one of the elements is a psychological state of a valuer.

Perhaps the concern is that subjectivism devalues intrinsic value, so to speak. As indicated already, some philosophers take the view that 'intrinsic value' literally refers to objective intrinsic value. They think that any subjectivist account of intrinsic value, such as I endorse, misunderstands the meaning of 'intrinsic value' (Green 1996: 31–4;

Korsgaard 1983). Thus it is suggested that subjectivism can accommodate only extrinsic value, which is a non-instrumental value that a thing possesses but only because it stands in a certain relation to the subjective states of some valuer. For instance, I might value the rainforest for itself and not because of any uses it has for me. I value it, therefore, non-instrumentally. Nevertheless its value is somehow dependent on my attitudes and so the source of the rainforest's value is not intrinsic to it but extrinsic to it. Others take the view that subjectivism truncates intrinsic value, by which they mean that subjectivist intrinsic value is less than robust, that it is worryingly weak, or that it in some way lacks the punch of objective intrinsic value (Callicott 1984, 1986 and 1992a). The thought here cannot merely be that subjectivist intrinsic value is not a real property. Given that psychological states are real states, subjectivist intrinsic value would certainly be a real property: it would be a natural property and would, of course, be empirically detectable. To say that intrinsic value is empirically detectable is just to say that the relationship in which an object stands to our attitudes is discoverable through introspection or reflection on our feelings, attitudes, beliefs and actions.

The basic thought behind the subjectivism objection seems to be that the distinction between 'intrinsic value' and 'extrinsic value' is the very same distinction as that between objective Moorean value and subjective value (Green 1996: 32; O'Neil 1993: 20; Rolston 1988: 115). According to those who endorse this view, to say that something has intrinsic value would be to say that it would have value in isolation, irrespective of what else there is; it would be to say that the thing's value emanates from it and it alone, independently of anything else, including valuers, in the universe. And something of the same idea is evident in the complaint that subjectivism, while it may well provide space for non-anthropocentric views, nevertheless offers only an anthropogenic account of value (Rolston 1994). While conceding that subjectivism does not entail that only what serves human interests has value, and so does not entail normative anthropocentricism, Rolston is concerned that it does nevertheless entail that value is dependent on human attitudes. While not necessarily anthropocentric in its normative values, subjectivism is anthropogenic (or, better, anthropocentric in its meta-ethics) because it endorses the slogan, 'No values without valuers.' In so far as subjectivism is anthropogenic, it is supposed to leave the value of wild nature on an insecure foundation, making it dangerously dependent on the particular views of valuers and on the very existence of valuers.

It is certainly true that if we take 'intrinsic value' to mean Moorean objective intrinsic value, then subjectivism does not support a theory of intrinsic value. If we accept this, then subjectivism will only yield a truncated version of intrinsic value, which some would call extrinsic non-instrumental value: a version which might mimic aspects of the more robust version but which is inferior to it in that it lacks a crucial ingredient, namely a peculiar objectivity. Some philosophers who take this view allow, nevertheless, that subjectivist intrinsic value accommodates the view that some things have value for their own sake or as ends in themselves. In other words they allow that subjectivism permits the view that objects have value irrespective of their usefulness to humans, and they have this value on account of the particular properties that they exemplify. Still, such critics take the view that this is not the strongest kind of value there could be, since it is value from some valuer's point of view and not abstractly, not, so to speak, from the point of view of the universe. This condemnation seems to be a condemnation of subjectivism as such rather than a condemnation of subjectivist intrinsic value.

So-called truncated intrinsic value does seem functionally analogous to objectivist intrinsic value. The difference emerges only when the background metaphysics is brought to the fore. So far as function is concerned I cannot see that truncated intrinsic value is deficient with respect to objective intrinsic value. To insist that 'intrinsic value' be defined so as to presuppose objective non-naturalism seems somewhat question-begging. At the very least, it is questionable to tie the idea of intrinsic value inextricably to the particular moral metaphysics advocated by Moore. What seems central to the idea of intrinsic value is valuing something for itself, for its own sake, as an end in itself. As far as I can see, subjectivism accommodates these notions.

Perhaps it is the naturalism of the indexical theory that is the problem. It might be thought that the indexical theory is flawed for the same reason that Moore thought that any theory identifying goodness with conduciveness to pleasure is flawed. Moore argued that such an identification would imply that to ask whether something that is conducive to pleasure is good is to ask an empty question, at least a question to which this identification provides an indisputable answer (Moore 1963). According to the theory, asking whether something that is conducive to pleasure is good is simply to ask whether something that is conducive to pleasure is conducive to pleasure. The question, however, is not obviously empty in this way, nor is the provided answer indisputable. This suggests that the alleged identity

25

does not hold. But this does not drive us to dismiss subjective naturalism.

The indexical theory does entail that it is an empty question to ask whether something that is in itself approved of by a valuer has intrinsic-value-for-that-valuer. This, however, is not analogous to Moore's case. The identification to which Moore objected fixed the answer to the question as to what properties are value-adding; only the property of being conducive to pleasure is value-adding in the example he considered. The identification proposed by the indexical theory leaves this question open: any property that is a possible object of approval is potentially a value-adding property. While a thing cannot have intrinsic value unless it is, loosely speaking, approved of, its being approved of need not itself be value-adding. For example, the rainforest is approved of because it is biotically diverse and it therefore has intrinsic value in virtue of its biotic diversity; it does not have intrinsic value in virtue of being approved of. The property of being approved of will itself only be value-adding if the fact that something is approved of is itself approved of. This is both contingent and independent of the indexical theory. There is nothing about the definition of 'good', or related terms that the indexical theory suggests, that makes it necessary that the property of being approved of is value-adding. To think otherwise is to confuse meta-ethical issues with normative issues. Or it is to conflate the question as to the nature of intrinsic value with the questions as to what properties are value-adding and as to what in fact has intrinsic value.

Thus the indexical theory is not open to the charge that normative anthropocentrism or, more generously, normative psychocentrism (as Katz 1987: 234–5 has it), both disavowed by environmentalists, is built into it. Intrinsic value is not restricted to psychological states, to the activities of sentient creatures, or to the products of sentient agency. Nor is it restricted to small-scale items, such as persons, animals, plants or rocks. Intrinsic value could be coherently attributed to ecosystems, to the biosphere, to the planet or even to the universe. Thus the indexical theory accommodates environmental holism. Value-adding properties may be possessed by ecosystems and natural systems as whole systems; such systems can have intrinsic value which is not merely the sum of the intrinsic values of the component individuals. Moreover, the value-adding properties are properties possessed by the things themselves and will include a multitude of intrinsic properties. So Jane values the wetlands in virtue of their naturalness and their biotic diversity and these are certainly properties of the ecosystem itself. Even the resultant intrinsic value is a property of the ecosystem itself, although of course it is an external relational property of the ecosystem. No doubt some environmental philosophers, such as Rolston who is concerned by its anthropogenic nature, will continue to be disturbed by this feature of the indexical theory. They will need, however, to indicate more clearly and exactly why this feature undercuts any environmental axiology it is called upon to support.

Some who are dubious about the adequacy of subjectivist theories of intrinsic value, and so of the indexical theory, suggest that there are core environmentalist claims, distinctive of the deeper, greener variants of environmentalism, that such theories cannot support. Their reasons are those earlier discussed in relation to Rolston's distinction between anthropocentric and anthropogenic values. They focus on the subjectivist's apparent endorsement of the slogan, 'No values without valuers.' So let us see how the indexical theory just might accommodate four claims that exhaust the kind about which there is concern. The claims are:

A Once upon a time there were trilobites, which had intrinsic value.
B At some time in the future, well after conscious organisms have become extinct, there will still be some biological complexity and it will have intrinsic value.
C Had the course of evolution gone differently, resulting in no conscious organisms but some biological complexity, the world would have had intrinsic value.
D Had the course of my psychological development gone differently, resulting in the development of no green values in my moral psychology, then wild nature would nevertheless have had intrinsic value.

These are certainly claims that would be endorsed by those with reasonably green normative views, and they are evident, explicitly and implicitly, in much of the environmental ethics literature. Certainly they are normative views I endorse and, I hope to show, consistently with my preferred meta-ethical theory. Since the intrinsically valuable states of affairs referred to in (A), (B), (C) and (D) do not, or so it seems, include the relevant valuer, then they are, critics allege, normative judgements that are not consistent with subjectivism. If this is true, then this is a tension between normative environmentalism and subjectivism. Those inclined to endorse both broad views would in this case have a problem, since, if the tension is real, they would either have to give up some presumably deeply held normative views or accept a theory of value that they may well regard as metaphysically abhorrent. Happily the tension is illusory, since a carefully framed subjectivism accommodates (A), (B), (C) and (D).

First of all, let us consider (A). According to the subjectivist, for me to say that the trilobites had intrinsic value is to say that I approve of their past existence. The fact of their having intrinsic value is the fact of their standing in this approval relationship to my attitudinal framework. My relevant attitudinal response does not require anything approximating direct causal connection with trilobites, although an indirect causal connection may be required.[17] What is required is that I be able to represent to myself, propositionally in this case, the fact of the trilobites' past existence. Contemplation of this representation of the past state of affairs triggers or provokes in me the valuing response; that is, an affect or feeling that is characterizable as a pro-attitude or a positive attitude or an attitude of approval towards the representation.[18] This all seems possible and so (A) seems accommodated. Perhaps, though, I have overlooked the tense in which (A) is cast. While my preferred meta-ethic allows me to say now that the existence of trilobites in the past has intrinsic value, does it really allow me to say that that state of affairs then had intrinsic value? Clearly I did not then value it since I was not around, but my valuing it now entails that it had value then. Certainly it is the existence of the trilobites in that past state of affairs that I value. This response may be helped by emphasizing a hypothetical element in my subjectivism. I can say that a thing has, and had, intrinsic value if, were I to contemplate it from the perspective of my present attitudinal framework, I would value it. The trilobites had, way back then, those properties in virtue of which my valuing response is now elicited and so they then had intrinsic value.[19]

Let us now consider (B). It is straightforwardly analogous to (A). If the future state of affairs is such that I would value it were I to contemplate it, then it has intrinsic value. Moreover there is no requirement that I be able to interact causally with a state of affairs in order to value it.[20] The valuing response can be provoked by some propositional or other representation of that state of affairs. And clearly it is possible thus to represent, although here it might be more accurate to say partially represent, a future state of affairs. I say 'partially', because my representation of the future state of affairs will lack much detail. The future is, after all, relatively obscure. Still, the past is often equally obscure, as is much of the present. Furthermore, my demise prior to the coming into existence of the valued state of affairs does not somehow entail that the future state of affairs suddenly loses intrinsic value. It remains the case that the future state of affairs stands in the approval relation to my attitudinal framework at the time at which the judgement was made. And that is a time prior to my demise. Indeed the judgement would not even have to be actual, given the hypothetical twist that may be given to subjectivism. Thus I might never have noticed that the future state of affairs had intrinsic value, never having represented it to myself and contemplated it. Nevertheless the structure of my attitudinal framework at the time could have been such that had I contemplated the future state of affairs I would have approved of it. That is all that is required for that state to have intrinsic value, understood as the indexical theory understands it.

Now consider (C), which is distinctive in that it involves a valuation of a world in which I do not exist at any time at all. The crucial question is how a subjectivism, which takes the valuer to be the source of value, could allow that a world in which the relevant valuer never exists could in fact contain value? There is no difficulty if we carefully state and think about the indexical theory. The relevant valuer makes the evaluation from his or her perspective in the actual world. From my perspective in the actual world, for example, I can review and evaluate other possible worlds, including worlds in which I do not exist. To say that such and such a world, or something it contains, has value is just to say that a consideration of some accurate representation of it would provoke the value response. My evaluations can range over possibilities: there is nothing strange in that. And, in evaluating other worlds in which I do exist, I might judge that the values I hold in those worlds are corrupt, just as I might judge the human chauvinist values I held in the past, or the human chauvinist values of many of my contemporaries, to be corrupt. And this, of course, shows why the subjectivist has no trouble accommodating (D). More, though, needs to be said about (C).

Some might insist that the account of (C) offered above is deficient because merely possible states of affairs have value only because I exist, because had I not existed the merely possible states of affairs would not have had value. In one way this observation is correct: my preferred meta-ethic implies it and not only for the kind of evaluation involved in (C) but for every evaluation made. This is, of course, because my attitudinal framework is required to fix intrinsic-value-for-me. So (C) creates no special problem for subjectivism on this score. Maybe, though, some critics of the indexical theory are troubled by the thought that it implies that had the relevant valuer not existed, nothing then would have had any value. But this thought is flawed. As a matter of fact, for better or for worse, I do exist. As a matter of fact I value both the trilobites and the future state of biotic complexity. Their having value is in one sense dependent on my valuing them but it does not follow that had I not existed they would have had no value. The reason is that my evaluations are not limited to past, present and future states of the actual world but pertain to the whole array of possible worlds (Elliot 1985 and 1992). So, from my necessarily human perspective in the actual world I can, and do, judge that wild nature has intrinsic value in those worlds from which I and my species, indeed any sentient species, are completely absent. The thought that there could be values even if no valuers had existed is, according to the subjectivist, just the thought that there are possible worlds which contain no valuers but which are valued (by me) from the perspective of the actual world.[21] All this means, according to the indexical theory, is that to say that a state of affairs has intrinsic value is to say that, from the perspective of my attitudinal framework, that state of affairs has value. Moreover, states of affairs in possible worlds may be judged and evaluated from the perspectives of my attitudinal framework. There is no mystery here.

So a subjectivist theory of value can accommodate the greenest of environmentalist values. This theory about value does not, by the way, imply that only I and others who are attitudinally like me are valuers. It allows that there are countless many other valuers, including, perhaps, some non-human valuers, who are doing something functionally proximate to what I do when I make evaluations. This subjectivism, moreover, leaves it a completely open question whether the evaluations of these others are, from my valuational point, of normative significance.

It might be urged, however, that while a technically subjectivist theory, such as the indexical theory, permits all core environmentalist judgements, there is nevertheless a contingency at its heart which is likely to erode the affective basis of such judgements. The idea is that the subjectivism somehow fractures and weakens the connection between judgements of intrinsic value and preparedness to act on the basis of them. Imagine, for example, that Jane, an adherent of the indexical theory, says 'Rainforests have intrinsic value.' According to the indexical theory, there is a straightforward sense in which the rainforests' intrinsic value is dependent on Jane's having the attitudes that she now does have. Jane knows that at some future time, after she is dead, she will have no attitudes at all, that nothing will then matter to her, that there will be nothing that will have intrinsic value in virtue of her attitudes. Jane might be tempted to think that intrinsic-value-for-Jane will disappear when she ceases to exist. Worse, she might be tempted to think that with certain possible changes in her attitudes, for example if she were subjected to powerful anti-environmentalist propaganda, the intrinsic value of rainforests would not merely be eliminated but would be transformed to intrinsic disvalue.

The indexical theory entails that Jane would be mistaken if she thought such things. While nothing in the further future would have intrinsic value in virtue of the attitudes she then has, things will have value in that future in virtue of attitudes she has now. Those things which possess intrinsic-value-for-Jane-now will continue to possess it independently of her future attitudes. In this sense their intrinsic value is fixed. Of course, the attitudinal framework that generates these intrinsic values will, after her death, be in the past. And of course certain changes to her attitudes could make it the case that these same things might not have intrinsic-value-for-Jane-tomorrow or could even come to have intrinsic-disvalue-for-Jane-tomorrow. Such changes in attitude, however, can not make it the case that those things which possess intrinsic-value-for-Jane-now will cease to possess it tomorrow. The point is that her attitude now to what transpires in the future is fixed, and this fixed attitude generates fixed, although indexed, intrinsic values.

Perhaps these thoughts are destabilizing. Perhaps the full realization that the intrinsic values are indexed, that they are not objective in the Moorean sense, will tend to cause Jane to cease caring about how things will be when she is no longer around, about how things might have been had she not been around and about how things will be if her evaluational attitudes change. Indeed, it might be suggested, her present attitudes will fade, weaken or become muted, with the result that she is no longer able to say with quite her past conviction that rainforests have intrinsic value. The thought seems to be that only Moorean objectivity can overcome an undermining contingency associated with subjectivism (Attfield 1994; Crisp 1994). What is supposedly so troubling is that the attitudes and preferences on which the value judgements are based have no more secure a foundation than the social, cultural and biological influences that have shaped the psychologies of those making the judgements; the judgements are not endorsed and somehow rendered objective by some deity, by the cosmos or by nature itself.

Perhaps there is an antidote to this way of thinking. Imagine that Jane comes to know that she will inevitably be caused, through psychological manipulation, to give up her environmentalist attitudes and adopt human chauvinist ones. She is, let us imagine, presently doing the preliminary work on a project that will lead to the restoration of a degraded forest only after this foreseen, forced transformation of her attitudes. Would her knowledge that these attitudes, which sustain her work on the project, will change, motivate her to give up the work? Will such knowledge weaken those very attitudes now, contributing to the transformation? Not obviously. In fact it might well have the opposite effect; it might move her to work harder; it might make her more determined to finish the project before the transformation begins; it might consolidate her environmentalist attitudes for the time being at least. Jane's reaction to the implications of the indexical theory could be like her reaction here. The difference between the cases, of course, is that in the former Jane's attitudes are not altered through manipulation; they do not change as the result of some identifiable coercive act. Still, it is arguably appropriate for Jane to take the same stance in the former case as in the latter, especially as her attitudes are not merely refined but are transformed. Those who are nervous of contingency will doubtless have a different take on this. They will say that in the example just discussed Jane knows that she is to be in some way deceived into having false moral beliefs. This, they would suggest, is why she would strive harder, become more adamant, more persistent. On this account it is Jane's belief that she is now aware of the moral facts that fuels her resolve. On the account offered by the indexical theory, it is Jane's felt conviction and depth of feeling that serves the same function. It is not obvious to me, however, why the latter account is less plausible than the former.[22] And, as we shall see later in this chapter, the view one adopts here has no real impact on the dynamics of normative belief.

Let us now move on to consider the relativism objection. The relativism objection, which is related to the subjectivism objection, seems motivated by two concerns. First, the fragmentation of intrinsic value conflicts with the moral phenomenology; in particular, the relativizing or indexing of value judgements fragments the concept of intrinsic value in such a way that genuine disagreement about attributions of intrinsic value are not possible. Second, the impossibility of disagreement means that rational discussion of attributions of intrinsic value is either impossible or pointless; it rules out the possibility of rational engagement. Certainly it does appear that Jane and John, in our earlier example, are making conflicting judgements, that Jane is saying that something is true which John says is false. Moreover, if Jane were to change her mind, then presumably it would seem to her that she was now in disagreement with one of her own earlier judgements. Interpersonal and intrapersonal disagreement about intrinsic value seems to be genuine cognitive disagreement about the presence or absence of some objective property. In other words, when we disagree with one another about matters of value, it very often seems to us as if there really is some particular thing about which we are disagreeing, just as when we might disagree about aspects of an accident we have witnessed. The indexical theory denies that disputes about matters of value are closely similar to disputes about matters of fact. As we shall see later, there is a point to which disputes about matters of value are similar to disputes about matter of fact. To the extent that they are, it makes sense to speak of someone being mistaken in the judgement they make. Ultimately, though, it makes no sense, on the indexical theory, to say that moral disagreement is cognitive disagreement.[23] The indexical theory claims, therefore, that we are to some extent misled by the phenomenology, by what it seems to us is going on when we are involved in disputes about matters of value and moral matters generally.

One response is to attempt to show how the phenomenology could plausibly have arisen even if the indexical theory is correct. An initial observation that helps this project is the observation that the indexing of intrinsic value is ultimately to attitudinal frameworks rather than to particular people. These, as was noted earlier, may be shared or exhibit substantial overlap from person to person. Similarly, they persist, or overlap, across time within the psychology of particular people. Indexing to attitudinal frameworks acts as a brake on the fragmentation of intrinsic value. We should also keep in mind the fact that the indexical theory does permit one kind of straightforward cognitive disagreements with respect to value judgements: for example, there can be disagreement as to whether some state of affairs does or does not stand in the approval relation to some attitudinal framework. On occasions we might not be altogether clear about what we approve of or disapprove of, or we might be self-deceived. Others might better know what our real attitudes are. They might be in a position to correct our judgements, speaking not from a perspective that is necessarily their own but taking what is essentially our own perspective. This is like a situation in which a friend, knowing our particular goals, is better able than are we to develop strategies for realizing those goals. Even though our friend does not share our goals, she or he may be better placed than are we to judge whether some strategy is the best strategy for us to adopt in order to realize them.

Apparent cognitive disagreement with respect to value judgements is, moreover, certainly connected with the very real likelihood of practical disagreement. While our value judgements might be made relative to an attitudinal framework, which, although shaped in a public domain in interaction with others, may be relatively idiosyncratic, our actions are performed in a material context that is thoroughly shared. Thus, if Jane and Jack make different attributions of intrinsic value, then they are likely to have conflicting preferences concerning what should be done. For example, if Jack intrinsically values species diversity he might be inclined to oppose forestry practices which threaten the existence of species. If Jane does not intrinsically value species diversity she might be inclined to support these practices, assuming that they produce outcomes which she does intrinsically value or concerning which she is relatively neutral. Real disagreement about what should be done can foster the illusion of disagreement about the inferred value beliefs underpinning the conflicting practical prescriptions or suggestions.

Moreover, as the intensity of the practical disagreement increases so too will the temptation to win the contest by connecting one's opponent's prescription with an allegedly false belief. An obvious candidate for the belief in question is the belief that something has unindexed intrinsic value, or Moorean objective value, which holds out the promise of a knockdown argument. But the indexical theory does not preclude the promise because it too allows that moral judgements can be mistaken. To pre-empt the reply to the second concern, intrinsic value attributions are made on the basis of beliefs about the presence or absence of value-adding properties, about which there can be real cognitive disagreement and about which one can undeniably be mistaken. If it could be shown that such a grounding belief for some intrinsic value attribution were false, then that would, in the absence of a functionally equivalent replacement, count decisively against the attribution. Consider, for example, a situation where Jack judges that a particular forest has intrinsic value. We ask him why he thinks this and he replies that the forest is a rich and complex ecosystem exhibiting considerable species diversity. In fact the forest is a single species plantation – a virtual monoculture. For whatever reason, this is some-thing which Jack has not noticed. So we can tell Jack that his attribution of intrinsic value is mistaken because he has a false belief that the forest exemplifies a value-adding property when, transparently, it does not.

We might also reflect on the functional role that judgements about indexed intrinsic value play in the psychologies of valuers where they do seem to agree. If Jane thinks that X has intrinsic value and Jack thinks so too, then, other things being equal, Jane and Jack are likely to behave in the same way concerning X, feel the same way about X and the like. In order for the two judgements to play the same functional role in the individual psychologies, it is not necessary that they be judgements about the same thing, let alone the same value fact. However, if there is such a distinctive similarity in functional role, then it may be tempting to Jane and Jack to think that their judgements are about the same fact. Sometimes Jane and Jack will be, in one way at least, right in thinking this. If their similar evaluations are driven by the same sets of attitudes then they share an attitudinal framework. In each instance, the judgement that X has intrinsic value is the judgement that X is approved of from the perspective of a particular, and here shared, attitudinal framework. Where their attitudinal frameworks are not shared it could still be that they approve of X. They approve of it for different reasons, since each thinks X exemplifies a different set of value-adding properties or, put differently, each thinks a different set of the properties the thing possesses are the value-adding properties. Here their judgements, that X has intrinsic value, are not made from the same attitudinal framework and so are not judgements about a particular object standing in the approval relation to the one framework. The contents of the judgements are different.

The second component in the relativism objection has to do with the possibility of rational discussion and rational adjudication of indexed intrinsic value judgements. This second component of the relativism objection is, moreover, difficult to disentangle from the subjectivism objection. And some of what has already been said in connection with the first component of the relativism objection points to ways in which rational discussion and rational adjudication of conflicting value judgements can proceed. So one reason that some people might baulk at the indexical theory is that they think that only a non-relativist objectivism provides scope for the rational discussion, and rational adjudication, of value disagreements. However, the subjectivism, which includes relativism, of the indexical theory is sufficiently sophisticated that there is no practical implication flowing from its adoption that would not flow from the adoption of objectivism, and vice versa. This subjectivism does not entail that value conflict cannot be rationally resolved, that convergence of belief on value matters cannot be helped through a process of giving reasons, listening to reasons and considering reasons. The process is exactly the same, moreover, for the subjectivist and the objectivist, although they would no doubt give differing accounts of what the process aims at and of what it involves. So the objectivist may say that the process aims at discovering mind-independent moral facts, whereas the subjectivist will say that it involves something like working through the implications, and reviewing or reflecting critically on the contents, of an attitudinal framework.

Consider the following case. Jack thinks that the rainforest has intrinsic value. Jill thinks so too. Moreover, Jack believes that there are objective values whereas Jill does not. So Jack thinks that the rainforest has a certain objective value property. Jill disagrees. Both Jack and Jill believe that the rainforest has intrinsic value in virtue of other value-adding properties it possesses, such as the properties of being biologically diverse, of being naturally evolved, or of being aesthetically pleasing. And presumably Jack believes that the objective value of the rainforest is perceived not directly but is somehow mediated by a perception of its value-adding properties. In other words, he is likely to believe that it is through his awareness of the value-adding properties that he comprehends or grasps the moral property. Analogously Jill will, she believes, have the valuing response in virtue of noticing, perhaps subliminally, the value-adding properties. There is every reason to think that in this case Jack and Jill will not find themselves in any practical conflict.

The situation might have been different of course. Had Jack disagreed with Jill as to the intrinsic value of the rainforest, there would have been some practical reason for them to engage in normative debate, perhaps because each is in a position to contribute to policy. Had Jack disagreed with Jill's value judgement, Jill might have invited Jack to consider those properties of the rainforest she took to be value-adding. And Jack might have consequently come to agree with Jill's value judgement. Here Jill and Jack would give different accounts of the process. Jack would say, falsely I believe, that the consideration of the rainforest's biological diversity permits him to comprehend that it possesses the further property of being intrinsically valuable.

Jill would say, correctly I believe, that when Jack's attention is suitably directed, when certain facts are drawn to his attention he begins to affectively respond as she has responded. Similarly, Jack might invite Jill to reflect again on the alleged value-adding properties of the rainforest in the hope that her attitudes of approval will diminish to indifference on such a reappraisal. And again each could give a straightforward account of the process in terms of her or his preferred meta-ethic. Jack would presumably give an account in terms of a better perception or comprehension of the moral facts leading to certain attitudinal adjustments. And Jill would give an account solely in terms of attitude modification. So, despite their different accounts of what is fundamentally going on, Jill and Jack make the same dialogical moves. For each of them, despite their meta-ethical differences, the dynamics of normative debate are basically the same.

Or again, imagine that Jack's judgement, that the rainforest lacks intrinsic value, is still intact after his reconsideration of its allegedly value-adding properties. In this case there are other moves that Jill might make in her effort to change Jack's mind. She might look for inconsistencies in Jack's overall normative position, which inconsistencies might be resolved by Jack's endorsing Jill's judgement about the rainforest. Jill might think of herself as making use of Jack's presumed desire for normative consistency, whereas Jack would think of her as making use of the presumed impossibility of inconsistent value facts. Alternatively Jill might strive to alter Jack's attitudes by educating him and refining his sensibility; she might try to excite in him something of the appreciation she has of the rainforest, partly by bringing him to a position where he can comprehend those natural facts about the rainforest that underpin Jill's attitudinal response to it. This might involve bringing Jack face to face with the rainforest, explaining its evolutionary history and its ecosystemic complexity. Here Jill will think of herself as bringing Jack's attitudinal framework into alignment with hers, partly by improving his perception of non-moral natural facts, whereas Jack will think of her as clearing away factors which had hitherto distorted his moral vision, his comprehension or perception of relevant non-natural, objective value facts.

It is possible of course that Jill will not persuade Jack to endorse her judgement about the rainforest. Jill might explain this in terms of Jack holding certain false non-value beliefs, which feed into, and distort, his value judgements; cognitive disagreement at one level is here leading to affective divergence at another level. Or Jill might explain their value disagreement in terms of basic attitudinal differences between herself and Jack, due perhaps to different patterns of enculturation and experience. Jack, however, is likely to see their disagreement as cognitive all the way down. He will think that there is some objective value fact, which at least one of them fails fully to comprehend. He will think not just that Jill and he disagree but that at least one of them is mistaken.[24] Again these rather different views of what goes on when they disagree have no significant practical effects.

The dialogical moves sketched above are standard moves in promoting convergence of moral belief, indeed all belief, and they are moves open both to the objectivist and the subjectivist. Although each would give a rather different characterization of the process and of its ultimate aims, there is no kind of move that either Jill or Jack, that either the objectivist or the subjectivist, could make that is not practically or functionally equivalent to some move the other could make. Note too, that even if Jill, like Jack, were an objectivist, there would be no additional leverage provided for bringing their conflicting normative views into alignment. Belief in objectivism, as such, does nothing by way of resolving Jill's and Jack's disagreement. Presumably they each reach a point where one can only say to the other that she or he is misperceiving or miscomprehending the value facts. So far as the dynamics of normative environmental debate is concerned the contest between objectivism and subjectivism is idle.

There is another kind of difference that the choice between objectivism and subjectivism might be thought to make; a motivational difference. Consider the case where Jack and Jill are both objectivists. If they think that their disagreement is cognitive all the way down, then perhaps they would be more likely to persist in the enterprise of achieving convergence of belief than they would if they thought their disagreement were in large part affective, and so did not threaten inconsistency or contradiction once the appropriate relativizations were signalled. What keeps the objectivists engaged – although what the continued engagement could amount to beyond a certain point except assertion and counter-assertion is not clear – is their commitment to uncovering a single truth. Something not too dissimilar, though, might likewise keep subjectivists engaged. Policy choices are guided by value judgements and often policies are mutually inconsistent. So strong preferences by different people for conflicting policies will, like the commitment to uncovering the truth, be likely to fuel continued engagement in the enterprise of achieving convergence of moral belief, or attitudinal framework.

There is a related point. Imagine that Jack is an objectivist and Jill is a subjectivist and that they make different evaluations of the rain-forest. Imagine that Jill is in a position to make policy and being of a liberal inclination has listened seriously to Jack's competing view. Given her subjectivism, she might conclude that there is no sense in which her evaluation is or could be objectively correct; she simply thinks of the situation as one in which her preferences conflict with Jack's preferences. She might think, being of a liberal inclination, that she should not disregard or discount Jack's preferences. Consequently the policy she institutes is not the one she most prefers on her own account but is some compromise with the preferences, as Jill sees them, that Jack has articulated. Had she not been so liberally inclined she might have allowed her preferences alone, especially if they were strongly held, to determine policy.

Now consider how things might be if it had been Jack who was in a position to determine policy. Imagine that Jack listens to what Jill has to say but that nothing she says persuades him that the rainforest has intrinsic value. It is possible that Jack thinks to himself that he appreciates the truth about this matter but that Jill does not. And this might well lead him to disregard or discount Jill's view. In other words, if Jack is an objectivist and believes there is some fact of the matter that adjudicates the conflict he has with Jill, and if he believes that he better comprehends the moral fact than does Jill, then he might well institute policy in accordance with his view without making any compromises in Jill's direction. This is analogous to the action of the illiberal Jill. But there is nothing about his objectivist view, as such, that pushes or even encourages Jack into this line of action. What would do the pushing or encouraging, if anything, would be Jack's belief that he is somehow better epistemically placed, with respect to moral knowledge, than is Jill.

The point is that Jack is just as likely, I would say more likely, to conclude that he has no reason to think that his angle on the value facts is any sounder than Jill's, although he thinks that Jill is mistaken in her account of what is occurring when she makes evaluations. This is especially likely if Jill and Jack have run through the various dialogical moves earlier mentioned. Since Jack cannot identify some point at which Jill has fallen into error, say on account of misper-ceiving the value-adding properties on which intrinsic value supervenes, surely he will hesitate fulsomely to endorse the view to which he, but not she, is inclined. Consequently, he is likely to be somewhat hesitant to impose the policy he favours over the one she favours. To do so would be illiberal in that it would be to disregard without reason the competing views of others; it would be a kind of epistemic disrespect (D'Agostino 1993). There seems no scope here, in any of the areas we have just discussed, for any clear pragmatic differentiation of subjectivism from objectivism.

The focus so far in this section has been on the question of pragmatic differentiation between subjectivism and objectivism. It has been assumed that the overriding motive that disputants have for settling value conflicts is that such conflicts help to fuel practical disagreement concerning actions and policies. Some might think that, in addition, there is a more abstract or theoretical motivation which is relevant. For example, where Jack and Jill disagree about some value matter, and where their disagreement has no practical consequence, Jack, the objectivist, might still want Jill, the subjectivist, to comprehend the truth. In other words, Jack may well be motivated to get Jill to agree with him, or get himself to come to agree with Jill, because he wants to get at the moral truth. This makes sense from an objectivist perspective. Moreover, there does not seem to be the same motivation for the subjectivist to secure agreement where nothing of practical significance is at stake. Perhaps it is where practical concern runs out that the differentiating characteristics of subjectivism and objectivism come into their own resulting in quite distinct normative dynamics. We should not, however, exaggerate the degree to which this might be so.

For one thing, Jill might be concerned that Jack's different value judgement may lead to some future practical conflict or she might think that it contributes to an overall value orientation which does lead to practical conflict. Or Jill may well be bothered by the fact that others are unlike her with respect to preferences that she thinks are extremely important. She might therefore be motivated to bring at least some of the preferences of others into alignment with her own. This will simply be a contingent fact about Jill's psychology with little in the way of a deeper explanation of it available. Perhaps one explanation that is plausible is that Jill sees disagreement in particular cases as a threat to her overall value orientation, which is one she prefers to maintain. In other words, she wants to guard against a change of attitude that, from her current perspective, she would count as inappropriate or inadequate. More significantly, Jill might well take Jack's disagreement with her as prima-facie evidence that she has perhaps not thoroughly reflected on the matter in dispute, something she, being a rational person, prefers not to be the case. In the end she may accept that there is a basic disagreement, that neither

Jack nor she is manifesting here any defect of rationality, but for a time at least she may be motivated to pursue their dispute in absence of any practical upshot. There is a fourth, related, point to make here. Many of our value conflicts with others result, as earlier remarked, not from a fundamental conflict at the level of basic values but from disagreements about various non-value background beliefs; for example different beliefs about the probabilities of leakages from stored radioactive wastes might contribute to conflicting value judgements about nuclear power. So questions as to the truth will enter into the picture for Jill as well as Jack.

Jack, for his, part, may not particularly care whether Jill has false value beliefs where nothing of practical consequence turns on their disagreement. His objectivism, of itself, seems to provide no motivation to pursue the dispute. What is likely to provide the motivation is his belief that Jill's disagreement with him is prima-facie evidence that he is mistaken. The fact of her disagreement may encourage him to check the relevant non-value facts, to attend carefully to the situation he is evaluating and so on. Having done these things he may decide that he is, after all, correct. There may be some residual motivation, perhaps having to do with some special value Jack places on knowledge, to lead Jill to see the moral truth but, importantly, the only means available to him for accomplishing this are the analogous devices, earlier discussed, available to both the subjectivist and objectivist for normative adjudication. So, even where practical conflict is not involved, the choice between subjectivism and objectivism does not seem to lead to very different, if at all different, normative dynamics.

Our deliberations so far have brought us to the point where the indexical theory of value can be seen to support various core environmentalist claims. It also shows how intrinsic value is grounded in the natural, objective properties that natural items exemplify. Moreover, it is a theory that gives content and substance to the claim that wild nature has intrinsic value. It has the resources to respond convincingly to the subjectivism and relativism objections, in particular allowing that there is plenty of scope for the rational adjudication of value conflicts, including conflicts concerning natural values. So we have a plausible theory of natural value but very little has been said about the requirements for action that it generates. This issue is taken up in the next chapter, where the connection between value and obligation is considered.

2

ENVIRONMENTAL OBLIGATION, AESTHETIC VALUE AND THE BASIS OF NATURAL VALUE

ENVIRONMENTAL OBLIGATION AND CONSEQUENTIALISM

Most of the discussion of the first chapter focused on the nature of value in general, and of natural value in particular. Various claims were made about how intrinsic value is to be understood and about the relationship between intrinsic value and value-adding properties. We might wonder where this leaves us with respect to constraints on action; with respect to what we may or may not do; and with respect to what policies ought or ought not be pursued. One central claim of this book is that if wild nature has intrinsic value, then there is an obligation to preserve it and to restore it. Some justification of this claim, which makes reference to the connection between value and obligation, needs to be given. Let us consider first how consequentialists would make the connection. Consequentialists provide something of a justification, since, as remarked in the first chapter, they define the obligatory as a function over intrinsic value. Considerations to do with intrinsic value exhaust the normative content of the consequentialist's principles of obligation and related notions. Some calculation that takes into account intrinsic values as the only distinctively moral component straightforwardly entails the consequentialist's views as to what is permissible, obligatory, impermissible and the like.

As its name suggests, consequentialism tells us to look at the consequences of an action in determining whether an action ought to be performed, ought not to be performed, is right, wrong, obligatory, permissible, etc.; specifically it directs us to look at the intrinsic values and disvalues attaching to those consequences. Consequentialism instructs us to behave in some way or another with respect to these values: for example, different varieties of consequentialism might tell us to maximize value, to minimize disvalue, to increase value, to reduce disvalue, to maintain value or, even, to reduce value. This last version is, obviously, perverse, endorsed only by those who seek to promote the bad at the expense of the good. Each variant expresses obligation as a function over value. Combine the function with the relevant values and an obligation is specified.

Traditional consequentialisms are usually maximizing. They tell us that an action is obligatory if, in comparison to the other actions which are open to an agent to perform, it maximizes the expected quantity of intrinsic value. They tell us, further, that only those actions that maximize expected intrinsic value are permissible. What is obligatory and what is permissible do not diverge, except in the unusual case where two or more actions equally maximize expected value. Consider a well-known traditional consequentialism, namely utilitarianism, which recognizes only pleasure or happiness as intrinsic values. Utilitarianism obliges us to do what maximizes expected pleasure or happiness. Any other action is impermissible, except in those cases in which two or more actions would equally maximize expected pleasure or happiness. In such cases it is obligatory to perform one of the actions and permissible to perform any one.

Utilitarianism is only one instance of a maximizing consequentialism. Other variants will be characterized by the particular intrinsic values they identify. And in all cases of consequentialism, the practical outcome of applying the principle is determined by these intrinsic values. There are plausibly intrinsic values other than pleasure and happiness, including, I would say, natural values. According to maximizing consequentialisms, if failure to preserve wild nature leads to a less than maximal increase in intrinsic value, then there is an obligation to preserve it. Most likely, I would think, such a failure would not merely fail to maximize intrinsic value but would lead to a loss of intrinsic value. In any case, in this example, it is obligatory to preserve the area of wild nature in question and impermissible not to preserve it. It would likewise follow that, if restoring a natural area that has been degraded maximizes expected intrinsic value, then there is an obligation to restore it. In the cases of maximizing and other serious variants of consequentialism, the support for environmentalist policies is strongest where wild nature itself is taken to have intrinsic value. The support will be exceptionally strong where natural values are the only intrinsic values recognized. A normative theory recognizing only natural values as intrinsic values will be controversial to say the least. Support will also be strong where, even though other values are recognized, natural values are taken to be the most important values. Again, the resultant normative theory is likely to be controversial. Support is weakened as the weight accorded to natural values in comparison to human-centred values diminishes.

It is important to remember that natural values may be instrumentally, as well as intrinsically, valuable. They are instrumentally valuable where their promotion leads to the promotion of other intrinsic values. This possibility opens an extra dimension in which consequentialism may generate support for environmentalist actions and policies. This is so even if it is denied that natural values are intrinsic values. Consider, for example, the extensive modifications to the natural environment that human activity has caused and continues to cause. Many of these modifications, such as the build-up of greenhouse gases, the depletion of the ozone layer, deforestation, land degradation, the elimination of species and the pollution of the atmosphere and of rivers and oceans, threaten the well-being, the likely pleasure and happiness, of presently existing and future humans. Such modifications are claimed by some even to render continuing human civilization tenuous if not improbable (Sylvan 1990). Others, although not envisaging such catastrophic outcomes, nevertheless warn of adverse impacts on human well-being and lament the destruction of natural resources which have important economic, scientific, medical, recreational and aesthetic uses. It is also sometimes urged that human well-being is more subtly dependent on the integrity of the natural environment than is suggested by such a list of instrumental values. Thus some have argued that human nature is such that humans can genuinely flourish only if they have frequent contact with wild nature (O'Neill 1993: 22–5; Thompson 1983).

One aspect of consequentialisms requires special emphasis: they permit trade-offs between quantities of the same intrinsic value and also between different intrinsic values. For example, if pleasure is the only intrinsic value, then a maximizing consequentialist would say that it is permissible, indeed obligatory, to reduce one person's pleasure or even to inflict pain, in order to achieve the greatest quantity of pleasure overall. It is easy enough to see how the basic idea is applied in such cases, even if we are doubtful that it is feasible to make sound interpersonal comparisons of experiences of pleasure and pain. A consequentialism which recognizes a plurality of intrinsic values is faced with an even more difficult task in making trade-offs. It has to make judgements not only concerning different quantities of the same value but concerning the comparative significance of quantities of different values. For example, the consequentialist who thinks both pleasure and the acquisition of knowledge are distinct values, has the problem of deciding just how much pleasure should be sacrificed in order to pursue some particular area of knowledge. Such judgements can be made, but they cannot be made according to any simple algorithm. A consequentialism that allows a larger number of intrinsic values becomes very much more complicated.

Because of the possibility of trade-offs across a plurality of values, it is more accurate to say that if something has intrinsic value it is prima facie obligatory not to destroy it rather than obligatory, all things considered. Noting that something is of intrinsic value puts us on a warning not to destroy it or degrade it unless it really is the case that such an action is going to maximize value. In cases where the increase in value is small it probably is not worth the risk of destroying or degrading in order to increase value. It is, moreover, always necessary to ensure that there are no alternative actions that might be performed that would increase value to a greater extent. The maximizing consequentialist would count as impermissible an action which achieved a small increase in value when there was an alternative action that could have been performed and that would have, with equal certainty, delivered a larger increase in value. What is more, consequentialism takes a long-term, not a short-term, view. Establishing that some action is permissible, all things considered, requires a serious attempt to assess its impact on the further future. And this is especially so when the action affects natural ecosystems and processes upon which all life and well-being depends.[1]

When all things are considered, and all relevant values and alternative courses of action are assessed and compared, we might discover that the loss of intrinsic value in one situation produces a significantly greater, offsetting intrinsic value gain in another. Thus the loss of intrinsic value through environmental despoliation could in principle be compensated for by increases of intrinsic value elsewhere. This is precisely the style of argument that is often deployed against green policies. It is often, for instance, claimed that the development of some wild area will result in substantially increased benefits for humans, typically by providing employment opportunities and increased material wealth. In the disingenuous discourse of populist politics, environmentalists might be asked whether they value trees more than jobs. The implication is that environmentalists have their value priorities wrong or that they are ignoring the substantial benefits that flow from environmental pillage. Such arguments typically exaggerate benefits for humans; underestimate adverse environmental impacts; ignore other, alternative means of achieving similar levels of benefits for humans, including alternative social arrangements; massively underestimate the costs of environmental despoliation and degradation to present and future humans and non-humans; and certainly fail to question the way in which benefits and wealth are measured (see Sylvan and Bennett 1994). Furthermore, the magnitude of the value attaching to wild nature is, where it is recognized, too often grossly understated. I shall indicate later some reasons for thinking that the intrinsic value attaching to wild nature is very intense, especially given the increasing rarity of ecosystems that are largely or relatively wild. That the value of wild nature is so intense implies that it is extremely rare that there genuinely is even approximate value compensation for losses of natural value. So an honest application of a maximizing consequentialist normative theory is highly likely to yield environmentalist policies, and where that theory endorses intrinsic natural values, it is certain to yield such policies.

As noted above, a distinctive feature of maximizing consequentialism is that it does not allow any deep distinction between the obligatory and the permissible. Except in cases where alternative actions would equally increase value, maximizing consequentialism says that any permissible action is also obligatory. Some variants of consequentialism, however, allow that actions which are permissible need not be obligatory. So assume that wild nature does have intrinsic value. Now consider improving consequentialism, which says that it is obligatory to act so as to increase, although not necessarily maximize, intrinsic value. Improving consequentialism will support a preservationist policy and a restorationist policy. Preserving wild nature will reduce the likelihood of failing to increase value, and so of acting impermissibly, and restoring wild nature will be a way of increasing value. But perhaps not any increase in value will do. As the earlier discussion indicated, there are cases where some environmental despoliation may lead to an increase in value, but in which some alternative action, not involving despoliation or the same degree of despoliation, would increase value to a greater extent. Improving consequentialism seems to leave open the possibility that the first course of action is permissible. This suggests that improving consequentialism may not be as likely to yield environmentalist policies as maximizing consequentialism. There are several reasons, though, for thinking that the implications of adopting an improving consequentialism are not, from an environmentalist perspective, quite so serious.

First, we should keep in mind that one reason advanced in favour of improving over maximizing consequentialisms is that the latter pitch the requirements of morality too high, that they yield obligations that, according to critics, are so onerous that they could not possibly be considered obligations.[2] Improving consequentialism does not require us to do the best we can but requires us only to improve matters to some degree. It is therefore less onerous. If, however, an agent is willing to make a particular degree of effort to improve things, we might reasonably require that she or he use that degree of effort to produce the best result possible. It is not outrageous to suggest that improving consequentialism be taken to have an efficiency principle built into it. The upshot would be a requirement not merely to ensure that an action improves value, but also to ensure that no alternative action involving the same degree of effort improves value more. An improving consequentialism that recognized intrinsic natural values and took them to be intense would thus strongly favour policies of preserving and restoring natural values.

Second, improving consequentialism, like maximizing consequentialism, takes a long-term view. While the former is less onerous than the latter, it still requires agents to take pains to ensure that their improving actions are improving in the long term. It does not in any way license a short-term view and it certainly does not underwrite the destruction or degradation of value for short-term improvements. Relatedly, improving consequentialism must engage in an honest appraisal of the actual consequences of those actions embarked on in order to improve value.

Third, the very fact that improving consequentialism is less onerous than maximizing consequentialism will likely serve to protect wild nature from destruction or degradation justified in terms of securing greater value. The improving consequentialist may simply think that the calculations involved in deciding whether some despoiling action is justifiable are simply too difficult. She or he might much prefer to improve value in ways in which the result, namely improvement, is clearly and unambiguously demonstrable. The maximizing consequentialist, in contrast, will be looking for every opportunity to maximize value, and thus may be inclined to take too great an interest, as far as environmentalists are concerned, in trading off natural values for allegedly greater values of other kinds.

Another, apparently even less onerous, variant of consequentialism makes it obligatory to act so as to maintain, although not necessarily increase, intrinsic value. Maintaining consequentialism will support a preservationist policy and a restorationist policy. Preserving wild nature will reduce the likelihood of failing to maintain value, and restoring wild nature will be a way both of guarding against, and of compensating for, losses of value. Maintaining consequentialism, because it is less onerous than the other variants of consequentialism so far considered, does not yield obligations to preserve and restore natural values of quite the same strength. We should not, however, think that it yields extremely weak obligations so far as preserving and restoring natural values are concerned, particularly in those variants that recognize intrinsic natural values and take them to be intense. It is not difficult, for instance, to imagine the maintaining consequentialist trying to maintain intrinsic natural value in the face of extensive and recurring acts of despoliation. The actions of others, including actions which impact directly on wild nature, will, all too frequently, depress intrinsic natural value. Restoration of despoiled areas might be an obvious way of compensating for the despoiling acts of others, which acts one is unable to prevent. There would obviously be an abundance of such restoration to be done. And the modifying comments made about improving consequentialism, such as those concerning efficiency of effort, will mostly apply in the case of maintaining consequentialism too.

The three variants of consequentialism that we have considered so far imply differing relationships between value and obligation, although they have in common the view that figuring out our obligations is nothing more than a matter of calculating values and plugging them into some function, such as a maximizing, an improving or a maintaining one. In the second case there is somewhat more looseness involved because improvements may be very large or very small. One of the reasons that we might have, though, for moving from an endorsement of maximizing consequentialism to one of the other variants is the thought, already mentioned, that the former is too stringent, that it directs us to act in ways that we simply know we have no obligation to act. Now the onerousness objection may be pressed even against maintaining consequentialism, since in a world in which the loss of value, particularly natural value, proceeds apace, the requirements of even maintaining consequentialism may prove exceptionally onerous. In the face of this real possibility, some might be tempted to draw a distinction between personal and impersonal consequentialism.

Maintaining consequentialism, for example, can be taken either impersonally, as prescribing that each person ensure that total intrinsic value does not diminish, or, personally, as prescribing that each person ensure that he or she does nothing to diminish total intrinsic value. Some philosophers, however, might contest the distinction between personal and impersonal consequentialism by arguing that omitting to restore intrinsic value to compensate for losses caused by others is an instance of reducing intrinsic value. If this is correct then it is difficult to see how a consequentialist, who recognizes intrinsic natural values, could avoid not only the preservationist obligation but the restorationist obligation as well. This would be a special instance of a general claim to the effect that omissions, or allowings to happen, are to be reconstrued as actions (Glover 1977). If we accept the distinction, then possibly another range of consequentialisms is up for discussion. I do not propose to discuss these possible consequentialisms, partly because I do not accept the distinction upon which they depend. As in the variants already discussed judgements as to intrinsic value directly yield principles of obligation; they directly prescribe and proscribe actions according to some function over intrinsic value.

It is worth making a further point, before moving on to a discussion of views which break the tight connection between value and obligation implied by consequentialisms. The point concerns improving and maintaining versions of consequentialism. Judgements as to intrinsic value will not be motivationally potent only through the application of a principle of obligation. If Jack judges that wild nature has significant intrinsic value, then presumably he would feel some compulsion to act in ways which, strictly speaking, he would count as supererogatory, that is, additional to what he believes is strictly obligatory. Imagine, for instance, that Jack subscribes to maintaining consequentialism. While he thinks that he is not obliged to increase, let alone maximize, value, he is strongly inclined to do much more than he is obliged to do. He exhibits no meanness of spirit, no moralistic minimalism: instead he allows his enthusiasm for natural values to dictate the course of his actions. Given the connection between attributions of intrinsic value and attitudinal states of valuers this would seem natural (Gaus 1990: 253–318). Even the least onerous of the personal variants of consequentialism, conjoined with the judgement that wild nature has intense intrinsic value, provides more than a minimal basis of support for policies of preserving and restoring wild nature. The strength of that support will increase if other variants are adopted, with the strongest support apparently offered by the impersonal maximizing variant.

ENVIRONMENTAL OBLIGATION AND DEONTOLOGIES

Thus far we have been discussing the connections between value and obligation that are afforded by consequentialist normative theories. It is time to consider connections afforded by deontological positions. Deontologies are distinctive in that they construe principles of obligation as something other than functions over intrinsic value. Thus they permit judgements that acts are obligatory independently of attributions of intrinsic value, although they do not necessarily exclude such axiological assessments. Indeed some philosophers argue that axiology reduces to deontology or that intrinsic value reduces to obligation (Chisholm 1978; Ewing 1959: 81–123) According to these philosophers, the claim that something has intrinsic value is reconstrued as the claim that one ought to prefer its existence to its non-existence. More importantly, irrespective of this reductionist view, there is no suggestion here that deontological assessments do not in fact depend, in most instances at least, on assessments of value. In other words, it is likely to be the case that complete deontological assessments require prior axiological assessments.

Deontologies claim that certain kinds of action are obligatory, permissible, impermissible, and so on, in virtue of specific properties of the action that an agent performs or could perform. While the properties in question need not include intrinsic value, they might. Thus it might be claimed that, since some object has intrinsic value, it is obligatory not to destroy it. The property of being destructive of a thing with intrinsic value would here be a wrong-making property. The relevant maxim would be: do not destroy things that have intrinsic value. But the assessment is not made in terms of calculating the loss of intrinsic value associated with the destruction of the object, either considered in itself or traded off against other intrinsic values consequent upon the destructive act. Rather the wrongness of the act can be established without looking beyond the fact that it is an act of destroying something of intrinsic value: there is no summation across resultant values that, through the application of some formula, yields a judgement as to the action's wrongness. So there is no suggestion that one ought to look to the consequences of such acts or that one ought to act in accordance with some function of the intrinsic value of the consequences of the act and that of its alternatives. There is, moreover, no suggestion that it is permissible to destroy a thing of lesser value in order to protect or create a thing of greater value. It may often turn out to be impermissible to act in ways that maximize, improve, or even maintain value, for example, in cases where the only available means of thus acting involves the destruction of something of intrinsic value.

These reflections provide a deontological basis for explaining the wrongness of acts of environmental vandalism: they are wrong because, among other things, they are acts of destroying things which possess natural intrinsic value. It should be emphasized that acts of environmental despoliation will be wrong for additional reasons that a deontologist should also find compelling. For example, such despoliation would wrongfully injure and kill non-humans and wrongfully impose costs and burdens on humans, including future humans. So a deontological view could support a preservationist policy. Indeed the support could be very strong given the general hostility of deontology to trade-offs. The crucial basis of this strong support would be the commitment to the principle that one ought not destroy things, including ecosystems, which have intrinsic natural value and, of course, the view that there are widespread intrinsic natural values.

A deontologist might also accept that it is obligatory to perform acts which restore value lost in violations of the obligation not to destroy things of value. This obligation may be binding not only on those who themselves were active participants in the despoliation, but also on those who have benefited from it. Nor is it completely implausible to suggest that present humans have an obligation to restore value earlier, and presently, lost through the destructive acts of others of their species, irrespective of whether they themselves have benefited from such acts (Sylvan 1994: 73–4). Here the restitutive element is important in maintaining the strictly deontological character of the view: the property of being an act which restores value for which one has some responsibility or from which one has benefited would be a right-making property.[3] These issues are discussed further in the next chapter. The point to note here, though, is that one assumption driving them is an axiological one; namely, that wild nature has intrinsic value. Much, therefore, depends on the ability of one's preferred theory of value to generate normative claims concerning natural values which sustain these kinds of deontological claims.

There is a problem with the deontological approach to environmental interference and intervention just now described, and it connects with a general objection that consequentialists have made against deontologies (Pettit 1991). The problem is that, taken literally, deontologies seem to render impermissible actions which do not really seem impermissible and which may even seem morally required. For example, the degradation of some small area of natural environment such as bulldozing a fire break, may be necessary to ensure the protection of some much more extensive area. If what we value is wild nature, then surely it is permissible to make the fire break; certainly that is so if what we fear is degradation through fire that results from human ignorance, negligence or ill-intent. In such cases the trade-off seems not just permissible but obligatory. Even where the trade-off is between natural values and other values, there will be cases where degradation of natural values will seem permissible. An example might be building a transport link between two population centres. Such a project will involve substantial destruction of natural values, both in the building process and in the fact that the transport corridor is an alien presence in some natural area. Still, there might be a case for it. Or there might be a case for minimal clearing of some flora and minimal disruption of some fauna to construct a dwelling, or for limited mining, or for sustainable forestry practices.

What such examples suggest is that a strict deontology is likely to deliver normative conclusions that are difficult to accept, justifiably. One response is to suggest a mixed ethic, containing both consequentialist and deontological components. Judgments based on these components must somehow be taken into account by moral agents and weighed against one another. If enough of value is at stake, then it may be judged permissible to act in a way that a strict deontology would proscribe. By the same token, the deontological component would act as a serious brake on consequentialist justifications of environmental degradation. In such mixed ethics the onus of proof would be on those who are urging action contrary to the deontological maxims, such as the maxim that we not degrade or destroy natural values. Shifting the onus of proof in this way reduces our susceptibility to the value-maximizing or value-increasing claims made on behalf of environmental despoilers (Sylvan 1994: 60–2). Recall, in this context, the earlier discussion of the requirement that consequentialist assessments be sincere, honest, complete, and involve comparisons of alternatives. Treating the deontological maxim as the default position, which we must be given compelling reasons for giving up, assists in ensuring that consequentialist assessments meet these requirements. Such assistance is bolstered if we add to our mixed ethic a further component to do with the so-called virtue of certain kinds of actions. Let us now consider this component.

VIRTUE, VALUE AND ENVIRONMENTAL OBLIGATION

It is tempting to say that acts of environmental degradation are van-dalistic in some morally pejorative sense. One reason we might say this is that we believe such acts destroy value. Their categorization as vandalistic is a way of alluding to the destruction of value. Moreover, the moral content of the categorization could be exhausted by the fact that the action destroys value. We might think, though, that in saying that an action is vandalistic we are saying more than that it destroys value and that the moral content of the categorization is not exhausted by the fact of value destruction. We might, moreover, think that the unexhausted content is not entirely accounted for by the fact that the environmental vandal acts contrarily to the maxim that pro-hibits the destruction of objects of intrinsic value. In fact we might think that, in condemning acts of environmental destruction and degradation as vandalistic, we are evaluating the motives and charac-ter of those who initiate and participate in such acts. According to this view, to say that people are environmental vandals is, in part, to say that they lack some virtue and exhibit some vice, that they have a defective character. Some have, furthermore, argued that this kind of evaluation of character can take us quite a long way in articulating our horror at environmental vandalism (Hill 1983; Passmore 1975). They believe, moreover, that one virtue of this virtue ethics approach to the evaluation of environmental degradation is that it avoids any controversial suggestion that there are intrinsic natural values. They believe that it provides a way of expressing deeply felt moral senti-ments concerning wild nature, and concerning its destruction by humans, within the framework of human-focused ethic; specifically an ethic that is focused on the appraisal of human character as exem-plifying ideals of excellence or virtues, on the one hand, and defects of character or vices, on the other (Pence 1991). The obligation to preserve, protect and restore natural value is turned into an obligation to cultivate virtue and to pursue ideals of human excellence.[4]

Thus Thomas Hill seeks to show that those who engage in envi-ronmental despoliation display a defect of character that can be condemned in terms of standards of human excellence. Hill's suggestion is that the indifference to the natural world that might dispose someone towards acts of environmental degradation, while not itself a vice, reflects traits which are vices. These could include ignorance, self-importance, lack of self-acceptance, lack of appropriate humility, lack of an aesthetic sense and lack of gratitude (Hill 1983: 222). Similarly, John Passmore speculates that if humans are able to free themselves from the view that nature exists only as something to be used, and to understand it as something also to be enjoyed, then certain notions, expressive of moral defects of character or vices, such as vandalism and philistinism, would seem obviously applicable to human relationships with the natural environment (Passmore 1975: 263). Sagoff likewise links concern for nature with the virtuous life. His view seems to be that we should respect nature as an appropriate expression of gratitude to, and love for, that to which we owe our existence and our happiness (Sagoff 1991). Sagoff, Hill and Passmore seek thus to provide arguments against environmental degradation and for the protection and preservation of the natural environment without attributing to it intrinsic moral value, focusing instead of what virtuous action would require.

The difficulty with this enterprise is giving content to the claim that acts of environmental degradation, exhibiting hubris, ingratitude, philistinism, vandalism or the like, are seriously morally flawed, without also accepting that nature in itself is morally considerable, of value, deserving, worthy of respect or the like. Consider an analogy that Passmore uses to help his claim about vandalism and philistinism with respect to nature (Passmore 1975: 263). He appeals to the extension of the notion of cruelty, a vicious kind of action, to assessments of our treatment of non-human animals. The idea seems to be that a moral notion, which has its central or initial application in the context of relationships between humans, quite naturally extends to human relationships with non-human animals. This extension, however, would seem to be underwritten by the belief that there are certain psychological states that a non-human animal may be in which have negative intrinsic value, such as pain or distress. Understanding that non-humans experience pain and distress is what makes the extension of the notion of cruelty to non-humans so natural. The reason, in other words, that one ought not to be cruel has to do directly with the disvalue that cruel acts bring about. And the reason that cruelty is a vice, a moral defect of character, is that those disposed to cruelty are inappropriately moved by the knowledge of the impact of their actions on non-humans. The notion of cruelty would not get a grip in the absence of the belief that non-humans experience acts of cruelty in a certain way, nor in the absence of the belief that their experiences are not too remote in content from the experiences humans would have if they were similarly treated.

We might ask, then, whether a similar point can be appropriately made concerning the vandalism, philistinism and other alleged moral defects of character that virtue theorists might appeal to in developing an environmental virtue ethic. It is not implausible to suggest that what makes the degradation of wild nature for some trivial, or even serious, purpose vandalistic, is that such degradation involves the destruction of natural value or at least that it involves the destruction of something that belongs to, might be enjoyed by, or used by others. Now it may be difficult to think of actual terrestrial cases that escape these qualifications, but it is possible to think of some hypothetical cases that do. Consider, then, the case in which some distant and insignificant celestial body is destroyed for no good purpose, say as a whim. Assume, too, that no interests of humans or non-humans are adversely affected by this destruction. A strong environmental ethic would condemn such an action (Rolston 1988 and 1994; Sylvan 1990). Is the action vandalistic in more than a metaphorical sense? If there were no natural values, then it is difficult to see why it would be vandalistic. In the absence of natural values, the action would seem no worse than merely pointless, which is hardly a resounding moral condemnation of it. The assessment in terms of virtuous or vicious character seems only to get a purchase if we already accept that there are natural values removed by the destructive act. Hill, in particular, resists this claim; he says that intrinsic value theory is neither helpful nor necessary in environmental ethics (Hill 1984: 369).

Hill thinks it is unhelpful because it fails to represent what is morally salient about acts of despoliation. He denies that what is salient is that such acts reveal a kind of value-blindness. The source of their moral repugnance derives instead, he says, from agents' failure to show care for things about which people should show care. So Hill invokes some ideal of human virtue or excellence of character. Moreover, Hill thinks the attribution of intrinsic value to nature contributes nothing to explaining why nature is something about which people should care. It is true, of course, that the attribution of intrinsic value would be unhelpful unless something is said about the bases of that value. So it will not do merely to assert that the natural environment possesses intrinsic value. Intrinsic moral value is a supervenient property and the literature abounds with suggestions about just which natural environmental properties sustain the moral property. It is the presence of those properties on which intrinsic moral value supervenes that explains why nature is something about which people should care. Later in this chapter some suggestions about the bases of such intrinsic value are defended. The attribution of intrinsic value is a way of expressing the moral salience of these properties. The value-blindness of environmental despoilers consists in their not recognizing the moral salience of these properties and, therefore, the appeal to intrinsic value does turn out to be helpful.

The appeal to intrinsic value is unnecessary, according to Hill, because it is not even needed, let alone helpful, for explaining our normative judgements about environmental degradation. The belief that we should not treat wild nature as a mere resource can be explained more directly by saying that we simply value nature for its own sake. What is involved in valuing something for its own sake is, Hill implies, different from attributing intrinsic value to it. Despoilers of nature may then be condemned because they have not acquired certain attitudes, valuing attitudes towards certain kinds of objects, which we expect virtuous humans to have (Hill 1984: 379). The view that Hill is advocating is reminiscent of one developed in Green (1996), and discussed in the first chapter. There is a distinction, as Hill suggests, between X having intrinsic moral value and X being valued for its own sake. Hill, though, seems to think that the distinction can be maintained only if intrinsic moral value is conceived of as some objective, non-natural property which is utterly independent of the attitudes and preferences of valuers. If this were so, then the intrusion of intrinsic value theory into ethics generally, and not just environmental ethics, could be criticized on the basis of the associated dubious ontology. There is, though, at least one other way of understanding intrinsic value which permits the distinction and which plays an important role in explaining our intuitions, inclinations, sentiments and the like as morally significant. This is the view, defended in the first chapter, that reduces a thing's having intrinsic moral value to a special instance of its being valued for its own sake.

Hill's claims about the superfluity of intrinsic value theory miss the mark. A plausible account of intrinsic moral value, which does not construe it as objective and marks it off from merely, or generically, valuing something for its own sake, permits explanations of the wrongness of environmental degradation in addition to ones couched solely in terms of ideals of human excellence. Accounts of the latter kind are distorting. There is a distinction to be drawn between, on the one hand, ways of treating the natural environment which we regard as admirable, desirable, constitutive of ideals of human excellence, and on the other hand, valuing the natural environment for its own sake in a completely non-instrumental way. In other words, there are at least two distinct sources of value, loosely speaking, relevant to environmental despoliation. There are the natural values which supervene on, but are not identical with, certain natural properties. There are also perfectionist values, for example values concerning ideal or virtuous character, which are undermined by the conduct of the environmental degrader. To emphasize the latter and to disregard the former is to be overly concerned with the human world.

Acts of degradation are appalling, then, for two reasons: first, because they reveal that many human persons do not meet perfectionist standards; and, second, because they remove from the world much that has intrinsic value, that is valuable for its own sake. Similarly we are appalled that there are some people who would think nothing of turning a fine building into a parking lot and we are also appalled that the building, a thing of value, has gone. The two things are distinct. Hill's error is to shift the focus of moral concern too far towards those who degrade and too far from the results of their acts. Appeals to the intrinsic moral value of the natural world shift the normative focus from less than perfect agents to significant features of the natural world. They are also helpful because they articulate part of the unease environmentalists feel in the face of environmental degradation: they emphasize the moral seriousness of certain losses from the world and the moral importance of preserving certain parts of it. Imagine, then, that some past negligent human act unintentionally caused the defoliation of all tropical rainforests. This environmental catastrophe would be appalling, and not just because a source of deep enjoyment is to disappear forever and certainly not because of what the act indicates about human hubris or other defects of character.

The evaluation of character depends on an evaluation of the consequences that actions in accordance with that character are apt to produce. Environmental degradation is genuinely vandalism because it results in loss of value. This is not, however, necessarily to turn considerations to do with character into considerations to do only with the value of the results of actions that particular kinds of character are apt to produce. Even if the acts of those inclined toward environmental vandalism were always thwarted at no cost or simply failed to produce the consequences aimed at by the agent, it might still be a disvalue for there to be such people around. But it would be a disvalue for there to be such people around if what it is that their characters incline them to bring about reduces value, and, in the case of environmental vandalism, reduces natural value.[5]

To be fair to Hill, there is an aspect of his virtue account that is worthy of endorsement. Consider what he says about environmental degradation and gratitude. The idea seems to be that in degrading the natural environment we display defects of character including ingratitude. Hill does not suggest that the object of our ingratitude is the natural environment. No doubt he thinks that only sentient creatures, or maybe only humans, can be objects of ingratitude. However, unless one is ignorant one should understand that we owe our existence and well-being to natural processes. We are the result of natural selection and the natural environment is what fundamentally sustains our well-being; we depend on it for our food, for our water, for the air we breathe, and even for our spiritual enrichment. If we understand these things, and the understandings involved do not necessarily have to be technical or scientific, then that understanding should trigger a mode of relating to wild nature rather like the appropriate mode of relating to those of our own kind to whom we ought to be grateful. The crucial point is that if one has a genuine capacity for appropriately showing gratitude, then, although strictly speaking wild nature is not a proper object of gratitude, one will seemingly treat wild nature with gratitude; in particular, one will not readily destroy or degrade it and one will be inclined to protect it and restore it. Now the understanding, or absence of ignorance, to which Hill's suggestion appeals, is really an understanding of aspects of nature that underpin its intrinsic value. Understanding the processes whereby the natural world has developed, evolved and unfolded, and understanding our own dependency on it as well as the pervasiveness and insidiousness of our impacts on it, is to understand features such as complexity, diversity and others mentioned earlier, which underwrite an informed aesthetic response to it, which in turn underwrites the attribution of intrinsic value. And it is difficult to comprehend how someone with this understanding could readily degrade or destroy wild nature: his or her insensitivity to natural value is a defect of character. It is appropriate now to consider the bases of environmental or natural value.

NATURALNESS AND OTHER BASES OF NATURAL VALUE

The intrinsic value that wild nature exemplifies supervenes on other of its properties. Thus environmental ethicists have drawn attention, variously, to its beauty, diversity, richness, integrity, interconnected-ness, variety, complexity, harmony, grandeur, intricacy and autonomy. Doubtless these properties do provide bases for natural values, and we shall return to some of them presently. There is, however, another property which warrants most attention, because it seems, to me at least, the key to the explanation of nature's intrinsic value. It is the property of being naturally evolved or the property of naturalness. At first glance this seems somewhat unilluminating and even circular: it seems to say that nature has intrinsic value because it is natural (Fairweather *et al.* 1994). There is more to the claim, so it transpires, than just this, but even if this were all there were to it, it would not follow that it was a hollow or uninteresting claim. Naturalness could well be a basis for value. It could be a brute fact about our attitudinal frameworks that it is on account of its naturalness that nature has value: the plain fact of naturalness could be what engages our prefer-ence structure. At some point in the process of uncovering bases of value there will be a stopping point, beyond which nothing more can be said by way of accounting for the presence of value. Appeal to the property of being natural might be such a stopping point. But more can, I think, be said.

Consider Bernard Williams's view that it is nature's otherness, its separateness and distinctness from creatures such as ourselves, who to a large extent, are produced and produce, within culture and tech-nology, that underwrites its intrinsic value (Williams 1992: 65). It is, on Williams's view, our comprehension of nature's otherness that sparks and sustains the valuing response. Wild nature is raw, says Williams, in that it is relatively unshaped by, relatively unmarked by, human intentions and human design. What we see in nature that impresses us and moves us is something that is there independently of the actions of creatures of our kind. While it is true that we ourselves are the result, ultimately, of natural processes, our own projects are often at loggerheads with nature's projects. And our projects are intentional in a way that nature's are not (Dennett 1987). Perhaps this is significant. When we view nature we do not find unordered chaos. We find patterns, dynamic relationships and processes, shapes that please us and inspire us, but these features are there indepen-dently of the actions of any creatures such as ourselves. What we see is ordered, although not the result of a plan; it is not an artefact. As Stan Godlovitch puts it, nature is 'primordially non-artifactual' (Godlovitch 1994: 18).

The otherness of nature as a whole, and in many of its parts, has to do with the absence of intentionality, the absence of contrived design (Brennan 1984). This absence of intentionality is consistent with the presence in nature of creatures with varying degrees of intentionality. Many creatures have evolved that act intentionally, purposefully, and whose actions shape nature. Their intentionality, however, is not played out through a framework of culture and technology as is the case with human agents. The otherness of nature, which underpins its value, stands in opposition to the human world of culture and technology. I shall say more later about the distinctiveness of nature, and try to give more content to the view that it is, in some deep sense, other. For the moment, let us accept the somewhat mystical suggestion concerning nature's otherness and ask whether it could plausibly provide the key to nature's value.[6]

Williams suggests one reason why it might not provide the key, for, as he implies, the sense of nature's otherness could engender pervasive and overwhelming fear (Williams 1992: 66–8). Williams's assumption seems to be that if something caused pervasive and overwhelming fear, then it would not be something of value. This might not be exactly true; that would seem to depend on whether the pervasive and overwhelming fear would crowd out any other response, such as the valuing response, whenever a valuer turned her or his mind to a contemplation of nature. It may be that fear of nature would dictate a negative evaluative response, perhaps like the response a valuer might have to some human agent who has committed numerous loathsome actions. It is possible, though, that something greatly feared might be valued, as evident in some theistic belief systems in which divine beings are both feared and valued. Even where the fear is, in Williams's terms, pervasive and overwhelming, there might be sufficient space for a positive valuing response. In the first chapter it was argued that intrinsic value is linked to considered evaluation, rather than to some immediate raw response. It is possible then, that in periods of calm reflection, one could positively value that which, when one were confronted by it, one would response to with pervasive fear. It is possible that one might relish the fact that an object of evaluation produced such fear. Still, Williams's point suggests that nature's otherness is not the unassisted or unsupplemented basis for nature's value.

The sense of otherness, an otherness that naturally evolves or comes into being, perhaps needs to be combined with another element in order to produce the valuing response, namely an appreciation of nature's aesthetic value. This aesthetic aspect of nature is manifested through properties such as diversity, stability, complexity, beauty, grandeur, subtlety, harmony, integrity, creativity, organization, power, intricacy, elegance and richness. And these are properties that ecology can assist us to perceive. Ecology invites, and assists, us to look beyond what might initially strike us in our observations of the natural and to notice relationships and qualities hitherto unnoticed. But it is not the mere fact of nature's aesthetic value that provides the basis for nature's intrinsic moral value. After all, there is much outside nature that has aesthetic worth, such as works of art produced by humans, but I hesitate to say that they have intrinsic moral value.

Nature's aesthetic value is a basis for nature's intrinsic value because the aesthetic value in question arises independently of intentional design, without purposive intervention. Indeed I endorse a view that Allen Carlson calls 'positive aesthetics'; namely, the view that all natural objects have aesthetic value (Carlson 1984). Ecology, as well as other sciences, helps us to comprehend the evolutionary and other natural processes that have led to natural organization, complexity, diversity and so on (Rolston 1995; Routley 1975). Thus ecology, as well as other natural sciences, contributes to the elimination of that fear of the natural that derives from bewilderment and the absence of understanding, and ecology, as well as other sciences, opens our senses and our minds to nature's distinctive aesthetic features. It is such features that are, in the first instance, the basis of nature's aesthetic value, although it needs to be stressed that nature's distinctive aesthetic value also derives from the fact that nature's organizational complexity is undesigned, unintentional.

The fact that nature's organizational complexity arises in the absence of intention and design itself contributes crucially to nature's aesthetic value. Moreover, this fact transforms the aesthetic value in question into the kind of aesthetic value that gives rise to moral value. The claim that there is such a transformation is fundamental to the advocacy of natural values, since in many contexts, outside the natural, aesthetic value does not yield intrinsic moral value. We might falsely infer from the fact that there is no general link between aesthetic value and intrinsic moral value that nature's aesthetic value could not be a basis for its moral value. Furthermore, the fact that non-natural aesthetic value generally is not a basis for intrinsic moral value weakens any attempted defence of the degradation of nature in terms of its usefulness in the creation of works of art and other valued, although not intrinsically valuable, cultural objects. Let us now examine the reasons for thinking that natural aesthetic value is indeed a basis for intrinsic moral value. A second important issue that emerges from the discussion above, namely the basis for the distinction between the natural and the non-natural, is dealt with in the final chapter.

AESTHETIC VALUE AND INTRINSIC VALUE

It is not difficult to accept that wild nature may be evaluated in aesthetic terms (Carlson 1992). Assuming that it can be thus evaluated, then clearly we might argue that it is generally impermissible to degrade nature because of the resultant loss of aesthetic value. Such an argument would have considerable force, certainly to the extent that the degradation of nature would reduce opportunities for aesthetic pleasure and aesthetic contemplation. Would the argument have force independently of such an appeal to human aesthetic interests? It would, provided that some connection could be established between certain aesthetic categories and moral categories. For example, if we thought that objects that are of positive aesthetic value are, in virtue of that fact, also of positive intrinsic moral value, then there would be a clear inference from the recognition that nature has aesthetic value to the conclusion that it is generally impermissible to degrade it. As it happens, I think that nature's aesthetic value does provide a basis for its intrinsic moral value, although, as I have already indicated, I do not think that aesthetic value generally is linked in this way to intrinsic moral value. I want, therefore, to consider an argument in favour of the general claim, an argument that suggests that the general claim is false, and then an argument for the special claim that natural aesthetic value is nevertheless a basis for intrinsic moral value.

Let us begin with an imaginary example discussed by Stanley Benn (Benn 1977: 17–19). The example is supposed to move us to take seriously the suggestion of a direct link between aesthetic and moral value. Benn begins by pointing out that at least part of our concern for the protection and preservation of works of art is that they give considerable aesthetic pleasure to humans who experience and contemplate them. While conceding that human-centred considerations might exhaust all of the moral reasons we might have for endorsing protection and preservation of such works and for abhorring degradation and destruction of them, Benn claims that it is at least plausible that the works have value in themselves which would make their destruction, certainly their wanton destruction or destruction for trivial reasons, wrong. In order to persuade us of the plausibility of this view, he asks us to imagine that our species is going to be destroyed in the very near future, along with some great works of art. Perhaps the last surviving human person destroys them on a whim just before he or she dies, or perhaps arranges matters so that they are destroyed in an explosion soon after his or her death. Benn suggests that, if we think about this scenario, we shall conclude that, while the extinction of our species would be unwelcome to say the least, the destruction of the works of art is a reason for additional regret. If, however, their value was entirely explained in terms of their capacity actually to satisfy human interests, then their destruction should be a matter of indifference, not the reason for additional regret that it seems to be. What supposedly underpins the additional regret is the thought that works of art are intrinsically valuable because they exemplify certain aesthetic excellences. The works of art are themselves directly valuable, or so it seems to Benn, having value over and above the value of the aesthetic pleasures they might engender. While the standards in terms of which such works excel depend on such things as human tastes, preferences, attitudes and the like, works of art objectively either do or do not excel. Whether or not some work counts as valuable relative to some largely culturally determined standard is an objective matter. Thinking that a work is valuable, according to the standard, does not make it so. Conversely, thinking that a work is not valuable according to the standard, does not make it not so. Benn's suggestion implies that aesthetic value is a basis for intrinsic value, understood in terms of the theory developed in the first chapter, although Benn himself might not necessarily see it in these terms.

Benn makes an analogous suggestion with regard to the value of the natural environment. In both the destruction of the work of art and in the despoliation of the natural environment what is bad-making is the destruction of an entity which exhibits a complex structural harmony and its replacement by a comparatively unstructured heap lacking the relevant excellences (Benn 1977: 21). While Benn says little about the criteria that define environmental excellence, it is reasonable to think that he has in mind the sorts of things mentioned earlier, such as complexity, richness, stability, diversity, connectedness, variety, subtlety, intricacy, ingenuity (in some suitably non-intentional sense), fragility and harmony, as well as properties that are less anchored in the intellectual representations of the environmental sciences, such as grandeur, magnificence, splendour, beauty, awesomeness. Take the case of a species extinction that might

63

soon be brought about by the actions of humans, say the extinction of the Indian tiger. How or why, on Benn's view, would this constitute a loss of value, and so be impermissible? It would constitute a loss of value in that it diminished the excellence-sustaining complexity, stability, etc. of the ecosystems of which the tiger is part. It would also be a loss of value in that it destroys individual tigers that exhibit the kinds of complexity, or other aesthetically relevant properties, that might lead us to regard them as natural, aesthetic objects.

Benn ties his argument to the success of his last person thought-experiment. So, let us pause for a moment and think about how that thought experiment is supposed to work. It, and others like it, might function in at least two ways. First, they might draw attention to discrepancies between our real moral psychology and the principles that we believe represent that psychology. Thus Benn's thought-experiment might bring us to see that we in fact have a particular moral belief concerning the destruction of works of art that is not accounted for in our systematized normative theory, that is, by the principles that we think describe or encapsulate our normative views. Second, they might generate changes in, or reshape, our moral psychology, thereby producing such discrepancies. The examples would, in this case, play something like an educative or developmental role. They would be an invitation to open ourselves to a new type of positive moral evaluation. Either way, Benn seeks to demonstrate that an adequate representation of our, perhaps dynamic, moral psychology requires the attribution of intrinsic moral value to works of art possessing aesthetic excellence, which value might underwrite deontic principles prohibiting destruction of such works. The example is, of course, intended to prepare the way for similar claims concerning the degradation of the natural environment. A similar argument, he suggests, might secure the same conclusion concerning the value of wild nature.

It is useful to summarize the structure of Benn's argument. He argues for the intrinsic value of aesthetic objects, tries to make the case for either an analogy between aesthetic objects and natural items or for the view that natural items are aesthetic objects, and concludes that natural objects, including overlapping ecosystems, arguably have intrinsic value. Thus he begins by offering a thought-experiment that he thinks might move us to accept that it would be prima facie wrong to destroy works of art. We are then offered an explanation of this which turns on linking aesthetic value with intrinsic moral value. The idea is that works of art possess intrinsic moral value in virtue of possessing aesthetic value. Benn's next move is to draw attention to significant features which works of art and wild nature have in common. He offers, in effect, an argument for viewing the natural environment, or parts of it, as aesthetic objects. We are then invited to respond evaluatively to the prospect of environmental despoliation in the way that, it is hoped, we earlier responded to the prospect of the destruction of works of art. Now the effectiveness of Benn's argument would seem to depend on our acceptance of the destruction of aesthetic objects, as depicted in the thought-experiment, as wrong because of the resultant loss of intrinsic value. It is only if we accept this that the overall argument becomes compelling as well as coherent. Furthermore, winning acceptance of this conclusion seems bound to involve describing and emphasizing what Benn takes to be the salient features of it and perhaps deploying similarly focused thought-experiments. No doubt many will be unmoved, regarding Benn's preferred view as at best coherent, although not compelling.

One such sceptic is Peter Singer. As Singer observes, Benn thinks the case for the intrinsic value of wild nature is more controversial than the case for the intrinsic value of works of art. But, Singer thinks, the allegedly less controversial case is, if one thinks about it carefully, very controversial. Singer thinks that a careful consideration of Benn's example, and others like it, will not support the conclusion that works of art have intrinsic value. He thinks that the value they have ultimately has to do with the interests of those who might appreciate and enjoy them. Thus he suggests that there would be nothing wrong with the last sentient being, out of boredom, destroying the Louvre and its contents (Singer 1979). There are familiar ways in which Singer's claims might be strengthened. For example, it might be argued that those who share Benn's view are not responding to the real question at issue, that they fail to take sufficient account of the fact that there will be literally no one around after the destruction of the works of art, and so no one who could possibly be deprived of any positive experience by their destruction. In actual cases where works of art are destroyed, the interests of humans are harmed and, arguably, it is the residue of sentiments based on this fact that produces the judgement in the last person case. It might also be argued that those sympathetic to Benn's position have failed to distinguish between two distinct things: first, the negative instrumental value that might attach to some envisaged future state of affairs in virtue of the present affective states, possessing negative intrinsic value, which present contemplation of the future state engenders; and, second, the negative intrinsic value attaching to possible future states considered in themselves. Singer would suggest that while the future state, or at least the contemplation of it, could certainly have negative instrumental value, it could not include negative intrinsic value. He would say that only certain psychological states of sentient creatures could possess negative intrinsic value. It might even be urged, furthermore, that Singer's view is the simpler, since it attributes intrinsic value to fewer kinds of things than does Benn's whilst explaining the bulk of our normative beliefs. And simplicity combined with that degree of explanatory power might persuade some that Singer's response is adequate.

There are two lines of reply to Singer's argument, that those sympathetic to Benn's reading of the last person example could pursue. The first is to reassert the view that it is the works of art themselves that have intrinsic moral value. So someone might insist that her or his response to Benn's example is a genuine response, that she or he has taken note of the suggestion that the response results from some misunderstanding of the example under consideration and that she or he has made the relevant allowances, and, further, that she or he has made the response the object of careful scrutiny. While it is certainly possible that people can be mistaken about their moral psychology or that they can be deceived about the basis of their moral judgements, the point cuts both ways. One might not implausibly suggest, against Singer and similar sceptics, that a desire for simplicity in moral theories, or a prior commitment to a certain variant of utilitarianism, may obscure elements of one's own moral psychology that one might otherwise notice. When Singer suggests that there would be nothing wrong with the last person destroying the Louvre and its contents, those sympathetic to Benn's evaluation might reasonably say that Singer has failed to notice that he does, in his heart, think the works of art in question have intrinsic, and not merely instrumental, value. And certainly they can, with justification, make this claim of themselves. Really all that Singer can do at this point in the debate is dispute the authenticity of the alleged response, and endorse an alternative.

The second line of reply against the sceptics is to explicate the function of the works of art analogy on which Benn's argument for the value of wild nature seems to turn and which is the initial object of Singer's criticisms. Benn first of all seeks to establish that it would be wrong to destroy some works of art in a last person case because some works of art satisfy criteria of excellence, and so have intrinsic value. He then suggests that the natural environment might similarly satisfy criteria of excellence, and so possess intrinsic value, and that it would similarly be wrong to degrade it. Now it is possible to concede that Singer is correct in claiming that artefacts do not possess intrinsic moral value in virtue of possessing aesthetic value and yet to hold that the natural environment possesses intrinsic value in virtue of possessing aesthetic value. In fact I think this is the correct view, since I am persuaded by Singer's discussion of Benn's last person case. But I think that if the last person were to set about destroying natural objects which possess aesthetic value, then she or he would indeed be destroying things of immense intrinsic value and that one basis for that intrinsic value is aesthetic value. I regard Benn's last person argument as a lever, that, once it has been used, may be discarded. His example reminds us that the natural environment can satisfy standards of excellence similarly to the way in which works of art can satisfy standards of excellence. Moreover, his discussion of the example suggests a form of argument that could be used to secure the view that wild nature has intrinsic value in virtue of its aesthetic value. We see how the argument is supposed to go in the case of artefacts, realize that it doesn't in fact succeed, but see that a variant of it succeeds in a different context. It is pertinent to invoke here the range of last person examples developed by Richard Routley and Val Routley (Routley and Routley 1980a: 121–3). The general idea is that some person, knowing that he or she is the last surviving person and in fact the last surviving sentient being, acts to ensure the destruction of the earth and its remaining ecosystems and landscapes after her or his demise. No bad consequences follow for humans nor for other sentient creatures since they will be, inevitably let us say, extinct. We are invited nevertheless to judge that the last person has done something wrong and that an appropriate explanation of this judgement is that intrinsic moral value attaches to the earth and its remaining ecosystems and landscapes.

Of course if we are to take this second response to Singer, then we need to specify some general feature of the natural environment that differentiates it from those aesthetic objects which are artefacts and that plausibly supports the view that it has value independently of the aesthetic pleasure it gives. Possession of aesthetic value is thus not by itself sufficient for possession of intrinsic moral value. However, in conjunction with some differentiating property it may be sufficient, and so it might be argued that if something can satisfy standards of aesthetic excellence, then, if it possesses some other significant property, it possesses intrinsic moral value. And of course, the obvious differentiating property is the property of being naturally evolved. The natural environment, although an aesthetic object, is literally a natural object, a product of evolutionary, geomorphological and other natural processes, whereas those aesthetic objects which feature in Benn's thought-experiment are artefacts, products of intention and design. The idea is that the natural environment has a certain autonomy and independence from humans which is not shared by artefacts and which is a determinant of the kind of value that it has. The distinction is represented illuminatingly by Carlson as the contrast between what is discovered and what is created (Carlson 1984: 31–3). Nature, unlike art, has a life of its own, independent of human purposes; it is autonomous in a way that artefacts, essentially shaped and controlled by human purposes, intentions and design is not. The fact that nature's projects are not intentional, that they are not the products of planning or design, gives its aesthetic properties a special characteristic not possessed by the aesthetic properties of artefacts. Humans create artefacts and create their value, and the value of those artefacts disappears when humans disappear. This is not so, however, with nature's aesthetic value. And that it is enduring provides the differentiation that allows us to say that natural aesthetic value is a basis for intrinsic moral value, whereas the aesthetic value of artefacts is not.

There are two qualifications that perhaps need to be made. For one thing, works of art could have instrumental value after all humans have ceased exist. The instrumental value possessed by works of art might extend beyond their capacity to serve human interests. Thus a piece of sculpture might provide a convenient nesting place for a bird. Perhaps more interestingly, as indicated earlier, the continued existence of particular works of art might be components of states of affairs that people no longer existing desired would exist after their demise. If we think that such objective, as opposed to felt or experienced, satisfaction of desires has intrinsic value, then works of art could continue to have instrumental value, in a way that connects with human interests, even after all humans have ceased to exist.

It should also be said that even someone who thought works of art had intrinsic value could endorse the view that that intrinsic value ceases to be exemplified when humans no longer exist, although the works of art themselves continue to exist. A possible view is that the aesthetic properties of artefacts are not sufficient for the intrinsic moral value of artefacts, and that an additional condition must be met. The additional condition is that the works must be such that humans will in fact enjoy and appreciate them. According to this view the fact that the works of art have instrumental value, here contributing to enjoyment, is a necessary, although not sufficient, condition of their having intrinsic value. When it is conjoined with the fact that certain standards of aesthetic excellence are exemplified, then the fact of their instrumental value yields intrinsic value. Admittedly this view is quirky. I mention it simply to indicate how someone who thought works of art have intrinsic value, in some circumstances, could agree with Singer's final assessment of Benn's argument.

There is a fundamental objection to the view that nature's aesthetic properties are a basis for natural intrinsic value, which requires comment. This objection, alluded to earlier, pursues the line that aesthetic properties are simply not the kinds of things that could have intrinsic moral value, that they are inappropriate objects of moral evaluation and that the evaluative mode appropriate to nature is purely nonmoral. Some who are sceptical of Benn's last person argument no doubt have something like this in mind. They could put their view by saying that the proper mode of environmental evaluation is aesthetic not ethical (Godlovitch 1994; Lynch 1996). Indeed they might even suggest that it is nonsensical, meaningless or incoherent to suggest that the non-sentient parts of wild nature, such as landscapes, forests, rock formations, are objects for moral evaluation or objects of moral consideration. It is important, though, to see that advocates of this view, which we might call 'the category mistake view', might still want to say that nature has intrinsic aesthetic value which constitutes a reason for protecting and preserving it. They concede, in other words, that the value of nature is not merely instrumental, consisting in something more than instrumental value deriving from the aesthetic pleasures it provides for humans. The thought here seems to be that nature has intrinsic aesthetic value that demands a nonmoral valuing of nature for its own sake. This intrinsic aesthetic value provides a compelling reason and powerful motivation for preserving wild nature. Importantly, though, it is claimed that the value in question is not moral value, that the relevant valuing response is not a valuing response of the moral kind.

It is difficult, though, to see why intrinsic aesthetic value provides a strong reason for condemning Benn's last person or the Routleys' last people (Godlovitch 1989: 177–9 and 1994: 16). Certainly it might provide a basis for our saying that we do not like what they are proposing to do and for establishing that the attitude of disapproval involved is anything but trivial. Certainly, their future actions thwart our preferences or desires concerning the state of things after our own demise. And, arguably, this objective, or unexperienced, thwarting of our desires is intrinsically bad. Maybe in Benn's example this is indeed all that can be said. However in the case of the destruction of natural aesthetic value, a rather stronger condemnation is elicited. This stronger condemnation, moreover, needs to focus on the destruction of nature and the direct intrinsic moral disvalue of that destruction, as against focusing merely on the disvalue of thwarted human desires.

The horror that I feel at the destruction of natural value seems to me to be a genuinely moral horror. What is proposed is not merely something that I do not like or even something that I intensely dislike, nor is it something that merely reduces the amount or degree of the intrinsic aesthetic value of the world. Rather it is something that I think is deeply wrong precisely because I think it would clearly drain intrinsic moral value from the world. In defence of the view that intrinsic moral value, and not merely intrinsic aesthetic value, is at issue, it is enough to refer to the account of intrinsic value developed in the first chapter. It is clear to me that the preferences I have concerning the destruction of natural value meet the requirements for sustaining a certain view about one basis for intrinsic value, namely, that intrinsic value supervenes on natural aesthetic value. Hesitation in endorsing such a view is caused, I think, from a human chauvinism that is reluctant to see moral value outside the domain of human experiences, feelings, character and so on, or from a more liberal animal chauvinism that is reluctant to see value outside the domain of the interests, experiences, feelings and so on, of sentient creatures. Thus Godlovitch cites, as the reason why non-sentient nature has no intrinsic moral value, the fact that nature has no point of view (Godlovitch 1994: 19). His thought seems to be that an action is apt for moral evaluation only if it impacts upon something that has a point of view from which the impact in some sense matters. The sense in question seems, for Godlovitch, to be tied to the possibility of experience. What matters, in the sense relevant to morality, is how things seem to individuals with at least a minimal capacity for experience.

But this is only a normative claim; it is not properly a claim about the conceptual boundaries of intrinsic value. The normative claim in question is the reflection, according to the account of intrinsic value advanced in the first chapter, of a particular valuer's attitudinal framework, according to which adverse impacts on the interests of, broadly defined, others, are at least prima-facie evidence of negative intrinsic value. The point of view that is relevant to defining the limits of what could have intrinsic value is the valuer's point of view. As a matter of fact, most human valuers are inclined to take into account how things seem from the varied points of view of others, including humans, animals and maybe even plants (Elliot 1978; Feinberg 1974). The initial valuer's attitudinal framework may, however, be such that intrinsic value for that valuer, and recall that intrinsic value did turn out to be relative, is not defined only in terms of how things seem from some or other point of view. What has intrinsic value for that valuer may well include the condition of, or the treatment of, objects that entirely lack, or do not contain anything with, a point of view, such as landscapes devoid of sentient or even goal-directed organisms. While the meta-ethical view endorsed in the first chapter is a variant of the view that there are no values without valuers, there is no entailment that all the values that exist are directly constituted by the subjective states of the kinds of organism that might conceivably be valuers, even of the most rudimentary kind.

I suppose that supporters of the Godlovitch view could simply stipulate that the boundary of intrinsic moral value falls where they claim. But this would be unreasonable if, as I think is the case, the structure of the allegedly nonmoral evaluations is similar to the structure of undeniably moral evaluations. Allowing the objects of the evaluations rather than their structure to call the tune is unjustifiably to blur the distinction between normative ethics and meta-ethics. Likewise if supporters of the Godlovitch view appeal to the way in which the notions of intrinsic moral value and intrinsic aesthetic value are typically deployed, there may well be unjustifiable blurring. The resultant conclusion about the mode of intrinsic-value nature would have been possibly driven by habit and normative prejudice.[7]

A positive aesthetic response to nature is entirely appropriate and desirable but such a response ought also to provide the basis for a positive moral response. Indeed, if we endorse the theory of intrinsic value proposed in the first chapter, the line between intrinsic aesthetic value and intrinsic moral value may well be blurred. It will be blurred to the extent that the characterization of the aesthetic attitudes that provide the basis for something's having intrinsic aesthetic value replicates or approximately replicates the characterization of those attitudes that provide the basis for something's having intrinsic moral value. One thing to keep in mind when thinking about this issue is the important distinction between modes of intrinsic value and the various sets of properties on which intrinsic value supervenes. We should beware of confusing varieties of bases of intrinsic value with varieties of intrinsic value. In other words, it does not follow from the fact that there are different sets, or types of sets, of value-adding properties, that there are several, mutually exclusive, notions of intrinsic value.

To say that nature or its components have intrinsic aesthetic value must be to say that they have aesthetic value considered in themselves, in virtue of their own properties, including such things as balance, harmony, tension, intricacy and beauty. These are some of the properties which provide the varying base sets on which the property of being intrinsically aesthetically valuable supervenes. These properties, moreover, could move us to the view that there is value in the objects exemplifying them continuing to exist, irrespective of whether they either have provided, or will continue to provide, humans with aesthetic pleasure. Imagine that we are so moved. This begins to look a lot like a moral attitude, an attitude concerning that which adds to the value of the world. Maybe some people are able to detect a sharp, exclusive difference between the aesthetic and the moral in this context. I am sure, though, that I cannot. And we must be wary here of allowing our actual normative views to call the tune concerning what could be of intrinsic moral value. Conjoined with the property of naturalness, intrinsic aesthetic value does begin to look normatively compelling as a basis for intrinsic moral value, rather than some quite separate category of intrinsic aesthetic value. It should thus be no surprise that aesthetic categories and concepts feature so centrally in the articulation of environmental ethics. Indeed this is a characteristic of the next chapter, in which the idea of faking nature, understood as not too dissimilar to faking works of art, is used to explore issues concerning natural intrinsic value and environmental obligation.

Before moving on, there is a final suggestion I would like to make concerning natural aesthetic value, namely that it is absolutely value-adding. To claim that a property is absolutely value-adding is to claim that its exemplification in some state of affairs makes that state of affairs better than any state of affairs in which it is not exemplified (Chisholm 1986: 93–4). So, if a property is absolutely value-adding, its non-exemplification cannot be compensated for by the exemplification of any other value-adding properties. This entails that the extinction of natural aesthetic value cannot be compensated for by any resultant intrinsic values such as those associated with human states, such as pleasure, or human achievements, such as high culture or knowledge. The claim that natural aesthetic value is absolutely value-adding needs to be carefully framed. The claim is not that the existence of any quantity at all of natural aesthetic value is absolutely value-adding. If this is the claim, then the depletion of wild nature might be thought not, in itself, to result in a loss of value. After all, it could be said that if some quantity of wild nature remained, then the necessary devaluation, which would result from the elimination of an absolutely value-adding property, would not occur. Instead, the claim must be framed in a way that allows the judgement that the necessary devaluations are produced to be made well before the point at which wild nature is eliminated or even much reduced. The claim is that, beyond a certain point, the elimination of any quantity of natural aesthetic value entails a transition from a more valuable state of affairs to a less valuable one no matter what else happens; it entails a loss of value, all things considered.

The interesting question concerns the point at which the entailed loss cuts in. Maybe it cuts in at the earliest possible point, so that any loss of natural aesthetic value entails a loss of value all things considered. Most people would find this view grossly counter-intuitive, since it entails that human civilization is necessarily value-depleting, depending as it does on the destruction of considerable natural aesthetic value. Myself, I find this view somewhat appealing. Another possibility is that the loss-entailing phenomenon cuts in rather later, when some large proportion of natural aesthetic value has been lost from the world. The thought here is that there is some vague or blurred threshold at which natural aesthetic value becomes absolutely value-adding. A perhaps similar idea is involved in the claim that value increases in something of a quantum leap when a species becomes endangered. Species loss to a certain point involves, so the suggestion might run, small incremental losses of value, but after a certain blurred point the loss of value associated with each further species member loss surges. While there is an unsettling arbitrariness in this view of natural aesthetic value as absolutely value-adding, it is not implausible to suggest that we have long passed the cut-in point.[8]

3

FAKING NATURE

THE REPLACEMENT THESIS AND THE RESTORATION PROPOSAL

The issues to be discussed in this chapter are best introduced through an example. Let us consider, then, the case of a mining company wanting to mine an ore-body using the open pit method. The pursuit of this project would devastate the surface ecology across a significant area and it would completely disrupt natural landforms. Understandably, environmentalists are concerned about the violent damage such mining will do. Individual creatures will suffer through injury, death and dislocation. Species may be threatened or rendered extinct. Geological formations will be destroyed and entire ecologies will be massively disrupted. There would, moreover, be adverse environmental impacts at some distance from the obviously disrupted site. For example, there could be changes to water flows, erosion patterns, rates of siltation in waterways and migration of fauna, to mention just a few.

The environmentalists are concerned that mining will destroy certain natural values associated with the surface ecology, which, they say, has hitherto been undisturbed by humans. Spokespeople for the mining company agree, perhaps surprisingly, that the mining process will extensively destroy natural values. They accept that if those values were indeed to be permanently lost, then the case against mining would be compelling and that it should not proceed. Indeed they do not even attempt to justify the immense disvalue that mining would produce by pointing to compensating benefits elsewhere. At this point there is, for example, no upbeat talk of job creation or of generally improving the quality of life for humans. Apparently the mining company agrees that there are no trade-offs of

74

values secured through mining that would compensate for the natural values lost.

Given this agreement, the environmentalists might think that their case is secure. They would be wrong: the spokespeople for the mining company, it transpires, do have an argument in favour of mining. They claim that those natural values that would be destroyed in mining can in principle be fully restored. The values are, they say, values that can be replaced as opposed to merely compensated for by the securing of different values. While it is true that restoration is a kind of compensation, in that the replacement of lost values allegedly compensates for the fact of their earlier loss, there is no suggestion that the compensation involves trading-off one kind of value for another, such as trading-off natural values for economic values. The mining company guarantees, moreover, to in fact restore the, temporarily, lost natural values. The spokespeople promise that the company will, once the relevant minerals are recovered, rehabilitate the mine site, re-create the original surface ecology and so, they claim, restore all natural values destroyed by the mining. Their argument is that because natural value can and will be restored, the case against mining is weak. They now support this claim with an account of the various economic benefits that will accrue to humans, at least presently existing ones, if the mining goes ahead. Once the restoration of natural values is guaranteed, the economic values become decisive. Or so their argument goes.

It is easy to imagine variants of this argument that seek to justify and defend various kinds of environmental despoliation. One famous example from the Australian context concerns sandmining on Fraser Island, a large and forested sand island off the coast of southern Queensland. Thus the Australian Deputy Prime Minister at the time, Doug Anthony, suggested that sandmining on Fraser Island could be resumed without controversy once 'the community becomes more informed and more enlightened as to what reclamation work is being carried out by mining companies' (Mosley 1980: 1). The implication of the remark was that the natural values about which environmentalists were concerned would not be irretrievably lost through mining, that they could be, in principle and in fact, replaced. Similar arguments are put by those engaged in destructive forestry practices, who attempt to deflect criticisms by environmentalists by emphasizing their replanting and regeneration activities and clothing these suggestions in the rhetoric of sustainable forestry (Katz 1992a; Maser 1988). In all of these cases the claim is that destruction of natural areas is permissible, because the value lost can be, and will be, restored. And usually this crucial claim is supplemented with an additional claim about improved well-being for humans.

This style of argument has some initial appeal, for it recognizes that there are natural values, values that directly emerge from or are associated with the intrinsic characteristics of wild areas, and that do not derive from the uses to which such areas might be put or from the benefits or pleasures they might provide for humans. In other words, the argument concedes a core claim of environmentalism, namely, that wild nature has intrinsic value. It also accepts that the existence of natural values generates human obligations towards wild areas based on the obligation not to reduce natural values. It accepts, moreover, that the presence of natural values constitutes a compelling reason for letting wild nature alone. It claims, though, that natural values can be restored and, moreover, promises to restore them. Indeed it avowedly recognizes that there is an obligation to do so. If natural value can be and will be restored, then the obligation to leave wild nature alone is weakened, perhaps to the point where it has little force, provided, of course, that restoration of natural values is later accomplished. Let us call the fundamental premiss in this chain of reasoning, the claim that natural value can be restored, 'the replacement thesis'. And let us call the policy response, that the replacement thesis underpins, the restoration proposal.

THE ANTI-REPLACEMENT THESIS
DEFENDED

The argument based on the replacement thesis is seductive to be sure, but it can be challenged at various points. First, it might be urged that the argument overstates the benefits which would result from environmental despoliation. Taking the Fraser Island case earlier described, it might be urged that the benefits to humans of sand-mining are exaggerated or that equivalent benefits can be achieved in some other way. But this response will have most bite if it is coupled with the claim that natural values cannot be restored. For even if the benefits of mining are exaggerated or even if there is some alternative way of realizing similar benefits, there is scope to discount considerably the significance of the loss of natural values, because they can and will be restored, or so it is claimed by advocates of the replacement thesis. Second, it might be urged that, even if natural values can in principle be restored, most likely they will not in fact be restored. In

76

the mining case it might be maintained that efforts at rehabilitation are almost certain to fail to create a surface ecology exactly like the one earlier existing. This might be because funds for restoration will not materialize, perhaps because the company concerned goes out of business, because companies simply renege on promises made or merely go through the motions, striving to do nothing more than provide an inferior restoration, or because management policies or government policies change.

Third, even where there is a serious, well-funded effort to restore natural values, the effort may fail owing to a failure of science and technology. It is important here to focus on some reasons that might be given in support of the claim that something of value would be lost if a certain bit of the environment were destroyed. This gives us some sense of the magnitude of the task involved in a restoration project that aspires to be anything like complete. It shows us why many actual restoration projects are rather less than complete restorations, aiming instead at some rough and approximate restoration. So it may be that the area supports a great diversity of plant and animal life, it may be that it is the habitat of several endangered species, it may be that it has a distinctive soil constitution, it may be that it contains striking rock formations, such as cliffs or caves, or fine specimens of a particular tree species. Perhaps there are steps that could be taken to ensure the restoration of species diversity and the continued existence of the endangered species. It might even be possible to restore the distinctive soil constitution and to ensure the development of the appropriate fine specimens. Other elements might prove rather harder to re-create. For instance, it will be no easy feat to re-create intricate rock formations, including such things as distinctive patterns of weathering and colouration.

Unless we are willing to settle for a less than complete restoration, this third response to the argument based on the replacement thesis should weigh very heavily with us. And there is a fourth response that should not be ignored. We should not overlook the fact that there will be a time, between despoliation and restoration, during which the relevant natural values are absent. Their absence, even for a relatively short period of time, is surely something which requires justification, since it reduces the overall natural value of the earth where this is calculated across time. Thus the value of the rainforest is not just the value it has at a single time but is at least the summed value that it has across all of the times at which it exists.[1] Restoration will not itself be able to compensate for this missing slice of natural value, so the other kinds of compensating value, such as economic value, must be substantial.

These four styles of response are important and should never be neglected. There is, however, a fifth style of response which does not depend for its force on contingencies such as current technological limitations or the inaccurate calculation of benefits. This fifth response is the argument that natural values can never be fully restored, not even in principle. The claim is that even if restoration is possible, such that, say, a surface ecology completely indistinguishable from the one existing prior to disruption is created, an important basis for natural values is missing. In what follows, this fifth response is defended and those natural values that cannot be restored are delineated. It is, moreover, a response actually made in the Fraser island case mentioned earlier. Thus J. G. Mosley reports that:

> The Fraser Island Environmental Inquiry Commissioners did in fact face up to the question of the relevance of successful rehabilitation to the decision on whether to ban exports (of beach sand minerals) and were quite unequivocal in saying that if the aim was to protect a natural area such success was irrelevant. . . . The Inquiry said: '. . . even if, contrary to the overwhelming weight of evidence before the Commission, successful rehabilitation of the flora after mining is found to be ecologically possible on all mined sites on the Island . . . the overall impression of a wild, uncultivated island refuge will be destroyed forever by mining'.
>
> (Mosley 1980: 1)

The Commissioners have here recognized a crucial point that underpins decisive objections to the replacement thesis, namely that natural value depends, in large part, on the presence of properties which cannot survive the disruption-restoration process. If this is correct, we will have a decisive reason for adopting policies of prohibiting the destruction of areas of wild nature. It will show that the resistance that environmentalists display in the face of restoration promises is not merely silly, sentimental, emotional, selfish or irrational (Elliot 1983). The basis of natural value appealed to by the Commissioners is also important because so much of the debate assumes that settling the dispute about what is ecologically possible automatically settles the value question. In short, if this fifth response is sound, it decisively defeats the seductive argument based on the replacement thesis and it shows the paucity of the restoration proposal.

It should be noted that there is another important argument

against despoliation, already alluded to in passing, which does not have to do with the question of whether natural values can be restored. This argument focuses on the felt suffering inflicted on living creatures as their habitats are disturbed or destroyed. Thus the mining project described above would drive creatures from their habitats, causing confusion, frustration, injury and death. It is possible at least to attempt to bracket the suffering of such creatures from the impact mining would have on the surface ecosystem through their elimination. And for present purposes that is what we should do. This is not to concede that their suffering is not morally significant; it is very significant. Rather it is just to make the point that it is a feature of the kind of case we are considering that the restoration thesis does not attempt to meet. And that in itself is an argument against the adequacy of the restoration thesis as a defence of ecosystemic destruction or disruption.

Let us now spend some time setting out the replacement thesis so that we are clear about what it involves. The thesis entails that the full value of some piece of the natural environment at any given time derives entirely from characteristics or properties that can be replicated, reproduced or re-created. So, imagine that an area of rainforest is cleared and later replanted and repopulated to create an environment exactly similar to the forest that was there earlier. According to the replacement thesis, the earlier and later environments necessarily have the same value. In other words, the restoration results in a full replacement of the value earlier lost. I shall argue, however, that some of the value of the earlier rainforest derives from a property it possessed that cannot possibly be replicated. Specifically, the distinctive, natural genesis or origin of the earlier rainforest contributed intensely to its value. The earlier rainforest had naturally evolved, whereas the later rainforest is the direct product of human artifice. This, I claim, makes for an intense value difference between them. A different example perhaps makes the point more graphically. Imagine two islands close by one another and exactly alike. One island is in every sense a product of natural forces, whereas the other island has been constructed by environmental engineers out of natural components. The former island is entirely natural; the latter island is an artefact. Let us assume also, for reasons that will become evident later, that it is a recently manufactured artefact. According to the replacement thesis, because the islands are exactly similar, they have the same value. I think this is false. I claim that the first island has more value than the second island. Indeed I claim that it has much more value than the second island.

In each of the examples two apparently natural objects are compared. They are indistinguishable in terms of their perceptible properties. If we took snapshots of the earlier forest and the later forest, and compared them, we would discover no differences. If we took snapshots of the two islands, and compared them, we would discover no differences. This is not surprising, since in each case the objects compared share all of their intrinsic properties. It is their relational properties, that is the relationships they have to objects and events outside or beyond themselves, that differentiate them. Thus the two rainforests have strikingly different histories. One is the product of natural forces, whereas the other is the intentional creation of human agents – a product of culture and technology. This factual difference between the two forests underpins an important value difference.

The genuinely natural forest, therefore, possesses a relational property that the other lacks and the relational property in question is an important determinant of that forest's value. Similarly in the case of the islands, the one island has a history of an entirely different kind from the other. Although their intrinsic properties are now the same, the processes by which they acquired them are utterly different. Again, a difference in relational properties underpins a significant difference in value. The relevant factual differences or differences in value-adding properties would not, in either case, be revealed by a snapshot; rather, they would be revealed by a video depicting the genesis and evolution of the two islands and of the two forests. The replacement thesis, it turns out, is flawed because it incorrectly assumes that the factual differences, upon which the value differences supervene, are all revealed by a snapshot. They are not. The particular history or genesis of something can be among those characteristics or properties upon which the value of that thing is directly based. That a thing's value can supervene on its relational properties, including its origin and subsequent history, is the conceptual basis for what might be called the 'anti-replacement thesis'. And that relational properties can be value-adding properties was established in the first chapter.

The anti-replacement thesis distinguishes between full value and equal value. Full value restoration would involve not merely creating something equal in value to something else that has been degraded or destroyed, it would also involve achieving that equal quantity of value by creating something with the very same pattern of value-adding properties earlier possessed by the thing degraded or destroyed. So the anti-replacement thesis leaves open the abstract possibility that restored nature could have value as great as original nature. This would be so if there was some feature of the restored forest, not present in the original, that somehow, to our amazement, compensates for the natural intrinsic value lost through the failure of the relevant relational property to be exemplified by the restored forest. Perhaps it would also be so if the values derived through despoliation were great enough to effect a similar compensation. I am hesitant to endorse this, even as a remote possibility, since it might give unwarranted assistance to those who would sacrifice natural values in order to advance human interests. Anyway, abstract possibilities aside, restored nature certainly would not have the same or greater value as original nature. This is partly because of the practical difficulties of restoring nature. More significantly, it is because the property of being naturally evolved, which is the property that crucially distinguished the original forest from the restored forest, is a value-multiplier or intensifier. This idea needs explaining.[2]

A value-multiplying or intensifying property is one that acts in concert with other properties to produce an overall value well in excess of the sum of the value of those properties, and, for that matter, the value-multiplying property, taken singly. Imagine, then, a naturally evolved object possessing only meagre value, such as a small meteor in space. The value of the meteor is meagre because there is no plausible value-adding property it possesses apart from the properties of being of moderate geomorphic complexity and of being naturally evolved. We might even hesitate to say that it has any value to speak of at all; certainly its value would seem of a magnitude that would allow many uncontroversial trade-offs. This might lead us falsely to infer that the property of being naturally evolved is not value-adding or only value-adding to a very small degree. We might conclude that the value of natural states of affairs, where they have significant value, is contributed by properties other than that of being naturally evolved. We can say, instead, that although the property of being naturally evolved is not value-adding in isolation, it nevertheless multiplies or intensifies the value that derives from other value-adding properties.

Consider the two islands earlier discussed. Both islands exhibit biological complexity, which we take to be a basis of value. One island exhibits biological complexity that has naturally evolved; the other exhibits biological complexity that has been intentionally created by humans. The value of the biological complexity in the first context is much greater than in the second, since the first exemplifies a property, namely the property of being naturally evolved, that intensifies its overall value. These claims concerning the property of being naturally evolved are discussed elsewhere. All that we need to understand in the present instance is how a value-multiplier would work and how the concept of a value-multiplier helps critics of the restoration argument based on the replacement thesis. And even if we come to reject the idea that there are value-multipliers, or that the property of being naturally evolved is one, we still have a basis, in the crucial relational property, for making a justified value discrimination between the original and restored forests and between the natural and artificial islands.

It is pertinent to flag an objection to the claim concerning the crucial relational property that has been advanced by various critics. Their general line is that the claim relies on an ultimately unworkable distinction between what is natural and what is not, between the natural and the artificial, between nature and culture, between the natural and the non-natural, or some such allegedly illicit dichotomy (Cowell 1993; Jordan 1994). The distinction between the natural and the non-natural requires detailed discussion: this is provided in the final chapter. Meantime let us assume a plausible suggestion as to how the distinction might be made good in a way sufficient to the present need. I shall take it that 'natural' means something like 'unmodified by human activity'. Obviously some areas will be more natural than others, according to the degree to which they have been shaped by human activity. Indeed most rural landscapes will, on this view, count as non-natural to a very high degree. And instances of even modest environmental restoration will be to some extent non-natural. So the distinction between the natural and the non-natural is not a sharp distinction: rather the contrasting concepts mark out opposite ends of a continuum. What is certainly true is that an area of wilderness in which there has been some impact by humans, for example through weed removal or the eradication of feral animals, is overwhelmingly natural, in contrast to even a leafy suburban precinct. Nor do I intend the natural/non-natural distinction to parallel exactly some dependent moral evaluations; that is, I do not want to be taken here as claiming that what is natural is good and what is non-natural is not, or that the natural is always better than the non-natural. The distinction between natural and non-natural connects with valuation in subtler ways than that. This is a matter to which we shall return.

So at the heart of the environmentalist's rejection of the restoration argument based on the replacement thesis is the belief that an area is valuable, to a significant extent, because it is a natural area, because it has not been modified by human activity, because it is undeveloped, unspoilt, or even unsullied or untainted. One way of fleshing out the suggestion and giving it some normative clout is to appeal to a notion from aesthetics. Thus we might claim that what the environmental engineers are proposing is that we accept a fake instead of the real thing. If the claim can be made good then perhaps an adequate response to restoration proposals is to point out that they merely fake nature; that in an obvious and dramatic way they offer us something less than was taken away. Certainly there is a weight of opinion to the effect that, in art at least, fakes lack a value possessed by the real thing (Goodman 1968: 99–122; Radford 1978). Let us now think about the suggestion that genesis matters in environmental evaluations much as it does in the aesthetic evaluation of artefacts.

THE NORMATIVE SIGNIFICANCE OF ORIGIN

Consider, first, the environmental engineer who urges that the exact intrinsic similarity that holds between the original environment and the perfectly restored environment leaves no room for a value discrimination between them. The engineer claims that if they are exactly alike, down to the minutest detail, then they must be equally valuable. The engineer assumes that value discriminations depend only on there being intrinsic differences between the states of affairs compared. But, it has been suggested, this is simply to discount the possibility that events temporally and spatially outside the immediate areas in question can serve as the basis of some differential value comparison. In particular, it discounts the possibility that the manner of an area's genesis has any role in determining its value. Maybe reflection on some of the examples discussed, such as the example of the two islands, has already persuaded us that the anti-replacement thesis has normative force. Perhaps it has only persuaded us that the normative issue is at least open. Perhaps earlier discussion has shown that there is conceptual space for rejecting the environmental engineer's suggestion. We might agree that genesis could play a role in determining value but we might nevertheless deny that it in fact does. If this is our view, then our argument is with the normative content of the anti-replacement thesis. If our position is the second or third, then we require some more discussion if the case for the normative force of the anti-replacement thesis is to be secured. Here, then, are some examples which suggest that an object's origins do affect its intrinsic value and our valuations of it.

Imagine that I have a piece of sculpture in my garden that is too fragile to be moved. The sculpture is a fine work and I judge it to be of considerable aesthetic merit. The local government authority, however, intends to lay drainage pipes just where the sculpture happens to be. Despite my protests they refuse to relent. The pipes, they insist, must go exactly where my sculpture is and consequently it will be destroyed. However, I am then told that really I have no cause to despair, no cause to lament the prospective loss of aesthetic value, because the destroyed sculpture will be replaced with an exactly similar artefact, with something identical in all its intrinsic properties to the original.[3] I am assured, moreover, that not even experts could tell the replacement was not the original, at least not without very carefully tracing the history of the object before them. Maybe I should doubt these assurances, but assume that I do not. Do I still have reason to be concerned? Do I still have reason to think intrinsic aesthetic value will be lost?

While I may concede that the replica sculpture would be better than nothing at all, it is utterly improbable that I would accept it as full compensation for the loss of aesthetic value resulting from the destruction of the original. Nor is my reluctance entirely explained by the monetary value of the original work. Indeed we can imagine that I am offered appropriate monetary compensation as well as the replacement sculpture. My reluctance springs, rather, from the fact that I value the original sculpture as an aesthetic object, which means that, among other things, I value it for its specific genesis and history. Indeed I may not even concede that the replica sculpture is better than nothing at all. I might take the view that the creation of the replica is demeaning, or disrespectful, of the original, and that the replica itself has negative value as a consequence. In this case the particular history of the replica, such as the fact that it is a copy and the fact that it was intended by its producers fully to replicate the aesthetic value of the original, acts as a value-subtracting or value-reducing property.

Now consider another example. I have been promised a Charles Blackman drawing for my birthday and on that day I am given a drawing which I take to be a particular Blackman that I once saw in a gallery. I am understandably pleased. My pleasure, however, does not last long, for I am told that the drawing I am holding is not a

Blackman but is really an exact replica of one destroyed in a fire. Any attempt to allay my disappointment by insisting that there just is no difference between the replica and the original misses the mark completely. This is so even if I am persuaded that not even the very best experts could tell, without conducting a careful investigation of the drawing's history, that it was not the original. I would say that what I had was not a Blackman possessed of particular aesthetic qualities but, instead, an object best thought of as a marvellously good print which represented, or attempted successfully to convey, the particular aesthetic properties of the original. While the replica may successfully represent the particular aesthetic properties of the original, and while it might well have positive aesthetic properties of its own, it does not itself have the particular set of aesthetic properties possessed by the original. There is a crucial difference between the original and the replica, which, once it is known, affects perceptions, and consequent valuations, of the replica. The difference of course is in the very different and distinctive genesis of the original.

It might be thought that genesis only matters in so far as it is perceived. For example, it might be thought that if the environmental engineer could perform the restoration quickly and secretly, then there would be no room for complaint. Of course, in one sense there would not be, since the knowledge that would motivate complaint would be missing. All that this shows, however, is that there can be loss of value without the loss being perceived. It allows room for valuations to be mistaken because of ignorance concerning relevant facts. Thus imagine that a real Blackman of mine is removed and secretly replaced with the perfect replica. I have lost something of value without knowing that I have lost something of value. This is possible because it is not simply the states of mind engendered by contemplating the drawing, by giving myself over to aesthetic pleasure and so on, which explain why it has value. It has value also because of the kind of thing that it is, and one thing that it is is a drawing executed by a particular artist with certain intentions, feelings and the like, at a certain stage of his artistic development, and living and working in a certain aesthetic milieu.

Similarly, it is not just those things which make me feel the joy that wilderness makes me feel, that I value. That would be a reason for desiring such things, but that is a distinct consideration. Thus I value the forest because it is of a specific kind, and one aspect of its specificity is that it is has a certain history which explains its existence. Of course I can be deceived into thinking that a piece of landscape has that kind of history, has developed in the appropriate way, when in fact it is the result of intensive restoration. The success of the deception, however, does not elevate the restored landscape to the value level of the original, no more than the success of the deception in the previous example confers on the fake Blackman the aesthetic value of a real Blackman. What has value in both cases are objects which really are of the kind that I value, not merely objects which I believe are of that kind. This point, as the discussion of the first chapter should have made plain, is appropriate independently of views concerning the subjectivity or objectivity of value.

I shall offer a final example to bring out the importance of genesis or origin in evaluations. Imagine that I am given a beautiful, delicately constructed, object. It is something I treasure and admire, something in which I see considerable aesthetic value. One day, however, I discover certain facts about its origin of which I previously had no inkling. I discover that it is carved out of a piece of bone taken from someone who was killed especially for the purpose of providing the raw material for the artefact. This discovery affects me deeply and I cease to value the object in the way that I once did. While I can still understand what it is about the object that underpinned my earlier positive evaluation, I now regard it as sullied. Its apparent beauty is, in reality, transformed, inverted and spoilt by the facts of its origin. The intrinsic properties of the object itself have not changed but, in response to the newly discovered relational property concerning its origin, my evaluation of it has. I have come to know that it is not the kind of thing I thought it was, and that my earlier evaluation of it was mistaken. The discovery is like the discovery that a painting one believed to be an original is in fact a forgery. The discovery about the object's origin changes the evaluation made of it, since it reveals that the object is not of the kind that I actually value. Like the earlier examples, the third example suggests that there is a compelling case for explaining at least part of an object's value in terms of its origins, history and genesis, in short, in terms of the kinds of processes that brought it into being.

The examples just now discussed focus on artefacts which have aesthetic value. It may be thought that the conclusion suggested by those examples, that genesis is a crucial determinant of value, does not carry over to the case of naturally evolved items. With this suggestion in mind we should consider a series of examples that do not involve fakes, replicas or copies of artefacts. So imagine, first of all, that Jill falls into the clutches of a utilitarian-minded super-technologist. Her captor has developed an incredible experience machine. Once its electrodes are attached and the right buttons pressed, the experience machine can bring one to have any kind of qualitative experience whatsoever. Jill is plugged into the machine. Her captor knows full well her love of wilderness and so Jill is given an extended experience as of canoeing down a wild river. This is environmental engineering at the limit. Jill really does believe that she is travelling down a wild river, witnessing natural systems of great intrinsic value. Because the experience is faked, though, Jill is being short-changed, and the value that she believes she detects is simply not there. Jill wants there to be wilderness and she wants to experience it. She wants the world to be a certain way and she wants to have experiences of a certain kind, namely veridical experiences of wilderness. Her experiences do not, however, have the genesis she wants them to have. As a consequence, we might say that, even though they are extremely pleasurable, they do not have the value she thinks they have. Moreover, the cause of those experiences, in this case the experience machine, does not have the value that Jill would attribute to the wilderness that she falsely believes is the cause of her experiences. The experience machine is the wrong kind of object to possess natural intrinsic value.

In our second example, Jill is abducted, blindfolded and taken to a completely simulated wilderness in which none of the components are even natural; every object out of which the simulated wilderness is composed is an artefact constructed from artificial materials. When the blindfold is removed Jill is thrilled by what she sees, smells and hears around her; the tall gums, the wattles, the granite boulders, the sounds of birds, the smell of the bush, and so on. At least that is what she thinks is there. We know otherwise. We know that Jill is deceived, that she is once again being short-changed. She has been presented with an environment which she thinks is of value but which, in her own terms, is not. If, for example, she understood that the leaves, through which the artificially generated breeze now stirred, were synthetic she would be profoundly disappointed, perhaps even disgusted at what at best is a cruel joke. Unlike in the experience machine case, here there are objects in the world that roughly correspond to her experiences, but the beliefs that she has concerning their nature, beliefs that are the basis of her evaluative response, turn out to be false. And so the synthetic wilderness lacks intrinsic value. Perhaps it even has intrinsic disvalue.

In the third example, Jill is taken to a place that was once devastated by open-cut mining. The vegetation that had grown there for many thousands of years had been cleared, rock formations smashed, the earth torn up, and the resident animals either killed or driven from their habitats. Times and attitudes have changed, however, and the area has been restored. The earth has been reshaped and has the sorts of contours it once had. Plants of the species which grew there before the devastation have been replanted and flourish once more, and the animal species that were once there have been reintroduced. Jill knows nothing of this sequence of devastation and restoration. She believes she is in pristine wilderness. Once again, she has been short-changed, presented with rather less than what she values most. What she values most is wilderness, natural ecosystems that have naturally evolved and that result from an unbroken continuity of natural processes extending into the past. What Jill sees around her may have some value but, because a crucial relational property to do with genesis is absent, what she sees around her has much less value than she believes it has.

In the fourth example, Jill is taken to an area that had once been cleared for farming. The forest which had stood there for some thousands of years had been felled. But that was long ago. The area is once again forested and a variety of creatures inhabit the forest. This happy situation, moreover, is not the result of human intervention. The devastated land has been reclaimed by nature and natural processes again determine the way it develops and changes. Jill knows nothing of this and thinks she is in a forest that has been there since before humans ever farmed. Once again, she has been short-changed, to some extent at least, and presented with somewhat less than what she values most. While what she sees has considerable natural value, it would have had more, had its continuity with past natural processes not been interrupted by human activity.

In none of these four cases does Jill get exactly what she wants or experience what she values most, although in each case she believes she does. If we can understand how she doesn't get what she most wants, then we can see how it is that a forest, which has naturally evolved and which has uninterrupted natural continuity with the past, has more value than one brought into existence through human contrivance, intervention or interference. Taking the first example, the experience machine provides Jill with certain of the experiences she values but because they are caused in so grotesquely a perverse fashion, there is little value in them. Indeed the underlying deception may function as a value-deflator or even a value-inverter, emptying the experiences of virtually any value that might attach to them as pleasing experiences or even guaranteeing that they have negative value. There is an analogy here with experiences of pleasure derived from sadistic acts. We might reasonably think that such experiences have no value at all, and not merely after we have subtracted the disvalue of the effects of sadism, or the disvalue of sadistic motives, from the positive value of the pleasure. Because the sadist's pleasure is caused in the particular way that it is, and embedded in a particular psychology, that pleasure, arguably, never had any positive value. The value-inversion phenomenon ensured that there never would emerge positive value attaching to the sadist's experiences. Arguably it is like this in the case of the experience machine because of the outrageous degree of deception, even though it is also the intention of the technologist to please.

The shift to the second example yields no value improvement to speak of. True, Jill's experiences are in this example veridical, being caused in the usual way by real objects in the real world. But it not simply that Jill wants her experiences to be veridical. She wants the real objects that cause them really to be of the kind she believes them to be. While Jill's experiences are caused in what we might think of as the normal way by real objects, there is, nevertheless, a huge element of deception involved that compels our regarding the second example much as the first, at least as far its exemplification of value is concerned. The main difference is that the synthetic environment functions to deceive through a different technology from that involved in the first example. Exactly the same comments about the values involved apply. If deception were not involved, if Jill were apprised of the facts about the synthetic environment, there may be some value in her experiences and there may be some value in the objects which, in conjunction with Jill's beliefs about their natures, histories and purposes, cause those experiences. I find it difficult to see, though, how art that mimics nature in quite this way would have any value at all. The thought that drives this judgement is difficult to articulate. One way of expressing it is in terms of the disrespect to natural values evident in their large-scale synthetic replication. There may even be some connection with the idea of blasphemy, although if that idea were to connect with the example I would want it to be somehow secularized. Or maybe the point is simply that people who commission, or take pleasure from such artefacts, are exemplifying some defect in their capacities for aesthetic judgement. Perhaps the way to focus on what is amiss is to consider analogies, such as the situation of those who would prefer to view a plastic reconstruction of a Mayan pyramid rather than the real thing. I shall not, though, pursue the issue.

Consider the third example. Here there is incomparably more of value than in the first and second examples. And clearly the value of the restored forest in hugely in excess of the value possessed by the earlier razed area. Without a doubt it is better that restoration took place than that the area remained wrecked. Still, it might involve somewhat less value than what would have been possessed by the pristine forest that Jill believes she is actually experiencing. The news of the actual forest's particular origin could justifiably cause her to make a significant reassessment of the natural values in her surroundings. The forest, though real, and composed entirely of natural items, is not completely what Jill wants it to be and believes it to be. It is to a large extent the product of contrivance and intervention. In other words, there is some scope for understanding its present broad characteristics in terms of the intentions and goals of humans, for understanding it, to some extent at least, as an artefact. If it were not in this sense a contrivance or product of human intervention, then Jill would value it more. The value that the forest actually has would to a large extent depend on just how many of its present characteristics are the product of natural forces and natural evolution. It makes perfect sense to think of nature regaining control of, or reclaiming, some area and making that area natural once more. Perhaps restoration work carried out after the mining had been completed kick-started the process and gave it a certain direction. But human control might thereafter not have been maintained, and natural selection and natural forces may have had a large hand in giving the area the particular ecological and geomorphological shape that it now has. Moreover, the degree of human control might not ever have been very great.

We should beware of over-estimating the degree to which restoration involves the sort of contrivance, the sort of shaping that occurs when, say, a town is planned or a building is constructed. Restoration work is often very basic, involving not much more than the laying of broad foundations, along with some nurturing and protection (see Baldwin 1994; Sylvan 1994). The degree to which the value of the restored forest approximates the value of the forest originally there is a function of the time that has elapsed since the restoration is achieved, particularly since the first occurrence of acts of restoration (Sylvan 1994: 65–6). The degree to which the value of the restored forest approximates the value of the forest originally there, is also a function of magnitude and intrusiveness of the human contribution during the basic restoration work. Given enough time, close to original value might be restored. Still, it makes sense to endorse the extreme view and to say that the passage of time does not restore full value because there is always something missing which is irreplaceable. What is missing is a natural provenance extending back to a time preceding the destructive impacts of human activity and thus rendering the present forest continuous with the forest that was cleared so that mining could proceed.

Lest these comments about the value-improving function of the passage of time give any succour to the restoration proposal based on the replacement thesis, we should keep in mind two crucial points. First, in restoration value is incrementally, and only eventually, restored. For example, mining followed by restoration removes a large chunk of value over some time: the proportion that remains missing at a given time decreases as the restoration proceeds, as natural processes take over and as human assistance falls away. Value is quantitative across time as well as at a particular time. That is almost too obvious a point to state, but it is an obvious point that is also too easily overlooked. The value that is, decreasingly, absent, must feature in the value accounting and clearly it cannot be redeemed through restoration. In saying this I am, of course, assuming that human activity cannot secure more significant natural value than would have emerged through natural processes. Compare the case in which Sally inflicts on George an injury that causes him protracted suffering and limits his mobility. Sally may care for George and nurse him back to health, ameliorating the suffering and assisting the return of mobility. Consequently the value in George's life later is much the same as the value much earlier, but the value lost in that intermediate period is lost forever. And so it is with natural value in cases of restoration. The second point we should keep in mind is the degree to which efforts at restoration are inadequate, half-hearted, botched, counter-productive, and the like (Sylvan 1994: 63–5). We shall return to these issues later in the chapter.

In the fourth example, the devastated area regenerates without the assistance of human intervention. In this example, human activity, destructive activity as it happens, features centrally in the explanation of how and why this regenerated forest, with its particular characteristics and its particular history, exists. That activity, however, does not extend into the period during which natural forces again take control and begin to shape the ecology of the regenerated forest. The regenerated forest, although resulting from massive human interference

91

with a pre-existing natural system, is not a human contrivance, except in the very unlikely circumstance of the forest's having been razed not simply to provide land for farming but also to provide a site for later regeneration, and it is only minimally a product of human activity. In judging the value of the regenerated forest we need to keep a comparative pathway in mind, namely the pathway in which the original forest had never been cleared and so in which no regenerated forest came to exist. In that pathway there never was a loss of value, and that remains, as in the case of the third example, a relevant evaluation regardless of whether, at some future point, the pathways exemplify roughly equal value.

We can say that it was an exceedingly bad thing, a huge diminution of value, that the original forest was cleared: and we can say this even though we accept that the value of the regenerated forest is roughly equal to the value of the original forest. Here, as with the third example, it is important to remind ourselves that value is quantitative across time as well as at a particular time. But even discounting the issue of loss of value over time, there is scope for saying that the regenerated forest has less value than the original forest. Although the former has regenerated of its own accord, it does not have the right kind of continuity with the forest that stood there initially, a value-enhancing continuity. That continuity has been interrupted by the earlier devastation, devastation carried out by humans.

There is an interesting question that arises here concerning value trade-offs. We might be in a situation in which we can intervene to assist the regeneration of an area from which forest cover has been cleared, perhaps by planting trees, providing appropriate cover, controlling weeds, reducing soil loss and erosion, and the like. Alternatively we might allow events to run their course without intervening in any way. We may be confident that nature will eventually reclaim the cleared land, although we might assume that what nature creates there will be rather different from what was there before clearing took place and from what would be there were we to intervene. We should also assume that nature unassisted will take rather longer to reclaim the spoiled area than would be the case were we to assist. What should we do? Should we intervene, thus speeding the process of reclamation for and by nature? Or should we simply stand aside? My view, held with some hesitation, is that we should intervene.

In justifying this view I would note two distinct value claims. The first is that natural continuity, reaching back into the past prior to the development of human cultures and technologies, is value-adding.

The second is the view that the development through natural forces of ecological complexity is, other things being equal, more value-adding than the development of that same ecological complexity assisted by human intervention. Now in the example being considered, the first value claim is not relevant because the clearing of the forest has destroyed the continuity with the past. So, in that example, human intervention threatens only the second value. It is not implausible to suggest that whatever extra amount of value the ecosystem that would come naturally to occupy the site of the despoliation would have possessed, is made up for by shortening the time span during which the despoiled site remains unreclaimed by nature and so relatively devoid of natural value. If intervention speeds things up, then the fact that natural values are more quickly restored overrides any concerns we might have based on the second value claim. And here we should also keep in mind the plausible view that the value-detracting force of human intervention decreases with the temporal distance between that intervention and a particular subsequent phase in the development and evolution of some natural system. The idea is that the passage of time and the lengthening domination by natural forces washes out the value-retarding fact of human intervention. Moreover the amount of value lost through human intervention is determined also by the magnitude of that intervention, rather than by the mere fact that it has occurred to some degree or other. So less value is lost if restoration involves not much more than seeding and weeding, than would be lost if restoration involves extraordinary technical manipulation.

In the course of my arguments so far, I have assumed or implied a broad analogy between faking art and faking nature. Part of my motivation was to use examples involving artefacts to highlight the important role that origin or genesis could play in environmental evaluation. Just as we might say that an artefact's value is partly determined by its origin, so too we might say that the value of an ecosystem is partly determined by its origin. We might say, furthermore, that just as an evaluation of an artefact must be revised because of some fact we discover about its provenance, for example that it is a fake, so, too, evaluations we might make about ecosystems must be revised if we discover that those ecosystems have resulted from human contrivance. There is no suggestion, however, that the concepts of aesthetic evaluation and judgement are to be carried straight over to evaluations of, and judgements about, the natural environment. Indeed there is good reason to believe that this cannot be done in a strict sense. For one thing an apparently integral part of aesthetic evaluation depends on viewing the aesthetic object as an intentional object, as an artefact, as something that is shaped by the purposes and designs of its author and his or her social milieu. Evaluating works of art involves, as was earlier implied, explaining, interpreting and judging them, in terms of their author's intentions; it involves placing them within the author's corpus of work; it involves locating them in some tradition and in some social milieu. Clearly these components of aesthetic evaluation do not feature in any evaluation of nature that does not appraise nature as the aesthetic creation of a divine being. Of course, this is not to say that certain concepts that are frequently deployed in aesthetic evaluation cannot legitimately be deployed in evaluations of the environment. We admire the intricacy and delicacy of colouring in paintings as we might admire the intricate and delicate shadings in a eucalypt forest. We admire the solid grandeur of a building as we might admire the solidity and grandeur of a massive rock outcrop. And of course the notion of 'the beautiful' has a purchase in environmental evaluations as it does in aesthetic evaluations. I think that it is clear that aesthetic appraisals of nature are possible, that our responses to nature are often aesthetic responses (Carlson 1984 and 1992; Lynch 1996). Nevertheless, arguments might be developed to drive a wedge between the two kinds of evaluation so as to weaken the analogies between faking art and faking nature.

One such argument appeals to the view that aesthetic evaluation has a cognitive element that is necessarily lacking in evaluations of uncontrived nature (Mannison 1980b: 212–16). This argument threatens the analogy by highlighting alleged differences between genuine aesthetic judgements and our responses to nature. The idea is that in making aesthetic evaluations we make judgements concerning the author's intentions and the like, in the way that was sketched above. These cognitive judgements mediate our response to the object of our evaluation. So, for example, the knowledge that a particular painting is not by the artist we at first thought, could well cause us to judge the work to be somewhat derivative in style and cause us to adjust our feelings about the painting accordingly. Now it might be claimed that nothing of this kind goes on in the evaluation of nature. While nature, like works of art, elicits any of a range of emotional responses in viewers, there is not, so the argument runs, a similar cognitive element. Certainly the aesthetic appreciation of nature does involve judgements to at least a minimal extent. Most obviously, we respond as we do because we believe that what we are viewing is real, rather than, say, a projection of images on to a screen. So the argument is not plausible if it claims that aesthetic response is completely devoid of a judgemental element, that it is, through and through, simply a raw emotional response to perceptions or sensations. But the claim may be that in the aesthetic evaluation of nature there can be only minimally a cognitive element, whereas in the evaluation of artefacts the cognitive element can be much more complex. The argument must be that since the cognitive or judgemental element in environmental evaluation is so minimal, then there is little content to the analogy between faking art and faking nature and indeed no rational basis to preferring real to faked nature when the latter is a good replica. This argument against the analogy between faking art and faking nature concedes, it should be stressed, that there is something to the analogy. It does not reject the analogy outright but suggests instead that it is not quite strong enough to carry the burden required of it.

One point that needs to be made at the outset is that in aesthetic evaluation quite generally there often is only a minimal cognitive element. Many who view paintings, for instance, do not make the sorts of complex judgements about intentions, technique, social milieu, and so on, referred to earlier. And certainly initial judgements about works of art will be like this. While they are partially informed, they are genuinely aesthetic judgements. Now the same is no doubt true of many people's aesthetic responses to nature. It is important to note, however, that many people who discern aesthetic value in wilderness do not do so merely because they enjoy soaking up scenery that is pretty, dramatic, spectacular, unusual or the like (Routley 1975). What they discern and value is much more than the superficial aesthetic qualities of nature. What they do see, and what they value, is very much a function of the degree to which they understand complex natural histories involving evolutionary processes and ecological, geological and other natural forces, that shape landscape, maintain it, and change it, and that both explain why, and determine that, it possesses the characteristics it does. Knowledge of this kind is capable of transforming a hitherto uninteresting landscape into one that is compelling. There are parallels, moreover, between the shaping of the aesthetic evaluation of an artefact by the evaluator's knowledge of the artist and her or his circumstances, techniques, situation in some tradition, and so on, and the manner in which knowledge of the particular circumstances and determinants of the creation of a natural area shapes the wilderness lover's responses to, and appreciation of, that area. For example, an understanding of the geomorphological forces, the climatic factors, the ecological progressions, and so on, that explain an area's present condition, will often intensify our aesthetic appreciation of the area. Understanding and aesthetic evaluation do go hand in hand: the responses people have to forests, deserts, oceans, wild rivers, and so on, are not merely raw, emotional responses. (Rolston 1975, 1986 and 1995; Routley 1975).

It would seem that the case for the view that nature cannot be a proper object of aesthetic evaluation is not secured by the argument concerning the role of judgement. Indeed some have argued that we should not think that what characterizes aesthetic responses to artefacts must characterize aesthetic responses to nature (Carlson 1984). According to proponents of this view, it is unreasonable to impose requirements concerning the aesthetic evaluation of artefacts, of objects which are the products of design, on an entirely different domain of aesthetic evaluation. In any case the effectiveness of the idea of faked nature does not depend on securing the conclusion that nature is an appropriate object of aesthetic evaluation. All that is required is that there be an analogy between faking art and faking nature, and there is. Understanding natural processes and the types of ecosystems to which they give rise enables the advocate of natural values to make discriminations that both give content to the analogy between faking art and faking nature and persuade us to take seriously the claim that faked nature is inferior to original nature. For one thing, it is important to make the point that only in fanciful situations dreamt up by philosophers are there no detectable differences between fakes and originals, both in the case of artefacts and in the case of natural objects. By taking a realistic example where there are potentially discernible differences between the fake and the real thing, it is possible to bring out the importance of the substantial cognitive element in responses to, and evaluations of, the natural environment.

Right now I may not be able to tell a real Blackman from a fake Blackman, though I might learn to do so. Similarly I might not be able to tell apart a naturally evolved area of rainforest from one that has been planted, but I might subsequently acquire the knowledge that would enable me to make the relevant judgement. Such a discovery would change my response to the forest. It was the thought that a forest, just like the one I had been viewing, would, and did, result from natural processes, that drove my very positive evaluation of it. The successor evaluation is more informed: it is informed and directed by beliefs about the forest, the type of forest it is, its condition as a member of that kind, its causal genesis and so on. Knowing that the forest is not a naturally evolved forest causes me to respond differently to it and to assign it less value than I would were it a naturally evolved forest. And this response is a rational response, motivated by the acquisition of new knowledge. The evaluation is not reversed as in the case of the bone sculpture earlier discussed; rather the value attributed to the forest is scaled down somewhat. There is still much of intrinsic value in the area of forest, much more than in a cleared area or an area under monoculture. Nevertheless, what is there at the time of viewing may be of less value than what would have been had the area been left largely to regenerate naturally, and certainly less than would have been there had the original forest not been devastated through human intervention.

Origin is important as an integral part of the evaluation process. It is important because our beliefs about it determine the evaluations we make. It is also important in that the discovery that something has an origin quite different from the one we initially believe it to have can literally alter the way we perceive that thing. The point concerning the possibility of detecting fakes is important in that it stresses just how much detail must be written into the claim that environmental engineers can replicate nature. Nevertheless, even if environmental engineering could achieve such exactitude, there is, I suggest, no compelling reason for accepting the replacement thesis.

FAKING, RESTORING, PRESERVING AND PROTECTING

It is useful to give some conceptual and terminological distinctions to provide a framework both for reflecting on and giving a sharper focus to the above discussion of the replacement thesis, the anti-replacement thesis and the restoration proposal. That discussion makes use of an analogy between faking art and faking nature, and the analogy plays a central role in justifying various evaluations of ecosystems. The analogy was employed in the paper from which this book developed and some discussants of that paper have been rightly critical of the way in which a broad range of activities were collapsed under the rubric 'faking' (Gunn 1991; Losin 1986; Sylvan 1994). They have suggested that many of the situations to which I ascribe differential value, helped by appeal to the analogy, are not really instances of faking nature. They have suggested also that the term 'faking' is normatively loaded. It is too easy a step, they suggest, from the claim that some process is a faking process to the claim that the resultant product is deficient or defective or of lesser value than the original. There is perhaps a little truth in the criticism that in the original paper the term did too much of the work better done by argument. The discussion above, I think, remedies that situation. It is, I think, clear that the judgement that faked nature has less value than original nature has a rational and plausible basis. What remains to be done is to consider the criticism that the faking analogy does not really embrace the full range of situations about which I make evaluations. Thus it is true that there is a range of activities, including faking, forging, copying, restoring and replacing, that were not sufficiently distinguished and given adequate individual consideration. The appropriate distinctions need to be drawn and the illicit reliance on the normative baggage of 'faking' needs to avoided. And, finally, some of the normative judgements made in, or implied in, the original paper are defective. As we shall see, the distinctions made below are useful in refining that view and framing it so as to meet fair criticisms and minimize normative defects.

Faking is an act of deception; at least it involves an aim to deceive, irrespective of whether or not it is successful. Faking is a kind of forging, as in 'forgery', in that it involves an attempt to pass something off as something that it is not. Maybe 'forging' has overtones of legal, if not moral, condemnation that are somewhat more resonant than 'faking'. Still, 'faking' is hardly a positive or even neutral term. To say that someone has faked nature is to say that she or he has produced or contrived some object, loosely understood, and deceptively represented it as a natural item, a natural process, a natural area or the like, when it is not natural, at least not to the degree that it is represented as being. The implication is that the act of faking is morally dubious and that the faked object is of, if not dubious value, then of lesser value that the original. While categorizing actions as faking or forging does imply a prima-facie negative evaluation, it is obviously true that in certain situations faking is morally defensible and even morally required. Thus someone might fake an emotion or a response in order to give some pleasure to another or in order to prevent some harm occurring. Similarly forging currency to subvert the enemy's war effort might be morally defensible or even required. The all-things-considered judgements that we might make in such cases, though, would depend on the judgements that we make about such things as motives, purposes, likely results and so forth.

Sometimes faking may involve deception only in a weak or super-ficial sense. Something faked may be intended to give an initial misimpression, although it might involve no attempt at continued deception. Thus someone might create a rainforest gully that at first glance, or even on close inspection, seems to be a natural rainforest gully, although it is not. If questioned about its provenance she or he might be completely willing to admit that it is constructed, and indeed express pleasure, or even pride, in her or his ability to have constructed such an object. Although wanting to create an initial misperception, maybe to establish a particular mood or to emphasize their technical skills, this person is not interested in any deep, con-tinuing deception. The faking is, in a straightforward sense, innocent. Her or his intention is not to deceive but, perhaps, to delight the beholder, or even to celebrate the natural through creating some-thing that seems natural. Obviously there are many possible motives such a person might have in addition to those already suggested. These motives are characterized, though, by the absence of any inten-tion of continued deception. Indeed one possible motive, which bears on the main normative issue discussed in this chapter, is to persuade the advocate of natural values that something at least close to the replacement thesis is true. The thought might be that some encounter with an initially successful fake will provide some justification for the claim that faked or, more mildly, restored, nature, can be as valuable as the real thing.

In some variants of the rainforest gully example, there will be no intention to deceive at all, not even initially. This would be a kind of copying, involving no forging or faking. It is true that copying can involve deception. This may be so even where copying is not clearly an initial step or an ingredient in faking or forging. For example, stu-dents might copy the work of others claiming it as their own. It is not completely clear that these students are involved in faking or forging. So, copying might, on its own account, involve deception and so have a normatively negative aspect. Copying, moreover, is redolent of lack of originality and consequently implies a negative judgement, not only of the copier but also of the copy. And, importantly, this might be so even where the copy is indistinguishable, in terms of its intrin-sic properties, from the original. This confirms the view, already defended, that origin is an important determinant of value. It is also worth noting that sometimes copying is not copying from an original but from an antecedent copy.

Sometimes, though, copying is completely innocent and may even be praiseworthy. We might say that someone has made an excellent copy of a piece of jewellery, where there is no suggestion of misbehaviour. There may also be some intimation of creativity in the process of copying and some suggestion that the copy is of considerable positive value. Innocent copying may even involve copying with the intention to deceive at least some people for longer than the medium term. Copying jewellery so that the owner may wear the copy while keeping the original under lock and key is possibly a case in point. The intention is to deceive some people and perhaps not merely in their initial judgements. How might copying be both innocent, or at least morally acceptable, and involve deception? Presumably because no one is unjustly harmed by the deception, the deception is well-motivated, and because the overriding intention is to protect the rights of the owner, because the copy is intended to please the wearer and to provide some aesthetic pleasure to onlookers. But the question is peripheral to present concerns and will not be pursued. The important point is that copying need not involve deception, that it may be an appropriate object of praise, and that the copy may be of significant positive value.

With forging, faking and copying, there is sometimes an attempt to replicate a particular object. This is the case when someone produces a copy of an actual painting and represents it as the original. The actual painting may or may not any longer exist, but the point of the forgery is to have people believe that the forged painting really is another particular object, namely the original painting. Let us call this kind of activity 'token-faking'. Token-faking will almost always involve attempting to produce a replica, or an approximately perfect copy, of an actual object. I say 'almost always' because there will be instances where some actual but imperfectly known object, such as a relic described in an old document, is faked. The defining feature of token-faking is that it involves producing a copy or replica of some actual, although not necessarily presently existing, particular object.[4]

Forging, faking and copying do not, however, always involve an attempt to replicate a particular object. Sometimes the effort is directed towards creating something in a certain style and representing it as having a certain provenance which it does not have. So, a forger might produce a work in the style of a great painter and represent it as the work of that painter. Here there is no suggestion that the forged work is a particular painting known to exist or to have existed; the suggestion is rather that the painting is a newly discovered work of the great painter. What is crucial in this kind of forgery is that a particular style is exemplified and a particular provenance, falsely, claimed. Let us call this 'type-faking'. The distinction between token-faking and type-faking carries over to forging and copying.

Forging, faking and copying, to varying degrees, are suggestive of wrongdoing. A closer consideration of the detail of particular cases might show that, as already claimed, particular instances are not in fact wrong or ethically dubious. There is, moreover, a related kind of activity, pertinent to any appraisal of the replacement thesis, that seems usually to carry no overtones of wrongdoing. This is restoration. In its most straightforward sense restoration implies that some actual object, which has fallen into disrepair, or which has been damaged or degraded, although not destroyed, is brought back to a condition that is much closer to its original condition. While this kind of restoration does not use a particular actual object as the model or template for the creation of another, distinct object, as token-faking does, it does use a past stage of an object as the model or template for shaping a later stage of that same object.

The difference between token-faking and what we might call 'token-restoring' is that, in the former case, there are two distinct objects involved, whereas, in the latter case, there is only one. Adding colour to a painting from which some patches of original colour have been stripped would be an example of token-restoring. Likewise, replanting along a track that has been gouged through a forest, would be an example of token-restoring. Token-restoring leaves intact the provenance of what is restored. It does not, however, necessarily improve, or even leave entirely intact, the value of what is restored. Indeed, in one special kind of case, restoration to a past condition will destroy rather than restore value. Thus some work of art might be produced with the intention that it alter over time, that it in fact will decay, fall apart, or something of the kind. The aesthetic object is not merely the work in its initial condition but the entire process through which it endures. In nature, too, there will be many instances where restoration to an earlier condition would destroy value. For instance, the kinds of flora that characterize particular locations will change over time as the result of natural forces, ranging from phenomena as subtle as natural selection to such catastrophic occurrences as fires, eruptions and floods. So the evaluation of instances of token-restoration must take account of natural processes and progressions spread over time. Restoration to an earlier condition will sometimes be at odds with such processes and progressions.

There is also an activity that we might call, without being too misleading, 'type-restoring'.[5] Type-restoring occurs where some particular object has been destroyed or so degraded that it cannot be token-restored. Type-restoring involves the recreation of a type of object previously instantiated through the creation of a particular object exemplifying the same type. The type in question would sometimes have to be vaguely defined, that is to say it would have to be defined in terms of relatively general characteristics, rather than defined down to the very last detail. In some cases type-restoring seeks to create a replica of some original, authentic object in the same location. For example, imagine that a particular building of great aesthetic merit has been destroyed but that the plans and specifications from which it was originally built are extant. A building is created in line with these plans and specifications and consequently the type that the original building exemplified is exemplified once more. Here the type that is restored can be very precisely defined. And creating a replica of a forest that has been clear-felled would be an example of type-restoration. Token-restoration does not necessarily improve, or even leave intact, the value of what is restored. Similarly, type-restoration might not result in something of much value, particularly in comparison to earlier exemplifications of the type.

Sometimes type-restoring might involve the creation of the replica in a location not occupied by the original. And sometimes this seems to make a difference to our estimate of the value that the replica possesses. For example, the creation of a replica building on the site occupied by the original would seem to have more value that the creation of a replica in some other location, such as theme park or even on some adjacent piece of land. Location might make a difference because we think that the value possessed by the original object is in part due to the relational properties it possesses, including its relations to other buildings in a particular precinct. The importance of the relational properties is a reason why same location type-restorations of even one particular object could vary in value. A same location type-restoration in a reasonably intact precinct could well have more value that one where other significant landmarks, buildings, streetscapes, and so on, have disappeared. We might think, moreover, that some locations, such as in a theme park, turn the type-restoration into a parody or joke, which is arguably disrespectful of the value of the original. This is not to say that some structures do not deserve to be parodied or joked about. Where they do not deserve such treatment we might judge certain type-restorations to be lacking in value, even to have negative value. And even where an entire precinct is replicated elsewhere, we might conclude, with some justification, that the replica has less value than a replica constructed on the original site. The same point can be made with the example of a rainforest. Recreating a rainforest where one was destroyed seems, on the face of it, to result in something of more value than the creation of a rainforest in a place where there never was one.

Usually type-restoration is pursued when token-restoration is no longer possible because the original exemplar of the type has been effectively destroyed. This need not be the case though. It is possible that type-restoration is pursued even where token-restoration is possible, perhaps because the latter is more costly than the former. And, of more relevance to our concern with natural values, an object might be destroyed intentionally, making token restoration impossible, with the concurrent intention of type-restoring it. This is what the replacement thesis allows in the extreme. Thus an attractive park might be flattened to provide a temporary car park for some public entertainment, but destroyed with the intention of type-restoring it when the event for which the parking is required is over. Or some surface ecosystem may be destroyed, in order to extract some mineral or in order to harvest timber, with the intention that it later be type-restored. Of course type-restoration does not require that there be any initial intention, on the part of those who destroy, to create a replica of the object. The destroyer might be compelled by public pressure to carry out a type-restoration. Or some other party might carry it out.

The distinction between token-restoration and type-restoration is not clear and unambiguous. Sometimes it might be difficult to classify a restoration as of the one kind or the other, not because there are certain facts of which we are ignorant that would determine the issue, but simply because there is no determinate answer. So, imagine a building that has been largely destroyed. The small parts of the original that remain are scattered around the site, but they are incorporated in rebuilding according to the original plans and specifications. Is the resultant building a new building with some left-over pieces of the old one or is it the old building with many and significant new parts? Maybe, given the example as I have described it, we would say that it is a new building, and so a type-restoration.

The determining factor would seem to be the relatively small number of original parts incorporated in the new construction. If, however, we increase the proportion of left-over parts we will inevitably reach a point where we would say that it is the old building token-restored. At some point in between there will be no determinate answer to the question as to whether we have a token-restoration or a type-restoration. Many restorations, including restorations of nature, may turn out to be of this type. Thus we can imagine a forest that has been considerably thinned, in which cattle have grazed for a long time, into which noxious weeds and feral animals have been introduced, and from which many indigenous species have disappeared. The changes the forest has undergone have dramatically reshaped its ecology; maybe so much so that we are tempted to say that the original forest, understood as an instance of particular type of ecosystem, has ceased to exist. The project of restoring the original forest might well be an instance of type-restoring. If, however, we begin to scale back the degree of interruptions to the original ecosystem, there will come a point where it is completely appropriate to think of the restoration as token-restoration. There will be a range of cases in between where the project is neither determinately the one species of restoration or the other.

Notice also that the distinctions between token-faking and type-faking on the one hand, and token-restoration and type-restoration on the other, are not strictly analogous. This is because token-restoring requires that the restoration be done on a specific object. The building is only token-restored if there is a single building postdating and predating the restoration and upon which the restoration is performed. Token-restoring, unlike token-faking, does not involve the creation of a replica, where this implies the existence, or even the possibility of the existence, at some time or other, of two relevant objects, namely the original and the replica. In token-restoring there is a single object. The token-restoration seeks to make that object more like it once was than it now is. Token-restoration presupposes continuity of a particular object which endures damage, and is then restored, while token-faking presupposes that something new, a replica, comes into existence. The point is worth labouring, since it provides a basis for discounting token-fakings with respect to token-restorings. Restoration, importantly, leaves us with the real thing. The fact that something is the real thing may give it a value not matched by the value of a replica, even where the replica is more like the restored object in its original state than that object is in its restored state. Originality or authenticity count for a great deal in value assessments; they do not make merely minor impacts on evaluations based on intrinsic properties alone.

These remarks make explicit an important point: not all restorations are complete restorations. Indeed some discussants might want to signal this fact by talking in terms of rehabilitation. The implication, it might be thought, is then clearer; namely that the process of improving value or restoring value does not always result in something exactly in the same condition it was earlier in. And then it might be added that partial rehabilitation is better than no rehabilitation at all. My use of 'restoration' is like this use of 'rehabilitation'; it admits of degrees. Nor should this talk of improving value be thought in any way to imply that nature can be improved by human intervention. It cannot. The improvement that is delivered through restoration or rehabilitation derives from the fact that these processes strive to follow natural designs, natural patterns: they strive to replace, restore or rehabilitate that which nature had created and which was subsequently destroyed or degraded by humans. It should also be pointed out that token-restoration, unlike token-faking, may or may not be deceptive. That token-restoration has been carried out may be something the restorer or others would want to hide from us, perhaps because they know we do not accept the replacement thesis and that we would judge the restored object to have less value than would be possessed by the object had it continued to exist intact. Or token-restoration may be explicitly acknowledged because of the value that it restores. Token-faking, in contrast, involves unambiguously the production of a replica which is then passed of as an original.

While there is no strict parallel between token-restoration and token-faking, there is, in fact, a somewhat closer relationship between type-restoration and token-faking. In the latter case an object is produced which exemplifies a great many of the intrinsic properties of some original object. The original object, if it still exists, could be placed beside the fake. Where the faking is well done, it would be difficult to tell which of the two adjacent objects is the original. The terminology I have suggested is, it turns out, a little confusing. The fake endeavours to reproduce a set of characteristics, in other words a type, exemplified by the original. This is what type-restoration seeks to do, except that in the case of type restoration the original cannot be put beside the replica. Type-restoration is analogous to that variant of token-faking in which the authentic object no longer exists. Type-faking, by contrast, does not try to exemplify some very extensive and determinate set of properties exemplified by a single authentic object, rather it tries to exemplify certain very general features exemplified by a group of authentic objects. Indeed the reason that the parallels go the way just now described is that token-faking, unlike token-restoring, is not a process performed on an original to put back value.

With this warning about possible confusion in mind, it is nevertheless helpful to continue using the suggested terminology.

It is useful to distinguish between three types of token-restoration. One type involves the removal of matter that has been added and that has spoiled the qualities originally possessed by the object of restoration. Imagine that a building has become discoloured by soot so that its overall aesthetic quality has been diminished. Assume that there has been no chemical interaction between the soot and the original building materials, so that the restoration really does involve only the removal of matter that has been added. Or consider the case of a painting over which a layer of varnish has been placed. Likewise the removal of the varnish would be an example of this first kind of restoration. The removal of very recently introduced feral animals would be an example of this kind of restoration, assuming that they had done no noticeable damage to the relevant ecosystem which itself had to be repaired. What is distinctive of this kind of restoration is that the original object is intact; it has not been intrinsically damaged, and its intrinsic properties have not been altered. Let us call this form of token-restoration 'extrinsic restoration'.

A second form of token-restoration involves the addition of matter where original matter has been lost or damaged. An example is patching a wall from which a lump of matter has been dislodged. In this second type of restoration the original object is intrinsically damaged, and the restoration involves a less superficial sort of intervention than in the first type of case. An example from the domain of the natural would be the reintroduction of a species into an area from which it had become extinct.[6] Call this form of token-restoration 'intrinsic restoration'. Intrinsic restoration will, of course, involve varying degrees of intrusion, ranging from the relatively small-scale, such as minor replantings, to the large-scale, such as putting meanders back into watercourses from which they have been earlier removed (Light and Higgs 1996: 228). In fact many examples of restoration will involve both extrinsic and intrinsic restoration, so yielding a third form of token-restoration. We might call this 'mixed restoration'.

There is also a kind of case that is not simple to classify in the terms provided just now. Consider a case in which feral animals are removed from an area only after they have done considerable damage. The damage, however, may be remedied by natural processes over some period of time without any further intrusive contribution from humans, provided that the feral animals once removed are kept out permanently. The damage is such that natural self-healing, so to speak, is possible. Something analogous to extraneous matter is removed and nothing is added, although it is true that the original object, here the ecosystem, is not completely intact. I am inclined to regard such cases as more like extrinsic restoration than intrinsic restoration even though the intrinsic properties of the area in question have been clearly and substantially altered. Indeed what this kind of example shows is that the line between intrinsic and extrinsic restoration is blurred, and some instances of restoration could properly be counted in either category.

There are links between restoration, preservation and protection that should be highlighted. It is easy enough to see that the preservation, say of a painting, could involve restoration. Preservation aims to keep some object in existence, without any further deterioration of its distinctive properties but it might also aim to repair the condition of the object to be preserved. It would seem consistent with preservation to take steps of a restorative kind as well. Ideally, though, preservation is pursued sufficiently early to ensure that there is no deterioration at all of distinctive properties. Preservation may also aim at some particular type of thing rather than all existing tokens of the type: preservation of a particular may be motivated by the goal of preserving the type, through some, as a matter of fact this, particular. Thus one building of a certain style might be preserved, not in order to preserve that particular building as such, but in order to preserve at least one example of the particular style of building. Likewise the declaration of a national park might be motivated by the desire to preserve at least one example of some distinctive kinds of ecosystems. And the preservation of natural areas might involve repair and restoration. An area might be brought back from a state of degradation so that it might, in its repaired condition, be preserved.

Continuing a mode already employed, we might distinguish between type-preservation and token-preservation. In the case of preservation, type-preservation will always involve token-preservation. The point of the distinction is merely to signal that there is a particular reason for some token-preservations, namely that they are, in addition, type-preservations. So one token-preservation may be more compellingly justified than another, because some type of ecosystem is threatened and would be made safer through that particular act of token-preservation. Token-restoration of various kinds is one way in which the type-preservationist goal might be secured. There is another obvious way as well, namely through protection. Erecting barriers between art works and viewers is one way of protecting, and so preserving, the former. Examples are placing glass against a photographic image or putting a cordon around a piece of sculpture. Such barriers prevent intentional acts of destruction and vandalism, and also prevent unintentional damage through such thoughtless actions as touching and probing. Likewise the banning of off-road vehicles from, or prohibiting the grazing of cattle in, national parks, perhaps materially manifest in a series of signs, fences and barriers, can protect a natural area from damage. Unlike intrinsic restoration, protection does not involve any interference with or alteration of the object itself, although there might be a relatively unintrusive contact such as the removal of feral animals. And unlike extrinsic restoration there need not be any contact with the object itself, except perhaps at the periphery. Even peripheral contact might be minimized through the use of buffer zones, rather than a sharp edge, to separate the park from degraded areas.

To sum up, the important distinctions that have been drawn are those between faking, restoring, preserving and protecting. Moreover, there is some degree of blurring and overlap between these categories. And, within them, there is the type–token distinction, and the intrinsic–extrinsic distinction. These distinctions are useful in making value discriminations between various kinds of human involvements with nature and between the results of such involvements. Some of these judgements have been made in passing. Most importantly, it is asserted that a restored natural environment, provided it accords with natural designs and is constituted by natural objects, may possess considerable intrinsic value, and certainly much more than the degraded environment which was the object of restoration. This judgement is entirely consistent with the anti-replacement thesis, and the value difference between the degraded and the restored environment provides a compelling reason to embark on a project of restoration. The point is important since the anti-replacement thesis has been read by some as implying that restored nature is of negligible value (Gunn 1991; Katz 1991 and 1992a; Sylvan 1994). Nor does the thesis strictly imply that an area of land that has been restored cannot eventually come to have the value possessed by that area prior to its degradation.

Restoration may assist nature to reassert itself and to take control of some area once more: human intervention, although initially quite marked, might diminish and disappear. It is even possible to make sense of this idea in the case of type-restorations. These, remember, are restorations in which there is no significant remnant of original nature remaining in some area and in which the type of ecosystem originally characterizing the area is reconstructed over time.[7] Here, all continuity with the past ecosystem has been destroyed but nature may come to take control of the area that has been artificially created in accordance with the relevant natural design. After a time, the area, preserved through restoration, certainly where token-restoration is the mode, may come to have a value very close to that possessed by the area originally there. As indicated earlier, in making such comparisons we need to keep account of the absence of natural value or reduced natural value during the intervening period. We also need to keep in mind that had degradation not taken place, and had restoration not then been necessary, the natural area that would have occupied the space of the restored area would have had a continuity with the past, a provenance, not had by the restored area. The anti-replacement thesis says that originality, naturalness and natural continuity reaching into the past are important determinants of natural value. The restored environment could eventually become a natural environment but its natural continuity with a distant past would have been broken.

It may be argued that it is misleading to think of the restored ecosystem as seriously artificial or to think of it as an artefact in any deep sense. Certainly the means by which the restoration takes place is at least partially artificial but there may be more to the issue than the naturalness or otherwise of the means. Human restorative activity is guided and structured by the designs of nature. The original ecosystem exemplified a specific ecosystemic type, instantiated by numerous natural objects and organisms in relationships with one another. This ecosystemic type is a natural product, a naturally evolved design. Successful restoration accords with this design and involves its instantiation by natural objects and organisms, for example rainforest trees and cassowaries, which, while they might be intentionally raised by humans for restorative purposes, are, for all that, natural items. Their natures, their essences are not artefacts. They, like the ecosystemic types they instantiate, are the design-products of projective nature. Taking this perspective, we might even say that type-restoration is not through and through artificial. This suggestion will be anathema to some who endorse the anti-replacement thesis. Katz, for example, claims that restoration does, of necessity, involve the creation of artefacts (Katz 1992a: 232). What he seems not to take account of, though, is the role that natural processes and natural design play in the restoration. Nor does he take account of the considerable replacement of value that restoration can achieve. His view seems to be that human intervention in some area of nature completely destroys the intrinsic value of that area, even though similar areas, that are not at all the result of human intervention, would have considerable intrinsic value (Katz 1991, 1992a, 1992b; Sylvan 1990: 67–9). My view is that they have a lesser value, although certainly not zero value. Natural continuity, uninterrupted by human activity, is a significant determinant of natural value but it is not a precondition for natural value. To be fair to Katz, he does not think that restoration should not be pursued where degradation occurs. He agrees, for example, that as a matter of policy, Exxon should indeed have been required to restore the Alaskan coastline that was degraded through its negligence (Katz 1992a: 240). He seems, however, to regard such efforts as merely producing a better appearance and not restoring natural value.

Quite some time has been spent discussing various pertinent types of what Sylvan so aptly calls 'mucking with nature' (Sylvan 1994: 48). It might now be helpful to attempt a classification of natural values across those various modes of mucking with nature.

These will be, of necessity, crude evaluations. They will not, for example, take account of the possibility that some areas may have more value than others, because, say, they exhibit greater complexity or natural variety. They do not take account of the way in which degree of rarity might determine the value of a particular natural area, one plausible suggestion being that increasing rarity increases value. The broad evaluations offered should be read as containing a clause to the effect that other things are equal. Actual judgements in particular cases will be complicated, with possibly many factors having to be taken into account. This said, however, faked nature, in the most literal sense, has less value than token-restored nature. Recall, also, that type-restorations are similar to some token-fakings, namely those in which the original no longer exists. While type-restoration may not involve the element of deception that characterizes faking, it would still seem that the type-restored product would have the same value as the faked product, other things being equal of course. What is crucial in the case of token-restorings is that there is at least some significant degree of continuity between the restored and the original areas. The greater the continuity, the greater the value of the token-restoration at the end of the restoration process.

We should note, though, that token-restoration might well be a continuing enterprise, with no sharp termination. So large-scale extrinsic, and even intrinsic intervention might diminish in magnitude over time to the point where only some small-scale extrinsic interventions are employed on a continuing basis. For example, it might be necessary to continue to remove weeds or feral animals from an area. Here restoration blurs into protection and preservation. Extrinsic restoration, furthermore, will tend to result in more value than intrinsic restoration. The underlying idea is that extrinsic restoration does less to disrupt natural continuities, and is less an imposition of human control and technology, than intrinsic restoration. Maybe there are exceptions to this general rule, as when we compare large-scale extrinsic restorations with utterly minimal intrinsic restorations. Token-restored nature, moreover, tends to have somewhat less value than nature that is preserved or protected, although not restored. Nature that is preserved or protected, although not restored, has the same value as unprotected nature. Again the underlying value-determinant is authenticity or originality, understood in terms of degree of uninterrupted continuity with earlier phases of the area in question.

Matters are, however, complicated by the claim, made earlier, about the diminishing value-subtracting force of interventions over time. The claim was that a restored area increases in value as the length of time between the intervention and the time of evaluation increases. The underlying idea here is that nature might completely regain control and wash out, so to speak, the value-subtracting force of the, very much earlier, intervention. Recall, though, that value calculations are made across time and not merely at a time. While there is a sense in which, over a sufficiently long time, token-restoration, and maybe even type-restoration, can restore full value, it cannot compensate for the value lost during the intervening period of decreasingly diminished value.

THE VALUE OF RESTORATION AND THE OBLIGATION TO RESTORE

It has been argued that restored nature may be, indeed usually will be, of significant value. To what extent does this provide a basis for the suggestion that we have an obligation to restore degraded nature? For one thing, in many instances where natural systems have been degraded there will be continued degradation: the situation will become worse and there will be a continuing diminution of natural values. There is an obligation to prevent loss of value, and it is particularly compelling where the costs of restoration and the effort required do not entail significant hardship. This is certainly the situation for many of us. Small redistributions of our resources and small adjustments to our lifestyles will often make a difference in ensuring that degradation does not continue and that degraded areas are restored. The impact of these small differences are magnified through collective effort. There is also some obligation to increase natural value, particularly where substantial increases of value can be achieved, as is the case with the restoration of degraded areas. The assumption, of course, is that natural values are comparatively intense and that other values lost through the costs and efforts of restoration are less significant. So, even without endorsing any obligation to maximize value, and endorsing only less ambitious principles, there is an obligation to restore degraded nature.

Obligations to restore become more compelling when we accept that much of the degradation that surrounds us is the result of our activity, in conjunction with that of others of our species, and that it is activity from which we have in many ways benefited. The obligation to restore value is not tied exclusively to the loss of value that restoration prevents or to the increase in value that restoration might achieve. The obligation is driven by a duty of restitution, here a duty to restore natural value, not merely because it is natural value, but because it was wrongly or impermissibly eroded in the first place. In such instances the restitutive act should aim to reintroduce not merely value, but value of the same kind as was removed. While we ourselves might not have participated in environmental despoliation, it is close to certain that we have benefited in many ways from such despoliation, past and present. It is, as I have remarked, certain that we have, however unwillingly, participated in a form of social and economic life that has contributed massively to the erosion of natural values. Where we repair specific damage that is clearly done by others and clearly not by us, our actions, therefore, can be seen as, in part, acts of restitution (Gunn 1991: 308; Sylvan 1994: 65–8; Taylor 1986: 186–92, 304–6; Wenz 1988: 287–91). We can make restitution for our roles in degrading nature in one place by contributing to its restoration elsewhere. And this is not a trade-off in which we establish credits, so to speak, for damage that we carry out in the former place. Thus a developer cannot justify clearing certain natural areas for housing by pointing to the value of restoration work she or he has funded elsewhere (Katz 1992a: 231). In trade-off situations, actions are generally permissible, although, perhaps, regrettable. In the kind of situation envisaged here, the destructive action is impermissible: the restitution is for something we should not have done, for something that was impermissible for us to do.

Restitution, it must be stressed, does not somehow render what was done retrospectively permissible or in any other way morally redeemed. The past action was, and remains, impermissible and that fact, moreover, generates present and continuing obligations to restore degraded nature. Since we have been complicit, in varying degrees, in a range of activities that have degraded natural areas, it is plausible to claim that we have extensive restitutive obligations to restore degraded natural areas. This is an instance of a general obligation to restore, where we can, value that we destroy or erode. Discharging the consequent restitutive duty is not only deontologically required, it also has positive value. In restoring natural values there is a comparatively very small bonus: not only do we recharge the world with some of the type of value that human activity has wrung from it, we generate value directly in virtue of doing something we are obliged to do.

It is important to stress that accepting the view that restored nature may be of significant value does not offer support to advocates of the replacement thesis or approximations of it. The reason, already mentioned, is that there is an obligation not to destroy value. Consequent restoration does not erase the wrongness or impermissibility of the despoliation. To say that one will replace what one destroys does not negate the fact that value has been destroyed. The despoiling act is impermissible and we may not perform it, even if there is something that we would later do, such as restoring an area from which we have drained natural values, that would maintain or even increase value overall. The point is that the value of the restitutive act may not be factored into any assessment of the permissibility of a proposed despoiling act at the outset. Restoration certainly can restore some value and it is certainly morally required as restitution for earlier impermissible actions, but this is a far cry from the conclusion that the possibility of restoring value means that despoliation is not quite so wrong as it at first seems, let alone not particularly wrong at all.

This conclusion must rely to some extent on ethical assessments which go beyond the purely axiological. In other words it must rely on principles of obligation which are not functions over value, which do more than merely tell us to act some way with respect to value. If we stick entirely to the axiological then some trade-offs, which are in fact impermissible, would probably be underwritten. Perhaps this is not so. Perhaps there are some very complicated value-adding and value-subtracting properties which would enable us to make all of the right judgements without going beyond axiology to independent deontological principles. If there are such properties I would not like to have to articulate them, although some are, arguably, described in the concluding paragraphs of this chapter. Perhaps it is possible to rely on the intensity of natural values or on the claim that they are absolutely value-adding. It seems neater to accept that there is, at least, a deontological principle that says that the degradation or destruction of natural value is wrong or impermissible. Indeed even if the judgement could be delivered on axiological grounds, it is still possible that it has a deontological basis as well.

This is not say that there may not be a few cases in which despoliation is morally defensible; where we think it is permissible to act, on the basis of some very good justification, to reduce natural value with, perhaps, restoration in mind. The default position, though, is that it is not permissible. The justification for this as the default position has three components: first, wild nature has enormous intrinsic value; second, the value-destroying activities of our kind have already devastated the surface ecologies of our planet; third, it is generally impermissible to destroy or degrade intrinsic value. What is more, in striving to establish whether some act of despoliation is permissible, because it increases value for a good reason, we must be especially careful to distinguish between the value of the restitutive act *qua* restitutive act, which must not count at the outset, and the value of the resultant restored environment, which may count at the outset.

An analogy helps here. Imagine that I am considering causing a person some pain. I believe that only by causing the person pain can I secure a desired outcome. I calculate, however, that the value of the outcome does not compensate for the disvalue of the pain. But then I note that sincere apologies to the victims after the pain has been inflicted usually has positive value. If this case were such a case, then, together, the value of the apology and of the desired outcome would compensate for the disvalue of the pain. This way of thinking about the situation, however, seems misconceived, partly because it is difficult to see how such an apology could in fact be sincere. An apology given in such circumstances would be at best of neutral value. This is so, plausibly, even in those cases where a person acts in this calculated way but later comes to see the inappropriateness of it, and really does sincerely apologize and feel genuine remorse. It seems that the value of the apology is reduced at least to zero if it is factored into the overall calculation of value at the outset. We cannot justify some act of despoliation by saying that we will later carry out restitutive acts. Destructive acts, moreover, have disvalue over and above the disvalue of their consequences and this must be offset against the value of later restitutive acts. So imagine that an act reduces value by destroying an area of wild nature. Here we have not only the disvalue of the environmental damage but additional disvalue attaching to the destructive act itself. This also partially explains why environmental damage caused by human acts produces more disvalue overall than is produced when similar damage is done by natural phenomena. The disvalue of the degradation of a forest through human activity, such as clearing, would be greater than the disvalue of the degradation of that forest through a natural phenomenon, such as a volcanic eruption.

The quantity of disvalue attaching to the destructive act itself is arguably also a function of the goodness or virtuousness of its motive. Thus destruction of natural value motivated by greed may generate more disvalue than similar degradation motivated by the desire to minimally provide for one's own comfort. The claim is not that the magnitude of the natural values lost through degradation can be intensified by the motives, or the like, of the perpetrators. The disvalue associated with motives, or the like, is discrete and additional. Of course, compared to the disvalue associated with the loss of natural value it is pretty insignificant, but not so insignificant that it deserves no mention. It provides us with another reason, not that one is needed, for rejecting any suggestion that the replacement thesis provides any leverage for those who wish to advance the restoration proposal. The rejection of the replacement thesis depends on there being a coherent and normatively interesting distinction between the natural and the unnatural or artificial. It is time now to argue that there is such a distinction.

NATURALNESS, INTRINSIC VALUE AND RESTORATION ECOLOGY

THE NATURAL, THE NON-NATURAL AND THE ARTIFICIAL

The idea of the natural, or of naturalness, plays a central role in the arguments of many environmentalists. Even when environmentalists are not particularly concerned to argue for the value of the natural, they frequently speak as if there's a clear line between what is and what isn't natural. However, it is usually the case that the notion is used in a way that gives it an evaluative dimension. In this respect it is rather like the idea of the beautiful. When something is judged to be beautiful there is an implication that it should be treated with care and respect, that it should be preserved. To say that something is beautiful is, prima facie, to give a compelling reason for restoring it, protecting it, caring for it and preserving it.

This feature of the use of the ideas of the natural and the beautiful does not itself entail that the natural or the beautiful is intrinsically valuable or, more accurately, that they are value-adding properties. There would be point in giving the natural a value dimension even if things which fell into the category of the natural were valued not for themselves but for the pleasure they give. The value here would, of course, be instrumental or extrinsic value. And we certainly have good reason to restore, protect, care for and preserve things which have such value. For the most part, though, environmentalists do seem to attribute intrinsic value to the natural in virtue of its naturalness. This, of course, was the view defended in the second chapter of this book, where naturalness or the property of being natural was identified as one basis or determinant of nature's intrinsic moral value.[1] And in the third chapter, the distinctions between the natural and the artificial, or between nature and culture, played a crucial

116

role in the development of the anti-replacement thesis. It is useful now to explore the notion of the natural and the bases of these distinctions, and then provide some additional discussion of the connection between naturalness and intrinsic value.

We might begin by asking just what is natural. One simple answer is that absolutely everything is natural. In one sense, undoubtedly this is true. All that happens in the universe is determined and constrained by laws of nature: the structuring of the universe and all that it contains is an extended natural process. Certainly humans, and other intelligent forms of life, are natural products, owing their existence to natural processes which determine their capacities and structures. On this, the broadest, view of the natural, everything that goes on within the universe is natural.[2] When a tree grows and flourishes nothing non-natural is occurring; when a species becomes extinct, even as a result of the degradation of wild areas by humans, nothing non-natural is occurring; when humans clear wilderness and build cities nothing non-natural is occurring. All of these processes occur because the laws of nature are as they are. Nothing that happens can, in this sense, be non-natural. Nothing that anyone ever does can, in this sense, be non-natural.[3]

It is clearly not this idea of the natural that environmentalists have in mind when they urge us to desist from polluting the air, from turning productive land into desert, from disrupting the ozone layer, claiming that, in some sense or other, these things are contrary to nature, or non-natural. Or so it seems. While it is possible to take the view that everything that exists and that every process that occurs has intrinsic value just in virtue of its existence or occurrence, that would not itself provide the basis for morally condemning some actions or attributing intrinsic value to some thing. The appeal to the natural, if it is to do anything like the normative work required of it, signals a notion of the natural somewhat more fine-grained. Indeed, in the last chapter, the distinction between the natural and the non-natural was made in terms of the distinction between what was and what was not a product of culture and technology.[4] While this is the basis for the distinction that I think is most plausible, there are some other options to be pursued before further discussing this view.

One way of trying to grasp what advocates of environmentalism do have in mind when they condemn certain actions and policies because they are non-natural, is through a consideration of the injunction that we ought to act in harmony with nature. There is a variety of ways of understanding this injunction. Let us start with the

117

most straightforward. Some of the policies we pursue do not in the long run contribute to the quality of human lives. In many instances the quality of human lives is diminished or threatened because of the way our actions impinge on the uncontrollable elements of the world around us. For example, it isn't pleasant to live in a city susceptible to photochemical smog. Photochemical smog results from a causal complex that involves certain of our actions and certain fixed uncontrollable elements in the local geographical and climate systems. Our actions are mediated by these environmental factors in such a way that they rebound adversely on us. We drive cars because it suits us to do so in the context of our economically driven conurbations and our present forms of life, because they enable us to lead mobile and interesting lives, and because they widen our choices about where to live, where to work, where to seek recreation and so on. These are some of the contextual benefits, but as we all know there are also costs. The costs arise because the world is as it is, because the laws of nature are such that if we do certain things, certain other things happen. And, in the case we are considering, what happens is not pleasant for humans and subverts their health.

To live in harmony with nature is, on this view, to maximize the quality of our lives by ensuring that our actions do not, by way of their effects on the environment, produce too many costs. Living in harmony with nature is merely making the best of the laws of nature. Here, living in harmony with nature is not driven by a concern to respect nature for itself but by a wariness about how our impact on it might threaten our own well-being. It is clear, however, that on this interpretation environmentalist objectives may be thwarted, since all that is required on this understanding of the injunction is that we take care not to harm our interests by 'harming' nature. If we could be sure that, for instance, environmental degradation, despoliation, would have no adverse impact on human interests, then there would be no obligation to refrain from such actions. If technology could guarantee that the dominance, and extensive exploitation, of nature by human beings would not harm human interests, then the harmony in question would be delivered. At the very least we could expect that there could be limited or contained despoliation that would have little adverse impact on humans.

Living in harmony with nature is often taken to mean something else. At the other extreme it may be taken to mean living in such a way that our actions leave an absolutely minimal impact on the environment (Jordan 1994: 26). This is to be understood in terms of minimizing, to the extreme, the causal role of our actions in shaping the landscape. This suggestion may seem too extreme to take seriously in a policy context, but it is one which does find advocates. Robert Cahn, for example, urges us, metaphorically one presumes, to leave only our footprints where we pass (Cahn 1978). Sometimes the injunction that we should take only photographs is added (Jordan 1994: 21). It is also the view that is expressed in the United States Wilderness Act of 1964 (Callicott 1991: 240). If such an injunction is to be taken literally, then our real-life actions are about as far from the implied ideals as they possibly could be. In fact it is just not possible for all of us, or perhaps any of us, to live this way. Even hunter-gatherers shape their environments, if only by making paths through the bush, by lighting fires, by clearing living areas, by cutting trees and so on. It is difficult to describe anything like a human social arrangement in which more than footprints are not left behind.[5] Surely this is not what those who enjoin us to live in harmony with nature have in mind. At most it is feasible only in areas not already, or only minimally, inhabited by humans.

Taken literally, the 'only footprints' injunction denies human beings what it allows other animals. Many non-human animals reshape their environments significantly. An obvious example is the beaver which modifies watercourses, alters plant life and alters freshwater marine life. Countless non-human animals do leave more than footprints where they have passed, and contribute to the shaping of ecosystems and landscapes. If leaving only footprints is what is required by the injunction to live in harmony with nature, then it seems that many non-human animals do not so live. Nor could it be that this strict reading of what is involved in living in harmony with nature expresses what environmentalists have in their minds when they appeal to the notion of the natural as a value-differentiator. While we may want to say that such activity by non-humans reduces the intrinsic value that a piece of the natural environment possesses, or that it degrades or destroys natural value, it is still difficult to see any point to the claim that the beaver's activity, for example, is non-natural. This shows of course that the natural and the valuable may not always go hand in hand, or that they do so in subtle ways. This is an issue to which we shall return below.

Nor is it only the activities of non-human animals that shape ecosystems. The behaviour of plants also contributes to the shaping of ecosystems, as when a bird drops a seed from one area into another area. And, spectacularly, natural forces such as wind, eruption, earthquake, fire, flood and glaciation shape environments. Usually this spectacular reshaping will involve a significant loss of natural value, although in many cases it will lay the foundation for the evolution of new bases of natural value. For example, a volcanic eruption may lay waste natural areas, extinguishing ecosystems that have developed over time. After the eruption, new ecosystems will develop as natural forces modify the landscape, as organisms fill new niches, as new species evolve, and so on. In many instances the destruction of natural value through natural forces gives rise to landscapes which we judge to be aesthetically spectacular, such as the Grand Canyon. One question to which these observations give rise is whether loss of natural value through natural forces can be fully compensated for by the subsequent creation of natural value. The compensation, moreover, might not be in the form of intrinsic value of subsequent landscape but in the sequence of changing landscapes. In other words we might ask whether there is a fundamental ethical difference between a sequence of destruction and recreation of value involving only natural forces as against a sequence of destruction and re-creation of value through human intention and design. This question is taken up again below.

Despite these points there is some appeal in the 'only footprints' view – in fact, I think, considerable appeal. Perhaps this is most easily understood as a reaction to the environmental havoc that our species has wrought. Perhaps it is partly a form of puritanism born of disgust and despair concerning our present way of life. But what strikes me as the particularly interesting question is whether the injunction, taken literally, can be built into a consistent ethical principle. In one sense of course it can: it does not oblige us to do anything that is logically impossible to do. It does, however, oblige us to pursue actions and policies which are for practical purposes close to impossible: it would seem, for example, to oblige us to massively reduce human populations, to massively reduce levels of consumption, and thoroughly to restructure our economic and social forms of life. Even if we are unable to do all that it obliges us to do, there are subsidiary obligations which we are reasonably able to meet.[6] Thus it is possible to cease our overt incursions into such areas of wild nature that remain relatively intact, to take steps to protect and preserve them, to rehabilitate at least some of those natural areas that have been so appallingly degraded, to flatten growth in human population and consumption, and to develop more environmentally sensitive technology.

120

Treating the injunction that we leave only footprints as a serious candidate for an ethical principle involves, I think, an implied suggestion that nature is in some way sacred, or at least worthy and deserving of respect. A secularized understanding of what this involves brings us back to the claim that there are natural intrinsic values and to the associated claim that naturalness is, perhaps in conjunction with aesthetic value, a determinant of the intrinsic moral value exemplified by nature. And this returns us to a question already raised, namely, whether there is a conceptually legitimate distinction to be drawn between what is natural and what is not, which is also capable of bearing the normative weight placed on it by the normative theory of natural values endorsed in this book.

Let us refocus, then, on the issue of the distinction between the natural and the non-natural through a consideration of the question of what human activities might conceivably count as natural. A plausible first suggestion is that activities that do not alter the natural environment except in minimal ways, are natural in the relevant sense: this is simply a variant of the 'only footprints' view. Collecting some wood for fires, taking some fruit from trees, killing some animals for their meat and skins, building very basic shelters, and the like, are perhaps natural. What seems necessary, in order to mark off the natural from the non-natural in the sense desired, is some coherent notion of the natural that gives results that fit reasonably neatly with what the 'only footprints' view seems intuitively to require. I doubt, however, that there is such a conception. One suggestion, mentioned above, rests on the idea of humans not modifying landscapes. But there are many mechanical processes, again referred to above, that surely have to count as natural in which this does happen. Perhaps the difference between the natural and the non-natural is to be understood in terms of modifications to the environment that are not brought about by inanimate agents. But this will not do either. There are a great many animals that do modify their environments substantially. Beavers, as I've already noted, do something that humans are often rightly criticized for doing, namely building dams.

The question to ask, then, is just how is most of what humans do non-natural? One suggestion is simply that the extent and force of humankind's modification of the environment makes it somehow non-natural. There have, however, been more than a few dramatic environmental modifications which have nothing to do with humans. For instance, the last ice age changed the shape of the environment extensively and, more dramatically in the short term anyway, the eruption of Mt St Helens in Washington state extensively altered a large area of land. It is true, of course, that humans do have a huge impact on the environment and important reasons for this are our levels of technological development, our cultural norms and our social organization. The extent of our consumption and the sheer size of human populations, which so obviously determine the degree to which we degrade nature, are functions of these things.

Another suggestion is that it is the fact that human actions, which modify the landscape so extensively, are intentional that makes them non-natural. This suggestion does not, however, permit any sharp differentiation between the modifying activities of humans and non-human animals. Whether or not non-human animals can intend anything is an issue I do not want to take up at this point, but I do happen to think that many kinds of non-human animals act intentionally. While some of these kinds of non-human animals lack the capacity for conscious forward planning, do not have certain outcomes in their mind's eye, and do not comprehend exactly how certain actions will result in those outcomes, there are nevertheless more limited forms of intentional action of which they will be capable. It is worth adding that the category of intentional action is probably blurred at the boundaries, with no sharp distinction between intentional and non-intentional action. And where the boundary is drawn will depend on how much consciousness or self-consciousness we build into intentional action (Dennett 1987).

What is more promising than the intentional actions suggestion is one which is connected to it, involving rational capacities more generally.[7] So possession of certain rational capacities may make us unique in a way that places us outside the natural order. We are able to control and dominate nature in a way unparalleled by other creatures: it is our use, driven by cultural and economic norms, of science and technology to transform the environment that makes what we do non-natural. It is not unhelpful to think of ourselves as functionally similar to an introduced species that is disruptive of its new environments, such as rabbits in Australia and possums in New Zealand. In both these cases, there is no naturally constrained ecological niche for these animals, no natural, evolved checks and balances on their numbers, and so no brake on their impact on their environments. In both instances they have caused great damage to environments that, before their introduction, were relatively stable. Their introduction throws developed ecosystems into unstable states, as the creatures in question rapidly occupy the open niches that are available. Likewise our rational capacity has placed us in a position where our disruptive influence on environments is considerable, causing disharmony and instability in natural systems. We leave nature through our culture and technology, so to speak, and re-enter it as an alien species. Furthermore, the contrast between what is natural and what is not is often drawn as the contrast between what is natural and what is artificial. This tendency to contrast the natural with the artificial reinforces the suggestion that what is natural is best thought of as what has not been modified as a result of people exercising their rational capacities.

On this suggested account of the natural, all humans fall outside the natural, including indigenous peoples living traditional lifestyles. Obviously such humans live in social arrangements with well-developed cultural forms and employ technology of varying degrees of sophistication. While their impact on natural environments is non-natural, in the same broad sense as that of contemporary humans in developed economies, the degree of disruptiveness of that impact is usually comparatively small, although not insignificant. Thus fire regimes employed by indigenous Australians may have contributed to significant vegetation changes and may have caused some species to become extinct (Clark 1990). Or again, there is much evidence to show that American Indians significantly shaped, through their cultures and technologies, including their use of fire, the landscapes in which they lived (Williams 1988: 22–49). But it is not the quantum of impact that is the basis for a useful and workable distinction between the natural and the non-natural. We should attend to the structure of the agency involved. Thus human agency is importantly different from other kinds of agency, such as the agency of non-human animals, of plants, of acids, of geophysical forces and the like. Human agency involves an array of higher-order intentional states, is mediated by a heavy intrusion of culture, social organization and highly structured economic arrangements and is exaggerated by technological capacities. While humans are the result of, and are embedded in, natural processes, including cosmological, evolutionary and biological processes, they have transcended the natural.[8] We shall return to this point below.

The anti-replacement thesis, defended earlier, presupposes a distinction between the natural and the artificial, between what nature produces through evolutionary, geomorphological, climatic processes and the like, and what humans, as creatures of culture and technology, produce. The thesis does not assume that the natural/non-natural or natural/artificial distinction marks a sharp dichotomy: it allows that there are degrees of naturalness, that some environments are more natural than others. Certainly many terrestrial environments have been massively reshaped by human activity. The anti-replacement thesis also accepts that no terrestrial environment may be entirely natural, given the perhaps completely pervasive effects of human activity. Thus the poisons of industrial activity can be found in the deepest oceans, and the pollutants generated by life in contemporary conurbations have left traces in the Antarctic ice (Gunn 1991: 297). These distant impacts will no doubt feed into evolutionary processes, causing mutations and altering the determinants of fitness in particular environments. They lead to what Jordan has illuminatingly called 'ecosystem drift' (Jordan 1994: 22).[9] Indeed the most compelling sorts of cases involve human impacts on climatic and weather systems, where changes wrought by human activity penetrate the entire biosphere with relative rapidity (Smith and Watson 1979: 64). The anti-replacement thesis can accommodate this point about ecosystem drift. It does not have to concede that wherever human activity impacts on nature, the natural is transformed completely to the artificial. It says instead that there are degrees of naturalness and, further, that, other things being equal, value increases as naturalness increases. And it implies that there are still extensive areas of the earth's surface that are relatively natural and so deserving of preservation and protection.

The argument concerning the elimination of wild nature through the pervasive influence of human activity reappears in a more subtle form. In this form it concedes that there are relatively natural areas remaining but suggests that in the very act of preserving and protecting them they are rendered substantially less natural and somewhat less valuable. The basic claim is that there is no longer any such thing as wild nature or wilderness, since the preservation of those bits of it that remain is achievable only by deliberate policy. The idea is that by placing boundaries around national parks, by actively prohibiting disruptive activities such as grazing, trail-biking, mining, logging and so on, we are turning the wilderness into an artefact. The thought seems to be that in putting a boundary around a wild area we are somehow subverting its wildness, and that in some indirect way we are creating an artificial environment (Birch 1990; Nash 1989: 10; Rodman 1977; Williams 1992: 68). The argument implies that it is not possible as a matter of policy to protect wild nature, at least not by prohibiting disruptive incursions.

The argument is, of course, flawed. What is significant about wild nature is its causal continuity with the past, its relationship with an evolving series or sequence of states that are the products of natural forces. This causal continuity is something that is not destroyed by, for example, demarcating an area and declaring it a national park. There is an important distinction to be made between the naturalness of the area within the park and the means used to maintain and protect it. What is contained within the park boundaries is, as it were, the real thing. Moreover, within the boundaries of the park nature unfolds, evolves, and continues largely through the action of natural forces. This remains true even if what would have gone on in the park, were there no boundary and were there juxtaposition with surrounding natural areas, is somewhat different from what actually goes on. That wild nature within the park may have developed differently were there more wild nature outside the park, does not mean that the area within the park is in any way non-natural.

An example might help here. Imagine that an impressive rock formation within an urban area is protected from defacement or destruction. This does not make it any the less a natural object: it certainly does not mean that although it was once a natural object it is now an artificial object. While environmentalists may regret that positive policies are required to preserve wild nature against human assault, the regret is not a consequence of the view that what remains is less natural or of reduced value. What remains is natural and of immense value, requiring policy and resources to ensure its continued existence. There is, furthermore, a significant value difference between preventing damage and repairing damage once it is done. In the latter case the product of the restoration may be less natural and so of less value than the original area would have been had it remained intact and naturally evolved. Whether it is less natural and of less value would depend on the mode of the restoration, on whether, for example, it involves intrinsic restoration. That is one major difference that leaves room for an argument in favour of a pre-emptive preservation policy over and above a restoration policy.[10]

There is a related argument that is usefully considered here. According to this argument there is something fundamentally incoherent in the idea that natural areas can be preserved. The thought is that nature is essentially dynamic, it changes in multiple ways over even short time spans. The idea inherent in preservation, it is claimed, is that nature should somehow be captured, held constant, prevented from changing. Consequently in preserving nature we are preventing it from expressing its dynamic, unfixed nature (Jordan 1994: 19). This, however, is really only a caricature of what preservationists typically aim to do. While some might desire to freeze in time, so to speak, particular representative ecosystems as items in a dispersed natural museum, this is not typical. What preservationists, as I understand them, aim to do is to preserve natural areas as, in part, areas that will undergo change, that will transform over time, as a consequence of natural forces and relatively free from human influence. They aim to preserve areas in which nature is allowed to be, to develop and to unfold according to its own dynamics, not withstanding the fact of the pervasiveness of human influence.

Much of the discussion above might be taken to imply that the natural occurs only in areas that are relatively non-humanized, in which human activity is minimal. But this is not so. The natural can and does coexist, in varying degrees of tension, with the artificial. Thus wild creatures of various kinds, such as insects, worms, lizards and birds, are to be found in cities, towns and farmlands, as are trees, shrubs, flowers and mosses. Of course I have in mind organisms that are not introduced to these areas by humans, but which are vestiges or remnants of what was there before. These natural elements in human places give credibility to the claim that naturalness is a matter of degree. Moreover, the value that they have as individual natural items is considerable, and is not lessened by the fact that they exist in relatively humanized places.[11]

There is a related problem that has been alluded to several times already and that should now be addressed. I have spoken in terms of nature taking back, or recolonizing, areas from which it has been excluded through human activity or in which its presence has been diminished. It is best to approach these cases through a case in which human activity more subtly affects the natural world. Take the case of global warming and concede that human economic activity is having an impact on such interrelated things as weather patterns, glaciation, water-levels and climate. As a consequence of global warming tree lines will tend to move upwards, some habitats will be altered, some characteristics of organisms will be less constitutive of fitness in the altered habitat than they were in the original habitats, species characteristics will change, speciation will take directions it would not otherwise have taken, and some species will become extinct.

Are these changes natural or are they non-natural? Well, it is undeniable that the causal explanation of these phenomena must make reference to human activity that is driven by technology and by social and cultural norms. In some loose sense they are brought about by human activity; had humans not acted in the ways they have, then these changes would not have occurred. Although these changes are provoked, so to speak, by human activity, they can nevertheless be seen flowing as from nature's responses to systemic changes produced by that activity. It is a case of a natural response to a non-natural stimulus. And it seems quite different from a situation in which some natural area is cleared for human habitation, farming, mining or some such. Of course the devastation of natural values involved in such cases is quite directly nature's response to the brutality of human activity. However, nature is here massively and suddenly assaulted and there is no substantial sense in which nature remains as a significant force in the area that has been cleared. Moreover, in such areas humans typically wage a continuing campaign to prevent and stymie the re-emergence of controlling, shaping natural forces. While nature may be retained or reintroduced in small and bounded quantities, there is no sense in which it reasserts itself and takes control.

An initial suggestion is that the two kinds of case are differentiated by the gross impact of the relevant human activities. In the one case but not the other natural systems are literally smashed. In the other case natural systems are altered but active nature plays a significant shaping role in determining the outcomes of human activity. There seems to be the basis for a sound distinction here between the two kinds of case but there are some worrying aspects of these means of attempting to make good the distinction. In particular, the effects of the first sort of case, the subtle and pervasive case, can well be more widespread and of greater long-term magnitude than the effects of the second kind of case, which, although painfully obvious, might be comparatively localized. The point might be underlined by the following twist on the global warming example. Imagine that a nation-state deliberately increases its output of greenhouse gases in order to increase global temperatures so that agricultural patterns will change to its benefit. Here there is a very precise human design to alter ecosystems, and a relatively subtle and pervasive mechanism is employed. It is a mechanism that achieves its design by causing certain natural responses with cascading effects. Is the resultant world system non-natural or natural; is it artificial or natural? I find this a tough question but I think the best answer is that it is a natural system with a non-natural or artificial cause. The key issue, though, is how this representation of the situation impinges on questions of value. We shall come to that shortly.

So, the anti-replacement thesis assumes a conceptual distinction between the natural and the artificial, such as was suggested earlier. This suggestion has been questioned by some, using a version of the view that everything is natural, discussed at the beginning of this chapter. Such critics generally take the line that humans are just another species acting in ways that modify environments, displace other species and so on (Callicott 1991: 241; Gunn 1991: 296; Sober 1986: 179–84). But, for better or for worse, we are not just another species. As creatures of culture and technology we have partly transcended nature, we have become apart from nature, and, while we are members of a natural species, animals with natural instincts, drives and so on, much of what we do is not natural. As remarked earlier, while humans are the result of, and are embedded in, natural processes, including cosmological, evolutionary and biological processes, it is not merely metaphorical to say that we have partially transcended the natural.

For one thing, we should note how differently information is transmitted in nature and in culture (Rolston 1991). In nature, information is transmitted genetically and it does not include acquired information. In culture, information is transmitted through language, theories, public belief systems, rituals, traditions and the like. What is thus transmitted is acquired information, and the conditions for its acquisition in the first place are overwhelmingly social, cultural and economic. Such information is transmitted comparatively fast, and not necessarily from parent to offspring and not necessarily only locally. And while there might be instances in the non-human world in which information is transmitted through culture, or at least through the social life of non-humans, the extent to which this occurs is extremely limited. Moreover, culture and technology insulate humans from natural processes, including natural selection. Thus we use medical technology to assist injured or ill members of our species, one result being increasing, and increasingly long-lived, human populations.

Clearly technology in general makes possible massive intervention in ecosystems and provides at least some temporary protection from the potential adverse impacts such disruptions could have for humans. Moreover cultural structures, such as economic and political systems, drive such intervention. Note also our capacity for active decision-making, involving, among other things, culturally constructed attitudes, desires and preferences. Our propensities are not as hard-wired as, and so are more malleable than, those of other organisms. In short, the differences between human agency and the agency of other living and non-living things is profound and provides the firm conceptual distinction the anti-replacement thesis requires. Given differences such as those sketched above, it is completely grotesque to think of humans as merely one more species subject to the forces of natural selection. It is simply misleading to think of ourselves as embedded in nature in the manner of other living things.[12] This is not to deny, of course, that the capacities that differentiate us from other things are capacities that emerged from natural processes: culture is a product of nature. But it is also true that culture has developed these capacities and contributed to the directions that they take. Technology is used to enhance and to complement human performance, and most of the goals to which we turn our capacities, while they may overlay certain natural drives, are, in their particular content and directions, culturally, socially or economically determined.

While the anti-replacement thesis clearly presupposes a distinction between the natural and the non-natural or artificial, between what nature produces through evolutionary, geomorphological and climatic processes and so on, and what humans, as creatures of culture and technology, produce, there is no assumption that the distinction marks a sharp dichotomy. As was noted earlier, the anti-replacement thesis acknowledges degrees of naturalness, accepting that some environments are more natural than others. Nor is there any assumption that the distinction marks a deep metaphysical divide. The anti-replacement thesis also grants that probably no terrestrial environment remains entirely natural. The impact of human activity is, after all, disturbingly pervasive and affects ecologies even in remote places.[13] Environments even slightly altered by human activity may follow different evolutionary pathways than would otherwise be the case. Recognizing degrees of naturalness, the anti-replacement thesis claims that value increases as naturalness increases and that value decreases as naturalness decreases.

Certainly the distinction between the natural and artificial is fuzzy at its boundary: certainly creatures other than humans instantiate higher-order intentional systems and arguably some exhibit culture, social organization and rudimentary economic arrangements. Such facts, however, do not erode the distinction. Rather they show that it is a distinction which is cashed in terms of non-contiguous parts of a continuum. Moreover the distinction between the natural and the artificial explicates an intuitive distinction many would draw

(Regan 1986: 210; Rolston 1988: 328–35). Furthermore, it would seem to underpin a value distinction that has some normative appeal. So, consider a case where a species becomes extinct because of a climate change that is not attributable to human activity and a case where a species becomes extinct because of a climate change that is attributable to human activity. Many would count the latter extinction to be worse than the former. While superficially one might see the latter as the natural displacement of one species by another, there is a fuller story to be told, involving the distinction between the natural and the artificial. Or again the barrenness of some island would stand in a different, better perspective if that were how nature made it, so to speak, and it was not brought about by human intervention. There is a case, as we saw earlier, for regarding naturalness, contrasted with the property of being artificial, as a value-adding property.

NATURALNESS AND VALUE

Let us now spend some time trying to trace more carefully the connection between naturalness and positive value. Alastair Gunn offers two cases which provide a starting point for this task (Gunn 1991: 306). In the first case, environmental engineers are replanting an area from which an earlier forest cover has been recently removed. They are guided in their replanting by a particular ecosystemic type; let us say it is the type of forest that was there before clearing. Consequently what they produce is a non-natural instance of an approximate natural type – approximate, because there are bound to be characteristics of the resultant area that would not have emerged through natural processes. What is produced, if the engineering is successful, is roughly the same kind of forest but not the same forest.[14] It is not the same forest since there is no continuity at all of natural, as opposed to technological, processes, that accounts for the similarity of the later forest to the earlier forest. In other words, the earlier forest possesses a relational property not possessed by the later forest, namely the property of being naturally produced. Moreover, what the engineers produce is distinctively different from what would have emerged had the forest regenerated naturally, which is to say, had a similar forest come to occupy the same area through natural causes. The regenerated forest is a natural object, whereas the replanted forest is an artificial object, although it is composed of countless natural parts. The anti-replacement thesis claims that the replanted forest has somewhat less intrinsic value than the naturally regenerated forest and much less intrinsic value than the forest originally there.[15]

The second case that Gunn discusses concerns some islands close to the coast of New Zealand. This case differs from the first in that environmental degradation has not been anyway near as extreme. In this case, restoration involves the removal of introduced flora and fauna and the reintroduction of native species. Not only is the restoration guided by a natural design, it is carried out on a substantially natural object, namely a minimally degraded ecosystem that imperfectly fits the loose design specifications. The restored ecosystem is to a large extent naturally continuous with the earlier undegraded ecosystem; it is the same particular ecosystem and close to the same kind of ecosystem. Of course the restoration cannot be explained in purely natural terms: reference must also be made to the intervention of human agents, their technology, and the cultural values that inclined them to embark on the restoration.

Given that the restored ecosystem is the same particular ecosystem as the earlier island ecosystem, we might be tempted to think that if the former is a natural object, then so too is the latter. It is more accurate to say that the ecosystem in its earlier phase was an entirely natural object, in the sense of being naturally produced, but that the ecosystem in its later, restored phase is to a degree a non-natural object, much more natural than the replanted forest but slightly less natural than in its earlier phase. We need also to remember the suggestion, made in the third chapter, that the significance of the small intrusion of the non-natural reduces over time, as natural forces take over the maintenance and evolution of the island ecosystems. Thus the restored ecosystem, which is the same particular ecosystem as was originally there, becomes increasingly natural as times goes on.

Naturalness, which can be a matter of degree, enters into evaluations of environmental restorations in several ways. First, we may ask whether a particular restoration accords with a natural design. If it does not, then the value of the allegedly restored environment is significantly lessened. For example, replanting sections of felled eucalypt forest with an alien species such as *pinus radiata*, puts trees back on the ground but not in accordance with a relevant natural design. There seems little value in such a restoration compared with a restoration according with the natural design. Indeed we might reasonably think that there is overall disvalue, since natural regeneration, which might have resulted in something like the original, is thereby ruled out. Second, there is the question of the degree to which a restored ecosystem is a natural object, a naturally produced instance of a natural design. My claim is that, other things being equal, value increases as naturalness increases. Furthermore, it was the normative significance of naturalness to which I sought to draw attention with the phrase 'faking nature'. An apparently natural ecosystem is faked, to some degree at least, if it does not accord with a natural design, is not constituted out of natural items and, crucially, is not the product of natural forces.

It is appropriate to return to a point alluded to earlier concerning the relationship between the natural and the valuable. There is some temptation to argue that what is natural is not necessarily valuable, indeed that sometimes what is natural has disvalue. This might seem to imply either that naturalness is not by itself value-adding, that it is value-adding only in conjunction with some other property, or that there is some property that, when co-instantiated with naturalness, defeats its value-adding tendency. My endorsement, in the second chapter, of positive aesthetics in the case of the natural and of the claim that natural aesthetic value is a (moral) value-adding property, does not sit easily with this suggestion. I seem committed to saying that naturalness is always value-adding. I stand by this view. It can, by and large, be squared with the examples critics have in mind when they dispute it.

To begin with, claiming that the natural is always value-adding is not to claim that natural phenomena never have negative intrinsic value. Intrinsic value in particular instances may be the resultant of a number of value-adding and value-subtracting properties. Consider the case in which I have a bacterial infection and feel some pain as a consequence. Imagine that the state that I am in is a natural state, and that is not an artefact of life in my particular social and cultural milieu.[16] Since my state is a natural state I seem committed to saying that it tends on that account to have intrinsic value. But my state also has an aspect, its painfulness, that is value-subtracting. It may well be that all things considered the state that I am in, although natural, is of negative intrinsic value. And there is another helpful way of looking at the situation. We can think of it in terms of intrinsic and instrumental value. So we might distinguish between the state of my body having a bacterial infection, which state we judge to be a natural state and so of positive value, and the distinct mental state of my experiencing protracted discomfort. The latter state has intrinsic disvalue, although it may also have positive instrumental value in motivating me to have the problem causing the pain attended to.[17]

The physiological state I am in is thus instrumentally bad. The resultant state, my pain state, which renders it instrumentally bad, may itself be of such a degree of negative value to justify the artificial alteration of the biological state which causes it. Natural values are not the only values. Even though they are very significant values, there are cases, as in the example under discussion, where they are trumped by other values. It is possible to accept that sickness and disease often are natural although not good.

The connection between the natural and the valuable can also be challenged, as was earlier implied, through reference to natural phenomena such as fires, hurricanes, earthquakes and volcanic eruptions. Such natural phenomena can totally alter landscapes and alter them for the worse ecologically speaking: species may be rendered extinct, ecological richness reduced, and habitats destroyed. Surely, it could be said, these are natural phenomena that are bad, not good. These cases might be treated employing the distinction between intrinsic and instrumental value. In particular, we should be careful not to blur our judgement concerning the intrinsic value or disvalue of the consequences of such phenomena with our judgement of the intrinsic value or disvalue of the phenomena themselves. Judging that the consequences are of negative intrinsic value might incline us to judge that the cause is of negative intrinsic value. But no such inference should be made. There is no inconsistency in asserting the positive value of the cause and the negative value of the result. Indeed if we contemplate the power, magnitude, awesomeness and so on of the kinds of natural phenomena under consideration we should find it easy enough to see their positive value. Moreover there is no inconsistency in judging the cause to be of intrinsic value and asserting that it would nevertheless have been better, all things considered, had the cause not occurred. This would be so where the summed values of the consequences and the cause is less than zero.

There is a further important mode of framing our evaluations of destructive natural phenomena. We should try to see such phenomena in the context of a larger scale than we are perhaps used to employing in our evaluations. Natural history is to a large extent a history of evolving ecological richness, destruction of that richness and its subsequent renewal and transformation. In other words, we should strive to keep in mind the larger natural history or natural pattern of which the various destructive phenomena are part. If we manage to do this we might come to appreciate the destructive phenomena as instrumentally good as well as instrumentally bad. We

133

might adopt the former view in so far as we understand the destructive phenomena to be essential constituents of a larger whole that we judge to be of immense intrinsic value. We are still, of course, able to consider and take account of their instrumental disvalue.

One thing we might have to decide is whether we should intervene, assuming we can, to prevent the natural destruction of something exemplifying natural value. Leaving things alone and letting nature be can amount to acquiescing in the reduction of natural intrinsic value. In such instances there is, perhaps, justification for interfering with natural processes utilizing our scientific and technological resources. Consider the threat that the crown-of-thorns starfish posed not so long ago to Australia's Great Barrier Reef. It was not entirely clear whether the starfish invasion of the reef was the result of human activity. If it was, then the interventionist policy of removing starfish infestations from the reef could be seen as protecting natural value. While the reef's natural values were threatened by a natural organism, the emergence of the threat could be sheeted home to human activity, which makes the threat artificial rather than natural.

What, though, if the threat was clearly not in any way a result of human activity? What if the starfish infestation was clearly an entirely natural phenomenon? Should we still intervene? The argument for intervention would presumably be based on the concern that the reef will become less ecologically complex, that species will be threatened, that natural aesthetic values will be degraded. The argument against intervention would have to focus on the naturalness of the starfish infestation and direct our attention to the bigger picture. Ecological change, often through the natural destruction of natural values, is an integral component of nature's development. It is a development in which natural value sometimes reduces and then increases once more, and it is an extended natural process which itself has positive value. To intervene to save the reef might be to thwart the unfolding of that process and so might be an undermining of one source of natural value. Failure to intervene likewise results in the elimination of another source of natural value. We need to remember that naturalness is not the only mooted natural value-adding property. Natural aesthetic value is a case in point. The artificial thwarting of some natural process does not transform the value-adding properties thus protected into non-natural properties. The aesthetic value of the reef would still be natural aesthetic value, since it was entirely a product of natural processes. We do not produce something by protecting or preserving it, or somehow, thereby, retrospectively alter its mode of production.

Which response counts for more in this situation: the interventionist response or the non-interventionist response? I am not really sure. One reason I hesitate to endorse the non-interventionist response is that, because of the pervasive impact of human activity, nature's capacity to re-create natural value may be to some extent impaired. And of course there would always be the lingering suspicion that the starfish invasion was the result of destabilizing human activity. Even so, I find the non-interventionist response quite appealing. Perhaps my response is mediated by the thought that in intervening we are dominating nature, holding nature captive, taking nature prisoner, incarcerating nature or some such, and probably for our own ends. As the intrinsic disvalue of the consequences of non-intervention compound, then intervention may become justified and, perhaps, obligatory. So, imagine that we could somehow have prevented the eruption of Mt St Helens. Here a natural process obliterates the results of earlier natural processes. The advocate of natural values might say here that the eruption had intrinsic value in virtue of being a natural process and that the outcome of the eruption had some intrinsic value in virtue of its naturalness of origin. It could be said, nevertheless, that all things considered the devastation caused by the eruption had disvalue. For instance, the resultant suffering of human and non-human animals, the destruction of natural systems with positive aesthetic value and the extinction of local species, involving loss of biodiversity, plausibly have disvalue which overwhelms the positive value associated with naturalness of origin. The worry, though, is that we will intervene without having adopted the larger perspective, without having distanced ourselves from our relatively short-term interests and concerns. Thus in the starfish example we intervene because we are concerned to protect a source of aesthetic pleasure, and of opportunities for enquiry and research, for recreational activities, and of course, for commercial gain. In neither case do we properly value the cycle of destruction and renewal, the cycle of value reduction and value enrichment – a cycle that itself is of immense value.

The stakes may be raised considerably if we think about a situation in which the entire biosphere itself is threatened by some natural catastrophe. Take William Grey's example of an asteroid on a collision course with the earth (Grey 1993: 470). If it hits the earth there will be complete species extinction. It is possible, though, for us to deflect the asteroid, thus preventing the imminent natural catastrophe. Should we? I think, in this case, that we should. While we might accept that what results from the collision, were it to occur, has some value in virtue of its naturalness, we would, nevertheless, be right in thinking that value overall is maximized by deflecting the asteroid. And here we might appeal might appeal to various value considerations, including the fact that the earth is to a large extent a natural system or product of natural forces, the fact that humans and non-humans would suffer, the fact that the re-emergence of life is not at all guaranteed, the fact that many natural items of aesthetic worth would be destroyed, and the not irrelevant fact that the asteroid is of significantly less value than the earth.

Indeed Grey has a general point concerning the scale employed in evaluations that might be usefully discussed here because of its bearing on an example just now discussed. Thus he observes that the Great Barrier Reef will probably disappear and reform several times during the next ten thousand years. He goes on to add that this fact does not seem relevant to our concern to preserve it now (Grey 1993: 467). And let us assume that it is preservation against a natural threat that is involved. Maybe Grey is simply saying that in deciding whether to try to preserve the reef now we are not moved by the fact that what we are striving to preserve is going to disappear anyway. That would be correct. But Grey, I think, is making a somewhat stronger claim. I think that he is suggesting that we could not be moved by that fact, not merely observing that we are not. The implication seems to be that there is something dubious, if not impossible, about value judgements that pertain to, or range across, processes of such extended temporal dimensions. But it is not clear that those moved by natural values will think the fact of disappearance and reformation is irrelevant to concerns to preserve it now. If the process of disappearance and reformation is a natural process, then some might say that value overall is maximized by permitting the occurrence of the process. They might regret their own temporal location in relation to the process, perhaps because they do not get to see the reef at its most aesthetically pleasing or ecologically interesting, but nevertheless they agree that value is maximized by allowing the process to unfold. The temporal scale of the process does not seem to rule out such evaluations. Grey has not shown that thinking about the matter in this way is somehow psychologically impossible or dubious or inappropriate for humans; rather he has, in effect, asserted a competing normative position in which naturalness of origin, or just naturalness, is not a value-adding property in a completely general sense. Others might agree that the process has value because it is a natural process, arguing, nevertheless, that it increases disvalue all things considered. For instance, the process destroys a natural product of considerable aesthetic worth, and deprives humans of certain enjoyments.

Let us now try to tie together some of our speculations concerning the natural and the valuable. First, the anti-replacement thesis does not entail that every naturally evolved state of affairs has positive value all things considered. At most it entails that a naturally evolved state of affairs will contain some intrinsic value. But it might also contain intrinsic disvalue which neutralizes or even outweighs the intrinsic value. For example, a naturally evolved state of affairs containing intense, continuous and widespread pain would almost certainly lack intrinsic value overall, although it might contain elements of great intrinsic value. It should be noted, moreover, that attributing overall intrinsic disvalue to a state of affairs does not preclude the judgement that, all things considered, it is good that it occurred. Such states of affairs may have considerable instrumental value, giving rise to large amounts of intrinsic value in the future or, more interestingly, contributing to cyclical patterns of natural devastation and natural reconstruction or renewal that possess immense intrinsic value. Still, the intensity of natural values and my endorsement of positive aesthetics underwrites the defeasible presumption that what is natural is valuable.

Second, the artificial, as opposed to the natural, destruction of natural intrinsic value is worse than the natural destruction of natural intrinsic value. It is useful to focus here on a comparative example. Imagine that Mt St Helens had been destroyed by a human-made explosion and that the consequent environmental damage was exactly the same as that produced by the actual volcanic eruption. In which process is there the greater loss of value, and if there is a difference where does it reside? According to the anti-replacement thesis, the artificial process involves more disvalue than the natural process. Moreover this claim is endorsed even after the disvalue of humans, actively embarking on such a destructive project or of being so negligent as to leave open the possibility of such an event, is factored out. The additional disvalue in the case of the non-natural destruction derives from the origin of the resultant state of affairs. The suggestion is that the disvalue of the result is intensified by the non-naturalness of the cause.

This, by the way, does not commit me to the view that the non-natural has disvalue; only to the view that non-naturalness of origin intensifies the disvalue of the destruction of natural values. It is also, perhaps, an open question whether the intensified disvalue associated with the destruction of natural values is always so great that value overall is reduced through the non-natural destruction of natural values. To assert that value overall is always reduced is to condemn human activity and human presence as such, since human activity and human presence inevitably reduces natural value. At least this is so if humans, including indigenous humans pursuing traditional forms of life, are grouped apart from nature. Even if some possible forms of human life fall entirely within the category of the natural, most of what most people do certainly does not. Perhaps one could assert the strong view: accept that overall value will for a long time be less than it could be, and work, within pragmatic limits, for the scaling back of human activity and human impacts on nature. Such a general policy might be pursued through attempting to reduce levels of consumption and population levels, and through promoting environmentally sensitive technology and practices. The chances of success of such policies is probably, if the truth be known, slim, and certainly the outcome horizon is quite distant. It would seem at least equally probable that the scaling back will be achieved through eco-catastrophe.

Many, however, will find this grudging distancing from the strong view insufficient. They will urge that in many instances human activity enhances value through the destruction of natural values. They might laud the larger, general accomplishments, such as they are, of human civilization. Or they might focus on the small scale, such as the shaping of a piece of stone into a sculpture, where, allegedly, the destruction of natural value makes possible the creation of superior value. Maybe human activity is in principle sometimes value-adding in instances where it reduces natural value. Whether it is value-adding in practice, given the increasing humanization of the natural and the pervasiveness of human impacts on the natural, is a separate issue. Sometimes, certainly, I am tempted to endorse the strong view and assert that the reduction of natural value always results in a decrease in value overall. Perhaps it is an unfortunate fact that our existence as creatures of culture and technology is at the price of reduced value overall. Still, one does not need to endorse such an extreme view in order to endorse most of the value claims that have been made so far.

Finally, let us consider the value dimensions of the sorts of difficult

138

cases discussed in the last section in which human activity shapes, pervasively and subtly, the direction that nature takes. Recall the example of the nation-state that wages economic war through the emission of greenhouse gases aimed at altering weather systems to its own advantage. I wanted to say that the resultant state was a natural state, engendered by natural responses to human activity that had quite specific aims. Similarly I wanted to say that the revegetation and rehabitation of areas that have been degraded through human activity results, given time, in a natural area, an area over which nature has regained control. As to the value of such resultant states of affairs, I would want to say that considered in themselves they have, so far as natural values are concerned, the same value significance. That their eventual shape is partly caused by human activity, quite intentionally in some cases, does not itself diminish their value. Nevertheless I want to say that value overall falls because of the redirecting influence of human activity.

In the greenhouse gas case, the redirection of nature may be comparatively gradual, although it might not be, since various threshold phenomena might trigger rapid change once certain levels of emission or accumulation are achieved. If the changes are gradual, there may not be any diminution of value between earlier and later stages in the process. But this does not mean that there can be no background or overlay phenomenon, in virtue of which the process as a whole has less value than would have been possessed by the process which would otherwise have unfolded. While impacting human activity does not necessarily contaminate, so to speak, the natural values in the various stages of the unfolding process, it does reduce the value of the process overall. The relevant value in the overall process is, furthermore, a natural value. It is the overall guiding hand of nature that is compromised and forced. The distinction between this kind of case and those in which human activity reduces the value of later states of affairs will not be a sharp distinction; the one kind of case will blur into the other. And that itself is further grounds for condemning the subtle manipulation or alteration of the course of nature. After all, processes that we think are not going to reduce natural value in later, contiguous states of affairs, may well turn out to do so.

The case of natural revegetation and rehabitation is quite different in one significant aspect. These processes take an extended period of time. The value of a degraded area in the period before the processes have substantially occurred is certainly less than the value of the area before degradation and after revegetation and rehabitation. So overall value is reduced in two broad ways: first, through the reduced value of later stages, and, second, through the reduced value of the overall process. We should, moreover, think about naturalness and its connection with the faking analogy of the previous chapter. We might find in the connection some basis for a value-ranking of the naturally restored environment that renders it less valuable than the environment that would have been there had degradation never occurred. In earlier attempts to explicate the value-adding force of naturalness, I spoke of the normative appeal of an unbroken continuity with the past and drew a parallel with the idea of provenance with respect to works of art. Maybe there are really two ideas here that need to be distinguished. The first is simply the idea that origin or provenance makes a difference to value. The second is the idea that antiquity of origin also makes a difference to value. The regrowth forest does not have a natural continuity reaching back into the past as far as that of the old growth forest. And even though the regrowth forest might properly come to be considered as natural, as much a product of nature, as the old growth forest, its natural connectedness with the past terminates at an earlier stage. So, we should perhaps distinguish in the idea of naturalness between the property of being a product of natural design and natural processes and the property of length of natural continuity with the past. Both factors might be seen as separately contributing to the importance of origin in environmental evaluations. Appeal to the second provides the basis for rating, for example, an old growth forest more highly on the value scale than a regrowth forest.

There is a further issue concerning naturalness and value that warrants some discussion. If there are degrees of naturalness and if naturalness is a determinant of value, then we might think that the more natural something is the more valuable it is, other things being equal. I am prepared to endorse some variant of this claim. I hesitate to endorse it unqualifiedly because there is probably a point at which naturalness in some degree simply fails to be value-adding: in other words, there would be some, no doubt blurred, threshold level of naturalness required before value is generated. Anyway, it does seem possible to rank areas value-wise on the basis of degrees of naturalness. We might also wonder whether quantity, as well as degree, of naturalness is a basis for value-differentiation. So, consider the situation in which we have two equally natural areas but where one is more extensive than the other, and focus, exclusively for the moment, on naturalness as the value-adding property. Does the larger area possess more value? I think that it does. Certainly where a very much larger area of wild nature is involved, then that larger area does have the greater value. We could, for instance, think of a situation in which either the smaller area or the larger area will be lost. While the loss of either area would involve massive value loss, the loss of the larger area would involve the larger value loss.[18]

There may be some reluctance in particular cases to endorse this last value claim. Where there is such reluctance I suggest it is because putative value-adding properties other than naturalness are introduced into the equation. Biotic richness might be such a factor, explaining why some might judge there to be more value in a small area of rainforest than in a much larger arid environment. Or again, there might be concern that certain areas are the last of their kind, and so a preparedness to judge a smaller area of remnant forest of some rare kind to be more valuable than an equally natural larger area of a different kind of forest. In the remnant forest example it may also be the case that a judgement about a certain kind of instrumental value, namely constitutive value, is merged with the judgement as to intrinsic value. So one thing that is highly valued is the continued existence of a representative range of natural ecosystemic types. The loss of the smaller remnant forest reduces the range. And while the intrinsic value of the smaller area of forest is less than the intrinsic value of the larger forest, its continued existence is a necessary constituent in the maintenance of the highly valuable representative range. While I do not agree that biotic richness is obviously a basis for value differentiation, I do think that the property of contributing to a representative range is value-adding. There may be some doubt as to whether it adds to the intrinsic value of the individual items that constitute the range, or to the range itself. I think that it adds to the value of both the individual items themselves and the range itself. So I think that rarity is value-adding or, more properly, value-intensifying in cases where naturalness is already present. As to whether biotic richness is value-adding in its own right, I might be persuaded that, other things being equal, an area that contains biota is of more intrinsic value than one that does not. So an area of the lunar landscape may have less value than an area of, say, the Antarctic landscape. The presence of life makes, arguably, a value difference, although more variety of life does not entail more value. And certainly the presence of life is not absolutely value-adding, as that term has earlier been defined.

The various value claims made above rely on the general claim

141

that naturalness is a source of intrinsic moral value. It is useful, therefore, to conclude the section with a consideration of one common objection to this general claim. This objection reasons from the ubiquitousness of naturalness to the conclusion that it yields vacuous value judgements (Thompson 1990). The thought seems to be that since so much is natural or exhibits high degrees of naturalness, then naturalness is a less than completely plausible basis for making value differentiations. I am puzzled, however, as to why the ubiquitousness of the natural should be thought to yield vacuousness, especially when we note that its ubiquitousness is not complete since many things are not natural on the account offered earlier. In any case, the judgement that everything which is natural has intrinsic value is hardly vacuous, uninteresting or unwelcome. Such a judgement would be substantive, indicating, among other things, why it is better that a universe exist, even were it to be devoid of human life or sentient life, than that nothing exist.

Perhaps the worry is that the view leads to the conclusion that no natural state of affairs is preferable to any other. While I am attracted to the view that no natural state of affairs is better than any other, subject perhaps to the qualifications discussed above, it is possible to reject that claim and consistently to endorse the general claim. This option is open to those who agree that naturalness is not the only value-adding property exemplified by natural objects. Thus one natural state of affairs might be better than another because, although both have some intrinsic value in virtue of being natural, one has additional value-adding properties not possessed by the other, such as species diversity or rarity. And to the objection that mention of the shared property can be dropped since it makes no value difference of practical relevance, it can be replied that there will be numerous cases where it does have practical relevance, such as in the comparison of cases of species extinction resulting from natural phenomena as against human activity. Nor does the exemplification of a value-adding property, such as naturalness, by something guarantee that it has intrinsic value overall, since it may possess value-subtracting properties. A natural state of affairs may, although not often, have negative intrinsic value overall, and indeed less intrinsic value than an artificial state of affairs, because the former exemplifies some massively value-subtracting property, such as widespread misery. These considerations also show that there could sometimes be axiologically based reasons for interfering with natural processes.

142

RESTORATION ECOLOGY: CONCLUDING THOUGHTS

By way of concluding and drawing together the various themes of this chapter and the preceding chapter, it is helpful to discuss several aspects of the philosophy of so-called restoration ecology. Some who speak on behalf of restoration ecology have questioned some of the claims made in these chapters, and at the same time have been themselves advocating, developing and implementing the technologies that aim to produce faked nature. Restoration ecology, as I shall represent it below, is in the first instance the theory and practice of restoring natural areas to an earlier state, a state preceding some ecological disturbance. The restored state aims at exemplifying the same ecological richness, species diversity and physical, biological and aesthetic characteristics of the earlier state. So restoration ecology might be taken to include returning a site to an original state after any significant disturbance, whether its cause be human activity or some unambiguously natural phenomenon such as volcanic eruption or meteor strike. Usually, though, restoration will aim at repairing damage done by humans. Restoration ecology, however, is more than merely the theory and practice of such restorative work; it has come to include philosophical, and certainly robust normative, elements. The chief examples of these elements are the claim that there is no significant normative or metaphysical distinction between nature and culture, the claim that natural value can in principle be restored in full, the claim that the value of natural areas may be improved by the involvement of human activity in shaping them, the claim that naturalness is not in itself value-adding, the claim that the manipulation of nature contributes to knowledge and understanding which is of intrinsic value, the claim that nature is to be thought of as a garden to be cultivated, shaped and manipulated to promote long-term human interests.

While not all restoration ecologists endorse all of these claims, they do nevertheless represent a good sample of the gamut of claims that have been made by restoration ecologists (Cowell 1993; Jordan 1986a, 1986b and 1994; Jordan *et al.* 1987; Katz 1992a; Losin 1984, 1986 and 1988; Morrison 1987; Risser 1987; Turner 1994). Indeed, to be fair, some who count themselves as restoration ecologists would endorse many of the views for which I have argued. One example is the view that restoration ecology should seek to repair landscapes that have been damaged and degraded in the past and that the

143

possibility of restoring landscapes should never be used to justify new disruption (Berger 1990: xvi–xvii; Sayen 1989). And even William Jordan, who has made some of the more extreme statements of the restoration ecology philosophy, does at times speak as if the restorationist perspective includes the preservationist perspective. He suggests that restoration complements preservation and, indeed, that restorationists are preservationists, sharing some of the ideals of wilderness preservation. But in virtually the same breath that these suggestions are made, Jordan makes remarks which undercut any thought that naturalness, understood as freedom from human manipulation through technology, is a key basis of natural value (Jordan 1985 and 1988).

Perhaps the restoration ecologist that I target below is really best thought of as an amalgam of, from my point of view, the worst of the views espoused by a number of restoration ecologists. But Jordan, Losin and Turner certainly do come close to espousing them all, and they are at times avowedly, although strangely, hostile to the preservationist position, especially where it includes the main value claim concerning naturalness that I endorse. Their criticisms of the preservationist position are posed from a perspective which sees no possible alliance, overlap or compromise between that position and restoration ecology (Kane 1994). One would think that they would be keen to prevent the continuing environmental damage that makes the possibility of restoration so important. Perhaps they have accepted most of McKibben's view, mentioned earlier, that terrestrial nature has to all intents and purposes come to an end, while declining to endorse his evaluation of this state of affairs. Not that restoration ecologists think that the end of nature is itself a good thing or even a natural thing; it is rather that they think that restoration has the potential to re-create the value that environmental degradation and destruction have eroded. And in a way I agree, as my earlier remarks about nature recolonizing restored areas indicate. These remarks, however, also made it clear that I think the resurrection of natural value in restored areas is dependent on the withdrawal of human influence. But that is not the view, or so it seems, of restoration ecology.

As I have just now implied, one of the greatest tensions between my views and the views of restoration ecologists concerns the basis of nature's value, particularly the claim that much of its value derives from its being naturally evolved. One reason restoration ecologists might dispute this value claim is that it might be thought to imply that successfully restored environments would have less value than original environments or that they would have no value at all. If this were so then my favoured value claim would entail a strong condemnation, at least no praise, for the practice of restoration ecology. Neither of these inferences would really be sound. For one thing, nothing that I have said implies that the restoration of degraded areas would have no value. I think that it would have value, as I have already made clear. It would serve, for instance, human interests, it would protect remaining relatively natural areas, and it would often involve only extrinsic restoration, which leaves areas relatively natural.

Moreover, the view I endorsed in the third chapter allows, as I have just now noted, that a restored area may be recolonized by nature in the fullest sense: it may once more become nature's domain where natural forces, and not human design, determine what occurs and what shape the landscape takes. Restoration ecologists often speak in terms of the continuing surveillance, management and manipulation of ecosystems (Jordan 1985 and 1994; Turner 1994). There is, as far as I can see, no suggestion that areas be restored and then left alone, to develop in accordance with natural forces, to be themselves. While it may be true that restoration is a long-term project, involving monitoring and minor interference, such as removing weeds and feral animals, long after the major restoration work has been done, the ultimate aim, implicit in the preservationist ideal, is to achieve a situation from which humans are absent, except as respectful, careful and unobtrusive visitors. Some time after that stage is reached we can say that nature has again taken control of the area. And restoration will have played a role in enabling this to occur. So, while it is true that the value of the restored ecosystem is less than the value of the original, the restored ecosystem may evolve into something which does have at least close to the same value as the original. There would, as I have noted several times, be a net loss of value over time, because of the period during which natural intrinsic value associated with the area in question was depleted, and, moreover, the newly natural area would not have the continuity through natural history with the remote past that some might value in addition to naturalness as such.

The philosophical point, though, is that restoration ecology disputes the claim that the restored environment has less value than the original environment. If this is correct then it could be argued that if the restored environment has the same value as the original, then naturalness cannot be a basis for the intrinsic value of wild nature. And this would bring restoration ecology into conflict with one of my main value claims. This inference would technically be flawed, though, since two states of affairs may well have the same value but the bases of that value might vary between the two states of affairs. Thus a natural area could have a particular value, in large part because of its naturalness, and a restored area could have the same value, in large part because of its value-adding properties apart from naturalness. Indeed those impressed by human creativity, ingenuity and the like, might say that the compensating value derives from the aesthetic properties of a human design wrought on the raw materials of the degraded ecosystem, or from the exemplification, in the restored environment, of scientific accomplishment.

All that would follow from this, however, is that the value of the restored and original environments, respectively, must have at least a partially different basis and naturalness could still be significantly value-adding. Still, this would not be an altogether happy result as far as my own preferred position is concerned. It would too readily allow that restored nature – and assume that it is intrinsic restoration that is involved – could have the same value, even in the short term, as original nature. While restored nature would, of necessity, lack one particular value-adding property, namely naturalness, there might be compensating value-adding properties it possesses. As was indicated in the third chapter, there is a difference between full value-equivalence and equal value: the former requires similarity in the value-adding properties and not just equality in the resultant values. It is important to affirm, at this point, that naturalness is a value-adding property that cannot straightforwardly be restored and that it is so intensely value-adding that the loss of natural value is not easily, if ever, compensated for through the generation of other values.

Let us briefly consider, then, some of the claims made by one prominent restoration ecologist, Peter Losin, concerning naturalness. Losin argues that the influence of humans on the landscape is not always bad or unnatural, and that, in fact, the human practice of restoration ecology can save natural values that would otherwise be lost (Losin 1986 and 1988). He goes on, seemingly, to question whether naturalness is a basis of intrinsic value. While there are things here with which I can agree, it is important to disentangle them from other parts of Losin's agenda that I would resist. Losin appears to make three distinct claims. First, he seems to be saying that human influences on the natural environment are not always bad. Second, he seems to be saying that human action should not always be seen as unnatural. Third, he seems to be saying that restoration ecology can preserve certain natural values. I shall discuss these claims in turn and ask whether any of them, to the extent that they are true, casts doubt on the claim that naturalness is a basis of intrinsic value.

The first claim is true in one way at least. After all, human influence can preserve nature through the designation of wilderness areas in which human activity is, through the enactment and enforcement of legislation, kept to a minimum. This might provide the basis for the argument, considered earlier, that went along the following lines. The value of nature within such a designated area is the same as the value of an exactly similar area of nature that was not preserved through human influence but which unambiguously naturally existed. Moreover, so the argument ran, the role of human action in preserving the first area subverts, if not destroys, its naturalness. We have, then, one area which is natural and one in which naturalness has been depleted, through the imposition of anthropocentric purposes. Since, however, the areas are of equal value, it might be inferred, naturalness cannot be the basis of nature's intrinsic value.

This argument, as we saw earlier, is flawed because it massively underplays the fact that artificial processes or human interventions do not directly generate or give rise to the shape of the ecosystems within the designated area but rather artificially prevent the destruction of something which has naturally arisen. To a large degree it is true that, within the boundaries of the wilderness area, ecological and other natural processes remain at work and that the ecosystems within the designated area are dynamic and evolve over time. And certainly the explanation of the structure of nature within the designated area is explicable without reference to human purposes: it is nature's project, not ours (Rolston 1988: 192–201; Sylvan 1990: 7–28). All that can be said about the role of human activity is that it partially explains how nature's project in this particular area continues. In the case of restored nature, by contrast, human purposes and human activity play a central role in explaining how the restored environment came to have the structure it has. It does not, then, seem that artificial protection compromises the naturalness of wilderness. We let nature alone by ensuring that nature is left alone, and that does not strike me as paradoxical. We can, furthermore, say that human influence in protecting nature in this way is, although unnatural, good. It is both good in itself, as a virtuous act, and instrumentally good, as a means of maintaining natural intrinsic value. However, admitting this does not in any way undercut the claims that naturalness is a source of value, that restoration cannot restore full value through restoring all

147

bases of value possessed by original areas, and that restoration rarely, if ever, restores equal value.

Turn now to Losin's second claim, that human action should not always be seen as unnatural. I think that this is to some extent correct, although not in any way that is particularly helpful either to the view that restoration ecology can in principle restore full natural value or to the view that naturalness, understood as that which is not the product of human technology and culture, is not intensely value-adding. As was allowed earlier, humans are certainly part of nature. There is also, as we saw, a clear sense in which humans have transcended nature or are outside nature. In so far as humans are creatures who make extensive use of technology and are thoroughly enmeshed in culture, they are more properly thought of as outside the bounds of the natural: human actions which employ technology and have a basis in culture are not natural. But Losin seems unhappy with this suggestion.

Losin's view, echoed by other restoration ecologists, seems to be that humans, even as creatures of culture and technology, are not apart from nature, are not in any deep way alienated from the rest of nature. Instead they are seen as natural inhabitants of ecosystems who transform those systems in the same manner that other creatures do (Jordan 1986b). And others complain that the distinction between the natural and the non-natural, on which my claim concerning naturalness as a basis for intrinsic value depends, reflects an affliction of the modern condition, namely an estrangement from nature, deriving from so-called Cartesian subject–object dualism (Cowell 1993: 27). This objection is sometimes associated with the view that restoration ecology has point in part because it involves an harmonious re-entry into nature. The thought seems to be that human intervention in the environment need not amount to laying waste to nature, or even to rendering the environment somewhat less natural, but may instead take the form of a co-operative transformation in a way that preserves certain values associated with nature, while involving a purposive role for humans in reshaping, even improving, nature (Callicott 1991 and 1992b). An example might be the purposeful introduction by humans of a species into an area in which it has hitherto not been present, perhaps in order to save that species from extinction because its original habitats are severely threatened, or in order to add to the biotic richness or diversity of an area. However, as I urged earlier in this chapter, there is a recognizable point to the distinction between the natural and the non-natural. There is, moreover, a recognizable point to the claim that even the harmonious transformation of nature drains it of significant intrinsic value, contaminating it with human purposiveness.

Losin's third claim is that restoration ecology can preserve certain natural values. Again I think that there is some truth in this, which is nevertheless consistent with the claim that restoration erodes one significant basis of intrinsic value, namely naturalness. Consider the restoration of a species through a genetic recovery programme and its reintroduction into areas from which humans earlier caused it to disappear. Its reintroduction may stabilize the ecosystems in question, preventing their unnatural simplification or collapse. The example compels the concession, argued for at various points, that ecosystems may be to varying degrees natural. The reintroduced species is in the ecosystem non-naturally but its being there stabilizes natural structures. Moreover, the recovery and reintroduction of the species amounts to a reinstantiation of a natural design. While the process is not natural, much of what it results in, and much of what it utilizes, is. While value is not fully restored, what natural value remains is preserved. And that is undeniably a good thing.

NOTES

1 THE NATURE OF NATURAL VALUE

1 For useful discussion of these issues see Goodpaster 1978 and 1979, Routley and Routely 1979 and 1980a.

2 See the discussion in Sylvan and Bennett 1994 and compare the idea of deontic experience in Birch 1993.

3 For a discussion of naturalisms generally see Pigden 1991, and of subjective naturalism in particular, see Rachels 1991.

4 Such a view can, I believe, be found variously put in Rolston 1994:16–19. It is also arguably evident in Rolston 1986: 73, 113–14, 132, and in Rolston 1988: 186–91. Unfortunately it is sometimes difficult to disentangle Rolston's meta-ethical views from his normative views. It should be noted, though, that this reading of Rolston is very controversial. For a more standard, although I think mistaken, reading, see Callicott 1992a.

5 Other terms might also be used such as the generic 'good-making' or the less well-known 'value-imparting' (Goodin 1992: 45).

6 There are various other distinctions that might be made here. For example, Moore makes the distinction between pure and mixed value neutrals. The former but not the latter have no value-adding or value-subtracting properties. Likewise there are pure and mixed goods and evils. See Chisholm 1986: 73–5.

7 See Chisholm 1986 for an excellent discussion of such phenomena.

8 Perhaps it is unusual for an ecosystem to survive the loss of species, even one or two. Perhaps, because of the complex interrelatedness of ecosystemic components, a small loss will soon compound to such a degree that the original ecosystem becomes another.

9 I say 'generally' because of some peculiar cases, for example the property of being unique. This is, arguably, a relational property that does not require the existence of anything else beside the unique thing.

10 See the useful discussion of the matter in O'Neill 1993: 13–15.

11 Ross (1930: 75), claims, echoing Moore 1966: 32, that if 'by calling a thing intrinsically good we mean that it would be good even if nothing else existed', then the property of being intrinsically valuable could not be a relational property as subjectivisms claim. One response is to dispute the semantic claim. A better response is to grant the semantic claim but to argue

that subjectivism allows that the preferences of actual valuers can extend to possible worlds not including those or indeed any valuers. So it would be possible both to insist that something has intrinsic value only if it were to have value if it alone existed and to insist that its having value in that possible world in which it exists alone consists in its being the object of an actual valuer's preferences. See Elliot 1985 for an extended discussion.

12 As Moore also points out, this category of meta-ethics does not exclusively include subjectivisms. Some naturalist objectivisms, such as the view that a thing's goodness is its fittingness to survive, fall into the category. See Moore 1922: 255–8.

13 For a full account see Elliot 1985. For a similar view see Callicott 1984; Routley and Routley 1980a: 152–65.

14 The former view, which is defended in Perry 1950, is on my view best understood as a normative theory.

15 That my view is relativistic is a criticism pressed in Attfield 1987: 191–2. Wong (1990: 615–16) retains the term 'relativism' for a view not dissimilar to mine. But the term too often comes with various bits of associated baggage, including the suggestion that relativism entails that truth itself is indexed to believers or that there are true contradictions. Wong's relativism, *qua* relativism, is no less innocuous than an account of indexicals, such as 'I', 'here' and 'now', that indexes them to utterers. Perhaps the term can be purged of unwanted associations but eschewing it might be the better policy.

16 The descriptor 'truncated' is used in Callicott 1986: 143, to emphasize the mind-dependence, or valuer-dependence, of intrinsic value, in contrast to the view, presumably false, that intrinsic value is an intrinsic, mind-independent property of the objects that possess it. I agree with Callicott that intrinsic value is mind-dependent but I would resist the implication that this somehow weakens the core of the Moorean analysis of what it is for something to be intrinsically valuable, namely valuable for its own sake, valuable in itself, valuable in virtue of the properties it possesses. Where Moore goes wrong is with the metaphysics of intrinsic value, not with the analysis of the concept. Of course, some of the metaphysics is going to seep into the analysis but my point is that the analysis can be disconnected from the metaphysics without significant conceptual loss. See also Green 1996 in which a summation like Callicott's is endorsed.

17 The reason that an indirect causal connection may be, indeed I would say is, required, is that my representation must be of actual trilobites. On the story to be developed in subsequent chapters, the intrinsic value of the trilobites has much to do with the fact that they are part of nature's evolutionary project; they are naturally evolved organisms. My knowledge of trilobites is causal knowledge. There is a causal chain that tracks backwards from my current belief state to actual trilobites. This pathway goes by the way of textbooks, the belief states of paleontologists, the fossil records and so on. It is not enough that I imagine a certain kind of creature with the intrinsic properties of actual trilobites and that that representation corresponds, fortuitously, to actual trilobites. That is not what it is to represent actual trilobites. The indirect causal link is required for that. And unless it is actual trilobites I represent, it is not those actual trilobites that I specifically value. Without the causal link and with only the fortuitous correspondence, all that

I would be valuing would be the existence of trilobite-like creatures. Or so it seems to me.

18 The account offered here is close to the affective-cognitive theory developed in great detail in Gaus 1990, Part 1.

19 For an illuminating discussion of this variant of subjectivism, see Lewis 1989.

20 Although it might be required that the future state is causally linked in an appropriate way to present states of affairs. That is implied by the argument of the third and fourth chapters.

21 This is a point which is very easy to overlook. See Attfield and Belsey 1994: 2: '[Elliot] shows that actual valuations made in our world could apply to worlds empty of valuers, but does not show how there could be values even if no valuers had ever existed or valued.'

22 See D'Agostino 1993 for a discussion of this, and related, issues.

23 The point could be made by saying that moral disagreement is not cognitive all the way down. And this view does find support in the common-sense view of many people. It is too easy to assume that the common-sense view of moral disagreement favours the claim that such disagreements are cognitive all the way down. It is not unusual to hear people in everyday contexts say that morality is, in the end, a matter of one's attitudes; that moral judgments are not judgments about objective moral facts. For further discussion of these issues see Williams 1985.

24 Here I discount the strange but interesting view that objective values are person-specific, there being objective values-for-Jack and objective values-for-Jill.

2 ENVIRONMENTAL OBLIGATION, AESTHETIC VALUE AND THE BASIS OF NATURAL VALUE

1 See the discussion of one particular consequentialism, namely utilitarianism, in Williams 1995. Williams reminds us that utilitarianism cannot discount future happiness with respect to present happiness. Utilitarianism is indifferent to the temporal distribution of happiness, attributing, for example, as much value to the happiness of a future person as to the similar happiness of a contemporary. In deciding how to act and which policies to endorse, the utilitarian will adopt the principle of maximizing expected benefit. A utilitarian may urge a policy with a high chance of a small benefit and condemn a policy with a very small chance of a substantial benefit. So utilitarianism may discount for the uncertainty of how things will turn out in the future, since, generally at least, we can be much more certain of the short-term effects of our actions and policies than of their very long-term effects. The greater the uncertainty, the greater the permissible discounting. One such discounting response is to treat presently competing actions and policies as having negligibly different consequences in the distant future. This response, says Williams, is completely inappropriate for evaluating resource use policies. Instead, she argues, utilitarianism combined with certain relevant facts of biology entails that choice between competing resource use policies should be guided by the principle of *maximum sustainable yield.* This entails a set of much more environmentally sensitive policy decisions.

2 See the relevant discussion in Smart and Williams 1973 and Pettit 1991.

3 It is sometimes difficult to discern when the deontological principle appeals to the axiological assessment. For instance, some who think that it is impermissible to kill innocent, unthreatening persons, explain this by saying that persons have intrinsic value or inherent value or inherent worth. These terms occur frequently in the environmental ethics literature but are used in divergent ways. For example, Taylor (1986: 72–5) defines them but notes different uses. His primary term is 'inherent worth', which he employs, I believe, to represent a deontological concept. Regan 1981, for example, uses it to represent an axiological concept. Anyway, such explanations can be read in at least four ways. First, they might be taken as tantamount to restatements of the impermissibility claim, saying, in effect, that certain acts are impermissible because they are impermissible. Second, they might be taken as gesturing towards some non-axiological property which makes acts having that property impermissible. In such cases more needs to be said by way of unpacking the relevant terms. So appeal might be made to the fact that persons are rational, autonomous, centres of self-reflective choice and so on. On this second reading, there is no suggestion that these properties are, in my sense, value-adding. Third, these properties are treated as value-adding but this axiological fact is taken as independent of the deontological requirement that agents not take the lives of beings who exemplify the properties in question. On the fourth reading, however, they are treated as value-adding, and the deontologically relevant feature of the act is that it is one in which a thing possessing value-adding properties is destroyed. While it is not a simple matter to discern which of these construals is correct in any particular context, it is clear that in many cases at least a preservationist stance would, for a deontologist, emerge in virtue of an attribution of intrinsic value to wild nature.

4 It is difficult to know whether it is completely appropriate to speak of obligation here, at least if one is developing a pure virtue theory from which axiological and, particularly, deontological components are missing. Presumably it is judgment as to the virtuousness and so on of character and action that provides the moral motivation: recognizing that some action would be virtuous would, for example, provide some motivation for performing it.

5 This way of putting matters does reduce, it would seem virtue theory to axiology, since it makes intrinsic value supervene on character. Virtue theorists, presumably, would resist this. The puzzle, however, is how to inject evaluation into plain judgments about character. There would seem to have to be an assessment of the value of particular traits of character. The problem is not unlike the problem of understanding how there could be an evaluative component in moral judgments if objective naturalism were true.

6 It might be suggested that this claim about the basis of nature's intrinsic value assumes that the universe itself is not created, and so assumes the falsity of many variants of theism. I think this is right. If there is a tight control exercised by the divine being over the details of its creation, then it is difficult to see nature as in any way autonomous. Tight control might be exercised by setting initial conditions and laws of nature such that the universe must be exactly as it is. Assume, moreover, that the divine being

engages in such fine-tuning precisely in order to achieve the effects that it will result. Disregard here any complications to this picture introduced by the view that humans are free agents whose actions are not determined, and who impact on the natural world. On this scenario nature is designed; it is the product of intentional action and the structure that it comes to have is explained by the divine being's intention to create a universe with just that structure. Arguably, the value it could then have, considered apart from the sentient creatures who inhabit it, is restricted to aesthetic value. But divine creation need not be so completely thought out. If the divine intention is simply to bring a universe into existence and to allow it to unfold and develop, then nature is not drained of autonomy and that universe is not through and through designed. A useful analogy is to compare a carefully and completely engineered garden, in which the gardener from the outset has very explicit and detailed intentions that determine all the fine detail that the garden comes to have, with a garden which is designed only in rough outline by the gardener and then allowed to develop with a large degree of autonomy. If divine creation is taken to imply only loose design, then it is not inconsistent with the claim concerning the basis of nature's value. This is not to imply that on the tight design model nature could not have intrinsic moral value. We might take the view that the very fact of divine design is a basis for such value. For the record, I do not believe that the universe results from divine creation. As Carlson points out, though, the view that nature is divinely created does open the way to the appreciation of nature as an aesthetic object, akin to the appreciation of human works of art (Carlson 1984: 17–21).
7 There is some helpful discussion of these issues in Brennan 1988: 40.
8 There is an interesting issue to do with scale that might arise here. Even if there are few planets in the universe with a biomass, there is nevertheless huge natural aesthetic value spread throughout the universe. Why should we be concerned that there is loss of natural aesthetic value in an insignificant part of it? Similarly we might regard the destruction of a very small quantity of natural aesthetic value on our planet as of no great concern if natural aesthetic value is largely intact. One plausible answer is that the distinctiveness of terrestrial forms provides the basis for concern: while natural aesthetic value is widespread, it is not widespread as a result of these particular natural geological, biological and ecosystemic forms existing.

3 FAKING NATURE

1 Indeed its value is, I think, more than the summed values, since the continuity and expanse across time of the rainforest itself increases value. In other words there is a value over and above the value of the summed parts that, arguably, increases at a rate more than directly proportional to the increase in the age of the rainforest. I am a little hesitant about the detail of this claim because it implies that older is better. Something of its plausibility is reflected in the special concern of many environmentalists to protect old growth forests. My reason for hesitating fully to endorse the claim is that I am also tempted to say that the value of a new, naturally evolved ecosystem, perhaps one that has developed in the aftermath of a volcanic eruption, is the same

154

as that of the old growth forest. Such comparative value assessments are difficult to adjudicate and I shall not pursue them.

2   Note that this is quite a different concept from that of an absolutely value-adding property. In particular, the former signals an interaction between singly value-adding properties.

3   If indeed self-identity is an intrinsic property, then not quite all intrinsic properties are shared. I say 'indexed self-identity' to signal the fact that both objects could be identical with themselves, although not with each other.

4   It is certainly possible to produce a fake of something that did once exist but no longer does. I think it is also possible to produce a fake of something that does not yet exist, even of a particular something that does not yet exist. For example, I may know that a particular piece of work is planned by a renowned artist, perhaps because of the widespread publicity it has received. Imagine that there is public knowledge of the broad outline of the planned work. Now if I produce something conforming to that outline and in the style of the renowned artist, and if I claim that it is in fact the work that had been earlier publicized, then I have, I think, faked a particular object that has not yet come to exist. I would, moreover, say this even if the artist, hearing of my activities, abandoned the project of producing the planned work.

5   It might be thought misleading because, literally, the type is not so much restored as re-exemplified.

6   It is worth asking here whether it is possible to re-create an extinct species, as opposed to merely reintroducing a still extant species into an area from which it has disappeared? I think that it is possible. A species is appropriately thought of as a spatio-temporally extended population, the members of which derive from a common ancestor and stand in a similarity relation to one another. The similarity relation is difficult to specify but presumably has to do with the functional (and structural) similarity of genotypes. Moreover, the shared ancestry causally explains the similarity relation. A species becomes extinct when the spatio-temporally extended population ceases to increase. It follows from this that judgments that extinction has occurred are a kind of prediction; they are predictions that extension will not increase or at least they are predictions that extension will not increase without some intervention by agents such as ourselves. So, in one sense, extinction is not necessarily forever, since means may be available or emerge which make such interventions possible. Gunn describes various means by which the process of increasing the spatio-temporally extended population may be reactivated (Gunn 1991: 301). Take the case of growing organisms from remnants of DNA. The resultant organisms will clearly be members of the species population on the above account. They will instantiate the similarity relation and the fact will be explained in terms of common ancestry. At least that will be a crucial part of the explanation. The use of genetic technology will be another part of the explanation. Importantly, the ancestry explanation distinguishes this case from cases of evolutionary convergence and from cases where genetic engineering mimics evolutionary convergence.

7   This suggests a variant case in which the line between token-restoration and type-restoration is somewhat blurred. In the variant there is some remnant of the original ecosystem remaining, although very little relative to

original coverage. An enlarged ecosystem is restored around, or extending out from, the remnant. Do we say that the restoration is a token-restoration or a type-restoration? I am inclined to say that it is the latter, and not simply because so little is left of the original. That is part of the reason; but also salient is the fact that the restored areas are not merely moderately degraded parts of the original, they are reconstructions on areas from which the original cover has been completely removed.

One thing that follows from all of this is that an organism need not itself be naturally produced in order to count as a member of a natural species. In the DNA remnant example, the species itself is a natural kind, since organisms with genotypes satisfying the functional similarity requirement have naturally evolved. However, the particular organism is technologically produced rather than naturally produced. We may thus draw a distinction between naturally produced members of natural species and non-naturally produced members of natural species. Cases of selective breeding to recover 'lost' species, such as Gunn's examples of the dusky seaside sparrow and the quagga, fall into the latter category along with the DNA remnant example. The example involving the storage of species-defining genetic information on a computer disk is a little more difficult to characterize. The important point is that the information describing the broad genotype that defines the species is electronically, not biologically, stored. Whether organisms later produced in accordance with that information are in the latter category or in a third category, namely non-naturally produced members of a non-natural species, will depend on what is built into the ancestry requirement. It is implicit in the discussion so far that the ancestry requirement does not entail that members of a particular species be the offspring of other members of that species. Such an entailment would rule out, for instance, selective breeding as capable of restoring natural species. At the very least the ancestry requirement entails a causal dependence between a later organism and an earlier organism of the relevant species. But some might incline to the view that the causal dependence must involve the transmission of genetic information via biological material. My own view is that causal dependence effected through any medium is all that is required. Would the species become extinct on erasure of the disk? I think it would have earlier become extinct, when organisms of the species, including seeds and gametes, were lost from ecosystems. The erasure of the disk is best thought of as ensuring that restorative intervention becomes impossible.

What goes for species goes for ecosystems considered as natural kinds or types: they too may be restored, re-created or brought back from extinction. A particular ecosystem may be thought of as an instantiation of an ecosystemic type. An ecosystemic type is a naturally evolved design, revealed through its particular instantiations. Ecosystem restoration aims at reconstructing instances of such designs. Sometimes there will be no remaining instances of the design and here ecosystem restoration is analogous to re-creating an extinct species. Sometimes there will be other instances of the design and here ecosystem restoration is analogous to reintroducing an extant species to areas from which it has disappeared. The specifications of the design must, of course, be fairly broad so as to allow particular ecosystems which differ in fine detail to count, nevertheless, as of the same kind.

Some particular ecosystems of a given type may be naturally produced, whereas others will be technological products.

4 NATURALNESS, INTRINSIC VALUE AND RESTORATION ECOLOGY

1 Put like this, the claim seems somewhat tautological, as some critics have remarked (Fairweather *et al.* 1994: 563). In a way it is, but the point is worth making because of the emphasis it gives to naturalness as a source of value. Really what is emphasized is that there is no explanation for at least part of natural value apart from naturalness itself. That nature has value is, so to speak, a brute value fact. Although the fact does not admit of further explanation, it requires emphasis and discussion in order to direct attention to its direct, unmediated, normative appeal.

2 Here I assume that there are no supernatural intrusions into the universe and that the universe itself is not the product of supernatural events such as divine creation.

3 This might be thought to raise certain questions about free will and determinism. It probably does. One could perhaps differentiate the natural from the non-natural along the lines provided by the distinction between free actions, that is, uncaused acts of will, and mere events. I do not want to do this, partly because I believe that determinism is true. Obviously I cannot defend the view here, although this way of drawing the distinction might come close enough in practice to the way of drawing the distinction that I do endorse below. My distinction, which is based on the contrast between the natural and the artificial, where the latter is understood as that which is produced by and through human culture and technology, might well track a distinction drawn in terms of events resulting from the acts of free agents and events which are not thus caused. Whether this is so will depend on whether one accepts or rejects the view that some non-human animals are free agents.

4 The distinction is also made this way, and similar normative weight placed on it, in Goodin 1992 and McKibben 1989, where it is a core component in their respective overall theses. Eric Katz does likewise in a series of articles (Katz 1985, 1991, 1922a and 1992b). And Eugene Hargrove comes close to endorsing a similar view. He notes that interference disrupts natural history, transforms natural objects into artefacts, and removes the distinguishing basis of natural value (Hargrove 1989: 165–205).

5 Interestingly, a lot of things people actually do that may be thought of as 'getting back to nature', 'getting involved with nature' or some such, fail to count as natural. For example, a camping expedition into a remote wilderness area is a high technology enterprise. Aluminium tent pegs and food containers are high-energy products. Plastic water bottles and synthetic tent fabrics do not biodegrade. And getting to the wilderness quite clearly breaches the 'only footprints' rule. People tend to get there in cars which burn fossil fuel and release exhaust fumes into the atmosphere. They drive along highways and roads which scar the landscape.

6 It is controversial, some might say incoherent, to claim that we have an obligation to do what is not possible. The issue is encapsulated in the slogan: 'ought' implies 'can'. While I accept that there is no obligation to do the

logically impossible or to do what is physically impossible, I hesitate to endorse the view that there is no obligation to do what is practically impossible. It is not appropriate to pursue the issue here, but those who dispute my view can recast it in axiological terms. They can read it as the claim that it would be better, value-wise, if such changes occurred, even though there is no obligation to produce them.

7 It is worth mentioning that advocates of restoration ecology, discussed below, allow that human rational capacities serve to differentiate humans from the rest of the natural order. Thus William Jordan highlights self-awareness as the key difference (Jordan 1994: 30). They attempt, however, to make the differentiation in a way that does not set humankind too much apart from nature. Certainly they place only minimal normative weight on the differentiation of humans from nature, resisting in particular the suggestion that human impact necessarily reduces naturalness.

8 See the interesting discussion in Smith and Watson 1979 of the notion of wilderness. They define it in terms that imply humans are apart from, or other than, nature, and in terms reminiscent of those used by the Royal Commissioners to characterize the wild character of Fraser Island (Mosley 1980).

9 There is an extreme form of this argument that says that ecosystem drift has been so pervasive and that human activity has impacted on, and altered, so much of the natural world, that we cannot say that nature still exists. The argument says that nature has literally come to an end. In one version the argument has been given a nasty twist. The suggestion is that even if we can sensibly speak of natural remnants, there is likely to be a reluctance to preserve them because they are likely to be regarded as clearly a lost cause upon which our efforts would be wasted (McKibben 1989: 211).

10 Relatedly, some might suggest that the understanding of nature afforded by the sciences is itself a kind of conquest, domestication and humanizing of nature. The concern might be deepened by the suggestion that the nature to which we seem to have access through our senses, and through their technological extensions, is not nature as it is in itself, there being no such thing.

11 See the discussion of these and related issues in Plumwood 1993 and Plumwood 1996. Plumwood is concerned to criticize the use of nature/culture dualisms in the defence of wilderness, emphasizing instead the continuity of nature and culture.

12 There are non-human animals which might not exactly be in nature either. For example, domestic animals, and many plant forms, are the product of human design and manipulation. And even where there is no overt design and no intentional manipulation, human cultural, social and economic norms to a significant extent determine the genotypes of these organisms. Natural selection occurs in the context of a thick layer of human cultural contributions. For example, culturally determined tastes in plant foods might lead to the emergence of plant species with particular characteristics, and fashions in companion animals might lead to a shift in the gene pools of dogs and cats.

13 Human debris is to be found in parts of our solar system beyond the terrestrial environment. Its presence there may not impact on organic nature, since that seems confined to the terrestrial environment, but it impacts on

the aesthetics of these distant places and, in a minimal way admittedly, on the shape and shaping of extra-terrestrial landscapes.

14 One suggestion is that the original ecosystem is restored if what is reassembled acts like the original (Jordan 1994: 20). The thought seems to be that ecosystemic identity consists in functional equivalence, presumably understood as involving not only the system as a whole but the various subsystems which constitute it. But that cannot be right, since it is conceivable that functional equivalence could be achieved through the use of highly artificial components including such things as synthetic rocks and genetically engineered species. While functional equivalence, or a close approximation to it, might be a necessary condition for ecosystemic identity, other requirements would need to be added. These would include such things as approximate geomorphological similarity, approximately similar distribution of species types, and approximately similar overall appearance. Certainly it would be too much to require exact similarity in every respect. Part of the reason that this would be too stringent a requirement is that ecosystems are dynamic and changes take place within then constantly. Their identity conditions are sufficiently fluid to allow such change without disruption of continuing identity.

15 These evaluations should not be seen as supporting policies of degrading unassisted regrowth forests or indeed replanted forests. While the value of the regrowth forest might be less than the value of the original, its value is still extremely high, and, as time goes by, its value will come to approximate if not equal the value of the original forest. And even the replanted forest might rapidly come under the sway of natural forces and be shaped without the intrusion of human design.

So, imagine that an ecosystem is impoverished by human depredation, that humans recognize that there has been a resultant value loss and that they strive to restore that ecosystem, for example by revegetating and reintroducing members of certain species. Imagine also that the restoration succeeds and that the ecosystem re-emerges as it once was. It would seem, however, that the restored ecosystem is not natural and that it therefore would have less value than the earlier unimpoverished ecosystem.

There are two replies available. First, it might be conceded that there is some basis of value which cannot be restored, but then argued that this diminution of value is comparatively small. The value difference between the impoverished and the restored ecosystem is vastly greater than the value difference between the restored ecosystem and the original. While it would have been better had the original not been impoverished it is also better that the ecosystem be restored rather than left impoverished. Moreover, intrinsic value might be generated by the fact that restoration is restitutive. An apt analogy is restitutive justice. Not only might the restituting state of affairs sustain intrinsic value but so too might the property of being an act of endeavouring to bring about such a state of affairs.

Second, it might be argued that it is misleading to think of the restored ecosystem as artificial. Certainly the means by which the restoration takes place is at least partially artificial but the following construal is possible. The original ecosystem exemplified a specific ecosystemic type, instantiated by numerous natural objects and organisms. This ecosystemic type is a natural product: it is, if you like, a naturally evolved design. Full and successful restoration accords with this design and involves its instantiation by natural objects and organisms, for example rainforest trees and cassowaries, which, while they might be intentionally raised by humans for restorative purposes, are, for all that, natural items. Their natures, their essences are not artefacts. They, like the ecosystemic types they instantiate, are the design-products of projective nature. Because human restorative activity is guided and structured by the designs of nature we can legitimately think of the restored ecosystem as exhibiting a continuity with the natural past, despite the fact that the continuity has been artificially achieved.

The situation is not unrelated to cases in which wild nature is artificially protected, for example through legislation protecting endangered species or the declaration of buffer zones around wilderness areas. In these cases I have no hesitation in denying that artificial protection compromises the naturalness of wilderness: the artificial processes do not generate or give rise to wild nature but rather artificially prevent the destruction of something which has naturally arisen. In the restoration case I am at least hesitant. I am inclined to think that the restored ecosystem, whilst having immense value, lacks some of the value of the original. I think this uncompensated loss results from the fact that the continuity with the past has been artificially achieved and from the fact that the processes which gave rise to the ecosystem were entirely natural processes. This yields a special reason for preserving wild nature. Not only does it possess intrinsic value, part of its intrinsic value is such that in fact it is unlikely ever to be restored.

16 While it is difficult to quantify such things, it would seem that a large proportion of the sicknesses, illnesses and diseases from which we suffer are at least in part products of our forms of life, of our modes of work, cultural practices such as diets, social norms and so on.

17 For some discussion and, it seems, a defence of the view that the pain has intrinsic value, see Callicott 1980.

18 Recall the discussion of the second chapter, suggesting that there is scope for deontological constraints that would entail the impermissibility of trading off the smaller area for the larger area. Also compare Mathews' comments on the arithmetic of natural value, where she suggests that the value of every possum in the forest is the same as the value of the forest itself, including the possums it contains (Mathews 1991: 129). Mathews' suggestion is that the intrinsic value of the possums individually, and of the forest as a whole, is infinite, and that each has infinite value because it is a self. I do not want to run a similar line concerning natural areas, according to which areas, no matter how extensive, would have infinite value and each sub-area making up an area would also have infinite value.

REFERENCES

Attfield, R. (1987) *A Theory of Obligation and Value*, London: Croom Helm.
—— (1992) 'Claims, Interests and Environmental Concern', in C. C. W. Taylor (ed.) *Ethics and the Environment*, Oxford: Corpus Christi College.
—— (1994) 'Rehabilitating Nature and Making Nature Habitable', in R. Attfield and A. Belsey (eds) *Philosophy and the Natural Environment*, Cambridge: Cambridge University Press.
Attfield, R. and Belsey, A. (1994) 'Introduction', in R. Attfield and A. Belsey (eds) *Philosophy and the Natural Environment*, Cambridge: Cambridge University Press.
Baldwin, A. D. (1994) 'Rehabilitation of Land Stripped for Coal in Ohio – Reclamation, Restoration, or Creation?', in A. D. Baldwin Jr., J. De Luce and C. Pletsch (eds) *Beyond Preservation: Restoring and Inventing Landscapes*, Minneapolis, Minn.: University of Minnesota Press.
Benn, S. (1977) 'Personal Freedom and Environmental Ethics: the Moral Inequality of Species', in G. Dorsey (ed.) *Equality and Freedom: International and Comparative Jurisprudence*, Leiden: Sijtof.
Berger, J. (1990) (ed.) *Environmental Restoration*, Washington, DC: Island Press.
Birch, T. (1990) 'The Incarceration of Wildness: Wilderness Areas as Prisons', *Environmental Ethics*, 12.
—— (1993) 'Moral Conservability and Universal Consideration', *Environmental Ethics*, 15.
Brandt, R. (1959) *Ethical Theory*, Englewood Cliffs, NJ: Prentice-Hall.
Brennan, A. (1984) 'The Moral Standing of Natural Objects', *Environmental Ethics*, 6.
—— (1988) *Thinking about Nature*, London: Routledge.
Cahn, R. (1978) *Footprints on the Planet: the Search for an Environmental Ethic*, New York: Universe Books.
Callicott, J. B. (1979) 'Elements of an Environmental Ethic: Moral Considerability and the Biotic Community', *Environmental Ethics*, 1.
—— (1980) 'Animal Liberation: a Triangular Affair', *Environmental Ethics*, 2.
—— (1984) 'Non-anthropocentric Value Theory and Environmental Ethics', *American Philosophical Quarterly*, 21.
—— (1986) 'On the Intrinsic Value of Nonhuman Species', in B. G. Norton (ed.) *The Preservation of Species*, Princeton, NJ: Princeton University Press.

—— (1991) 'The Wilderness Idea Revisited: the Sustainable Development Alternative', *The Environmental Professional*, 13.

—— (1992a) 'Rolston on Intrinsic Value: a Deconstruction', *Environmental Ethics*, 14.

—— (1992b) 'La Nature est morte, vive la nature!', *Hastings Centre Report*, September–October.

Carlson, A. (1984) 'Nature and Positive Aesthetics', *Environmental Ethics*, 6.

—— (1992) 'Environmental Aesthetics', in D. Cooper (ed.) *A Companion to Aesthetics*, Oxford: Blackwell.

Chisholm, R. M. (1978) 'Intrinsic Value', in A. I. Goldman and J. Kim (eds) *Values and Morals*, Dordrecht: Reidel.

—— (1986) *Brentano and Intrinsic Value*, Cambridge: Cambridge University Press.

Clark, R. (1990) 'Ecological History for Environmental Management', in D. Saunders *et al.* (eds) *Australian Ecosystems: 200 Hundred Years of Utilization, Degradation and Reconstruction*, Proceedings of the Ecological Society of Australia, 16.

Clark, S. R. L. (1979) 'The Rights of Wild Things', *Inquiry*, 22.

Cowell, C. M. (1993) 'Ecological Restoration and Environmental Ethics', *Environmental Ethics*, 15.

Crisp, R. (1994) 'Values, Reasons and the Environment', in R. Attfield and A. Belsey (eds) *Philosophy and the Natural Environment*, Cambridge: Cambridge University Press.

D'Agostino, F. (1993) 'Transcendence and Conversation: Two Conceptions of Objectivity', *American Philosophical Quarterly*, 30.

Dennett, D. (1987) *The Intentional Stance*, Cambridge, Mass.: MIT Press.

Duffy, C. and Meier, A. (1992) 'Do Appalachian Herbaceous Understories Ever Recover from Clearcutting?', *Conservation Biology*, 6

Dunk, P. (1979) 'How New Engineering Can Work with the Environment', *Habitat Australia*, 7.

Elliot, R. (1978) 'Regan on the Sorts of Beings that can have Rights', *Southern Journal of Philosophy*, 16.

—— (1982) 'Faking Nature', *Inquiry*, 25.

—— (1983) 'The Value of Wild Nature', *Inquiry*, 26.

—— (1984) 'Rawlsian Justice and Non-human Animals', *Journal of Applied Philosophy*, 1.

—— (1985) 'Meta-ethics and Environmental Ethics', *Metaphilosophy* 16.

—— (1989) 'Environmental Degradation, Vandalism and the Aesthetic Object Argument', *Australasian Journal of Philosophy*, 67.

—— (1992) 'Intrinsic Value, Environmental Obligation and Naturalness', *Monist*, 75.

—— (1994) 'Extinction, Restoration, Naturalness', *Environmental Ethics*, 16.

—— (1994) Ecology and the Ethics of Environmental Restoration', in R. Attfield and A. Belsey (eds) *Philosophy and the Natural Environment*, Cambridge: Cambridge University Press.

—— (1996) 'Solidarity, Property Rights, Redistribution and the Great Apes', *Etica & Animali*, 8.

Ewing, A. C. (1959) *Second Thoughts in Moral Philosophy*, London: Routledge and Kegan Paul.

Feinberg, J. (1974) 'The Rights of Animals and Unborn Generations', in W. T. Blackstone (ed.) *Philosophy and Environmental Crisis*, Athens, Ga.: University of Georgia Press.

Fairweather, B., Gibson, S., Philp, G., Smith, S., and Talbot, C. (1994) 'Report on the Conference on Philosophy and the Natural Environment', *Journal of Value Inquiry*, 28.

Fox, W. (1984) 'Deep Ecology', *The Ecologist*, 14.

Frankena, W. (1979) 'Ethics and the Environment', in K. E. Goodpaster and K. M. Sayre (eds) *Ethics and Problems of the 21st Century*, Notre Dame, Ind. and London: University of Notre Dame Press.

Gaus, G. F. (1990) *Value and Justification: Foundations of Liberal Theory*, Cambridge: Cambridge University Press.

Glover, J. (1977) *Causing Death and Saving Lives*, Harmondsworth: Penguin Books.

Godlovitch, S. (1989) 'Aesthetic Protectionism', *Journal of Applied Philosophy*, 6.

—— (1994) 'Ice Breakers: Environmentalism and Natural Aesthetics', *Journal of Applied Philosophy*, 11.

Goodin, R. (1992) *Green Political Theory*, Cambridge: Polity Press.

Goodman, N. (1968) *Languages of Art*, New York: Bobbs-Merrill.

Goodpaster, K. E. (1978) 'On Being Morally Considerable', *Journal of Philosophy*, 75.

—— (1979) 'From Egoism to Environmentalism', in K. E. Goodpaster and K. M. Sayre (eds) *Ethics and Problems of the 21st Century*, Notre Dame, Ind. and London: University of Notre Dame Press.

Gorchov, D. (1994) 'Natural Management of Tropical Rainforests', in A. D. Baldwin Jr., J. De Luce and C. Pletsch (eds) *Beyond Preservation: Restoring and Inventing Landscapes*, Minneapolis, Minn.: University of Minnesota Press.

Green, K. (1996) 'Two Distinctions in Environmental Goodness', *Environmental Values*, 5.

Grey, W. (1993) 'Anthropocentrism and Deep Ecology', *Australasian Journal of Philosophy*, 71.

Gunn, A. S. (1991) 'The Restoration of Species and Natural Environments', *Environmental Ethics*, 13.

Hare, R. (1981) *Moral Thinking*, Oxford: Oxford University Press.

Hargrove, E. (1989) *Foundations of Environmental Ethics*, Englewood Cliffs, NJ: Prentice-Hall.

Hill Jr., T. (1983) 'Ideals of Human Excellence and Preserving the Natural Environment', *Environmental Ethics*, 5.

—— (1984) 'Review of R. Elliot and A. Gare (eds) *Environmental Philosophy: a Collection of Readings*', *Environmental Ethics*, 6.

Jordan III, W. (1985) 'On the Imitation of Nature', *Restoration & Management Notes*, 3.

—— (1986a) 'Restoration and the Re-entry of Nature', *Restoration & Management Notes*, 4.

—— (1986b) 'Restoration and the Dilemma of Human Use', *Restoration & Management Notes*, 4.

—— (1988) 'A New Society: "A Second Precaution", and Restoration as a Strategy for Selling Ecology', *Restoration & Management Notes*, 6.

—— (1994) '"Sunflower Forest": Ecological Restoration as the Basis for a New

Environmental Paradigm', in A. D. Baldwin Jr., J. De Luce and C. Pletsch (eds) *Beyond Preservation: Restoring and Inventing Landscapes*, Minneapolis, Minn.: University of Minnesota Press.

Jordan III, W., Gilpin, M., Aber, J. (eds) (1987) 'Restoration Ecology: Ecological Restoration as a Technique for Basic Research', in *Restoration Ecology: a Synthetic Approach to Ecological Research*, Cambridge: Cambridge University Press.

Kane, G. (1994) 'Restoration or Preservation? Reflections on a Clash of Environmental Philosophies', in A. D. Baldwin Jr., J. De Luce and C. Pletsch (eds) *Beyond Preservation: Restoring and Inventing Landscapes*, Minneapolis, Minn.: University of Minnesota Press.

Katz, E. (1985) 'Organism, Community and the "Substitution Problem"', *Environmental Ethics*, 7.

—— (1987) 'Searching for Intrinsic Value: Pragmatism and Despair in Environmental Ethics', *Environmental Ethics*, 9.

—— (1991) 'Restoration and Redesign: the Ethical Significance of Human Intervention in Nature', *Restoration & Management Notes*, 9.

—— (1992a) 'The Big Lie: Human Restoration of Nature', *Research in Philosophy and Technology* 12.

—— (1992b) 'The Call of the Wild: the Struggle against Domination and the Technological Fix of Nature', *Environmental Ethics*, 14.

Korsgaard, C. (1983) 'Two Distinctions in Goodness', *Philosophical Review*, 92.

Lewis, D. (1989) 'Dispositional Theories of Value', *Proceedings of the Aristotelian Society*, Supplementary Volume 63.

Light, A. and Higgs, E. (1996) 'The Politics of Ecological Restoration', *Environmental Ethics*, 18.

Losin, P. (1984) 'Thinking About Restoration', *Restoration & Management Notes*, 2.

—— (1986) 'Faking Nature: a Review', *Restoration & Management Notes*, 4.

—— (1988) 'The Sistine Chapel Debate: Peter Losin Replies', *Restoration & Management Notes*, 6.

Loucks, O. (1994) 'Art and Insight in Remnant Native Ecosystems', in A. D. Baldwin Jr., J. De Luce and C. Pletsch (eds) *Beyond Preservation: Restoring and Inventing Landscapes*, Minneapolis, Minn.: University of Minnesota Press.

Lynch, T. (1996) 'Deep Ecology as an Aesthetic Movement', *Environmental Values*, 5.

McCloskey, H. J. (1980) 'Ecological Ethics and its Justification: a Critical Appraisal', in D. S. Mannison, M. A. McRobbie and R. Routley (eds) *Environmental Philosophy*, Canberra: Research School of Social Sciences, Australian National University.

—— (1983) *Ecological Ethics and Politics*, Totowa, NJ: Rowman and Littlefield.

McKibben, B. (1989) *The End of Nature*, New York: Random House.

Mackie, J. L. (1977) *Ethics: Inventing Right and Wrong*, Harmondsworth: Penguin.

Mannison, D. (1980a) 'A Critique of a Proposal for an Environmental Ethic', in D. S. Mannison, M. A. McRobbie and R. Routley (eds) *Environmental Philosophy*, Canberra: Research School of Social Sciences, Australian National University.

REFERENCES

—— (1980b) 'A Prolegomenon to a Human Chauvinist Aesthetic', in D. S. Mannison, M. A. McRobbie and R. Routley (eds) *Environmental Philosophy*, Canberra: Research School of Social Sciences, Australian National University.

Maser, C. (1988) *The Redesigned Forest*, San Pedro, Calif.: R. and E. Miles.

Mathews, F. (1991) *The Ecological Self*, London: Routledge.

Merchant, C. (1986) 'Restoration and Reunion with Nature', *Restoration & Management Notes*, 6.

Moore, G. E. (1922) 'The Conception of Intrinsic Value', in *Philosophical Studies*, London: Routledge and Kegan Paul.

—— (1942) 'Reply to My Critics', in P. Schilpp (ed.) *The Philosophy of G. E. Moore*, Evanston, Ill.: Northwestern University Press.

—— (1963) 'Goodness as a Simple Unanalysable Property', in P. Taylor (ed.) *The Moral Judgement*, Englewood Cliffs, NJ: Prentice-Hall.

—— (1966) *Ethics*, Oxford: Oxford University Press.

Morrison, D. (1987) 'Landscape Restoration in Response to Previous Disturbances', in W. Billings, F. Golley, O. Lange, J. Olson, H. Renmert (eds) *Landscape Heterogeneity and Disturbance*, New York: Springer-Verlag.

Mosley, J. G. (1980) 'The Revegetation "Debate": a Trap for Conservationists', *Australian Conservation Foundation Newsletter*, 12.

Naess, A. and Rothenberg, D. (1989) *Ecology, Community and Lifestyle*, Cambridge: Cambridge University Press.

Nash, R. (1973) *Wilderness and the American Mind*, New Haven, Conn.: Yale University Press.

Nash, R. (1989) *The Rights of Nature*, Madison, Wis.: University of Wisconsin Press.

O'Neill, J. (1993) *Ecology, Policy and Politics: Human Well-being and the Natural World*, London: Routledge.

Partridge, E. (1986) 'Values in Nature: Is Anybody There?', *Philosophical Inquiry*, 7.

Passmore, J. (1975) 'Attitudes to Nature', in R. S. Peters (ed.) *Nature and Conduct*, London: Macmillan.

—— (1980) *Man's Responsibility for Nature*, London: Duckworth.

Pence, G. (1991) 'Virtue Theory', in P. Singer (ed.) *A Companion to Ethics*, Oxford: Blackwell.

Perry, R. B. (1950) *A General Theory of Value*, Cambridge, Mass.: Harvard University Press.

Pettit, P. (1991) 'Consequentialism', in P. Singer (ed.) *A Companion to Ethics*, Oxford: Blackwell.

Pigden, C. (1991) 'Naturalism', in P. Singer (ed.) *A Companion to Ethics*, Oxford: Blackwell.

Plumwood, V. (1991) 'Ethics and Instrumentalism: a Response to Janna Thompson', *Environmental Ethics*, 13.

—— (1993) *Feminism and the Mastery of Nature*, London: Routledge.

—— (1996) 'Wilderness Scepticism and Wilderness Dualism', in J. B. Callicott and M. Nelson (eds) *The Great New Wilderness Debate*, Athens, Ga.: University of Georgia Press.

Rachels, J. (1991) 'Subjectivism', in P. Singer (ed.) *A Companion to Ethics*, Oxford: Blackwell.

Radford, C. (1978) 'Fakes', *Mind*, 87.

Regan, D. H. (1986) 'Duties of Preservation', in B. G. Norton (ed.) *The Preservation of Species*, Princeton, NJ: Princeton University Press.

Regan, T. (1981) 'The Nature and Possibility of an Environmental Ethic', *Environmental Ethics*, 3.

—— (1992) 'Does Environmental Ethics Rest on a Mistake?', *Monist*, 75.

Risser, P. (1987) 'Landscape Ecology: State of the Art', in W. Billings, F. Golley, O. Lange, J. Olson, H. Renmert (eds) *Landscape Heterogeneity and Disturbance*, New York: Springer-Verlag.

Rodman, J. (1977) 'The Liberation of Nature', *Inquiry*, 20.

Rolston III, H. (1975) 'Is There an Ecological Ethic?', *Ethics*, 85.

—— (1982) 'Are Values in Nature Subjective or Objective?', *Environmental Ethics*, 4.

—— (1986) *Philosophy Gone Wild*, Buffalo, NY: Prometheus.

—— (1988) *Environmental Ethics: Duties to and Values in the Natural World*, Philadelphia, Pa.: Temple University Press.

—— (1991) 'The Wilderness Idea Reaffirmed', *The Environmental Professional*, 13.

—— (1994) 'Value in Nature and the Nature of Value', in R. Attfield and A. Belsey (eds) *Philosophy and the Natural Environment*, Cambridge: Cambridge University Press.

—— (1995) 'Does Aesthetic Appreciation of Landscapes Need to be Science-based?', *British Journal of Aesthetics*, 35.

Ross, W. (1930) *The Right and the Good*, Oxford: Clarendon Press.

Routley, R. and Routley, V. (1979) 'Against the Inevitability of Human Chauvinism', in K. E. Goodpaster and K. M. Sayre (eds) *Ethics and Problems of the 21st Century*, Notre Dame, Ind. and London: University of Notre Dame Press.

—— (1980a) 'Human Chauvinism and Environmental Ethics', in D. S. Mannison, M. A. McRobbie and R. Routley (eds) *Environmental Philosophy*, Canberra: Research School of Social Sciences, Australian National University.

—— (1980b) 'Social Theories, Self-management and Environmental Problems', in M. A. McRobbie and R. Routley (eds) *Environmental Philosophy*, Canberra: Research School of Social Sciences, Australian National University.

Routley, V. (1975) 'Critical Notice of Passmore's *Man's Responsibility for Nature*', *Australasian Journal of Philosophy*, 53.

Sagoff, M. (1991) 'Zuckerman's Dilemma: a Plea for Environmental Ethics', *Hastings Centre Report*, 21.

Sayen, J. (1989) 'Notes Towards a Restoration Ethic', *Restoration & Management Notes*, 7.

Sayre-McCord, G. (ed.) (1988) 'Introduction', in *Essays on Moral Realism*, Ithaca, NY: Cornell University Press.

Schiffer, S. (1990) 'Meaning and Value', *Journal of Philosophy*, 87.

Singer, P. (1976) *Animal Liberation: a New Ethics for our Treatment of Animals*, London: Jonathan Cape.

—— (1979) 'Not for Humans Only: the Place of Nonhumans in Environmental Issues', in K. E. Goodpaster and K. M. Sayre (eds) *Ethics and Problems of the 21st Century*, Notre Dame, Ind. and London: University of Notre Dame Press.

Smart, J. J. C. and Williams, B. (1973) *Utilitarianism: For and Against*, Cambridge: Cambridge University Press.

Smith, P. and Watson, R. (1979) 'New Wilderness Boundaries', *Environmental Ethics*, 1.

Sober, E. (1986) 'Philosophical Problems for Environmentalists', in B. G. Norton (ed.) *The Preservation of Species*, Princeton, NJ: Princeton University Press.

Sylvan, R. (1990) *Universal Purpose, Terrestrial Greenhouse and Biological Evolution*, Canberra: Research School of Social Sciences, Australian National University.

—— (1994) 'Mucking with Nature', in *Against the Mainstream: Critical Environmental Essays*, Canberra: Research School of Social Sciences, Australian National University

Sylvan, R. and Bennett, D. (1994) *The Greening of Ethics: From Human Chauvinism to Deep-Green Theory*, Cambridge: The Whitehorse Press.

Taylor, P. (1986) *Respect for Nature*, Princeton, NJ: Princeton University Press.

Thompson, J. (1983) 'Preservation of Wilderness and the Good Life', in R. Elliot and A. Gare (eds) *Environmental Philosophy*, St Lucia: University of Queensland Press.

—— (1990) 'A Refutation of Environmental Ethics', *Environmental Ethics*, 12.

Turner, F. (1994) 'The Invented Landscape', in A. D. Baldwin Jr., J. De Luce and C. Pletsch (eds) *Beyond Preservation: Restoring and Inventing Landscapes*, Minneapolis, Minn.: University of Minnesota Press.

Wenz, P. (1988) *Environmental Justice*, Albany, NY: State University of New York Press.

Weston, A. (1985) 'Beyond Intrinsic Value: Pragmatism in Environmental Ethics', *Environmental Ehtics*, 7.

—— (1987) 'Forms of Gaian Ethics', *Environmental Ethics*, 9.

Williams, B. (1985) *Ethics and the Limits of Philosophy*, London: Fontana.

—— (1992) 'Must a Concern for the Environment be Centred on Human Beings?', in C. C. W. Taylor (ed.) *Ethics and the Environment*, Oxford: Corpus Christi College.

Williams, M. (1988) *Americans and their Forests: a Historical Geography*, Cambridge: Cambridge University Press.

Williams, M. B. (1995) 'Discounting versus Maximum Sustainable Value', in R. Elliot (ed.) *Environmental Ethics*, Oxford: Oxford University Press.

Wong, D. (1990) 'A Relativist Alternative to Antirealism', *Journal of Philosophy*, 87.

INDEX

aesthetic evaluation: cognitive element in 13, 94–7; and evaluations of natural environment 93–7
aesthetic judgement, or moral judgement 4, 62–73
aesthetic value: as absolutely value-adding 72–3; and intrinsic moral value 60–2, 68, 72–3; and intrinsic value 62–73, 121; natural 134–5; and otherness of nature 60–2
aesthetics: and fakes 83, 84; positive *see* 'positive aesthetics'
Alaskan coastline, Exxon and the 110
American Indians 123
animals: cruelty to 54–5; domesticated 158; felt suffering in habitat destruction 79; intentionality of actions 122; reshaping their environment 119
Antarctic ice, pollutants in the 124
Anthony, Doug 75
anthropocentrism, normative 24–6, 27
anthropogenic account of value 24, 27
anti-replacement thesis 117; defended 76–83; and natural/artificial distinction 123–4, 128–9; on regenerated versus replanted forest 130–1; and restoration 108–11
approval relations, to attitudinal frameworks 16–23
artefacts 68; origins of 93; *see also* works of art
artificial: against the property of being naturally evolved 79–82; coexistence with the natural 126–30; destruction

vs. natural destruction 137; the natural and the 115, 123–30
asteroid on collision course with the earth example 135–7
Attfield, R. 3, 31
attitudes: changes over time 31–2, 37; filtering and convergence of judgements 20–32; forced transformation by manipulation 32; and future non-existence of the individual 30–1; and motivation to act on them 30–2; second-order 21–2
attitudinal frameworks: approval relations to 16–23; moral and aesthetic 70–2; and naturalness 59; overlap of 20–2, 33–4
Australians, indigenous 123
authenticity 104, 111
axiology 50; defined as the theory of value 4; and deontology 4–5, 113–14

bacterial infection with pain scenario 132–3
Baldwin, A.D. 90
'beautiful', the 94, 116
beliefs, and evaluations 94–7
Benn, Stanley 62–6, 67
Bennett, D. x, 46
Berger, J. 144
biological complexity: as basis of value 81–2; future 27, 28–9
biosphere, threat of natural catastrophe to 135–7

biotic richness 141
Birch, T. 124
Blackman, Charles, example of drawing
    84–5
blasphemy 89
Brennan, A. 60

Cahn, Robert 119
Callicott, J.B. 24, 119, 128, 148, 151
Carlson, Allen 61, 62, 68, 94, 96, 154
cars, costs and benefits of 118
Cartesian dualism 148
categories, moral and aesthetic 4,
    62–73
'category mistake view' 69
causes, versus consequences in
    evaluation 133, 137
chauvinism x, 70
Chisholm, R.M. 12, 13, 14, 50, 72
Clark, R. 123
Clark, S.R.L. 1
cognitive disagreement, and moral
    disagreement 33–41
cognitive element, in aesthetic
    evaluation 94–7
compromise 39
consequences, versus causes in positive
    or negative evaluation 133, 137
consequentialism: defined 42–3; and
    environmental obligation 42–50;
    objection against deontologies 52;
    personal and impersonal 48–9;
    trade-offs in 44–6; and value and
    obligation 42–50; varieties of 43; see
    also improving consequentialism;
    maintaining consequentialism;
    maximizing consequentialism;
    preference consequentialism
constitutive value 141
continuity: interrupted viii, 91–2, 140;
    natural 109, 110, 111, 125; and
    token-restoration 104, 110–11;
    value-adding property of natural 92,
    111
copying, innocent or to deceive
    99–100
core environmentalist claims xi, 76;
    and indexical theory 27, 30–2, 41
Cowell, C.M. 82, 143, 148

Crisp, R. 3, 31
crown-of-thorns starfish, on Great
    Barrier Reef 134, 136
cruelty, to animals 54–5
culture: freedom from impact of
    human 12; and nature 116, 123–30;
    as a product of nature 129
culture and technology 148; human
    relations with 59, 60; insulate
    humans from natural processes
    128–9
cycles of destruction and renewal 135,
    137

D'Agostino, F. 40
deception: by environmental
    engineering 87–92; faking as an act
    of 98–9; and token-restoration 105
defects of character, alleged moral
    53–5, 57–8
degradation: obligation to restore after
    111–15; as a result of human activity
    112, 114–15; wrongness of viii,
    114–15
Dennett, D. 59, 122
deontology 114: and axiology 4–5;
    defined 4–5; and environmental
    obligation 50–3
destruction: artificial versus natural
    137; of natural value, moral horror
    at 70
determinism 157
devastated land: reclaimed by nature
    88, 91–2; restored by environmental
    engineering 88, 90–1
disease, as natural though not good
    133
disrespect, epistemic 39–40
disvalue: of consequences and non-
    naturalness of the cause 137–8; and
    motive 115; see also intrinsic disvalue
DNA, growing organisms from
    remnants of 155, 156
Duffy, C. x
Dunk, P. ix

ecological change, as part of nature's
    dynamic 125–6, 134–5
ecology, contribution of 61

economic values, and natural values 75
'ecosystem drift' (Jordan) 124, 158
ecosystem restoration 156
ecosystem restoration, functional
  equivalence in 159
environmental degradation: and
  ingratitude 58; as vandalism 53–5,
  57–8
environmental engineering, deception
  by 87–92
environmental ethics viii; and intrinsic
  value theory, Hill's claim 55–8
environmental holism 26–7
environmental obligation: and
  consequentialism 42–50; and
  deontologies 50–3; virtue and value
  53–8
environmental restoration, technology
  of ix–x
environmentalist, use of term xi
equal value, and full value 80–1, 146,
  148
evaluation: consequences versus causes
  in 133, 137; importance of origin in
  83–97; knowledge and 95–7;
  motivation and 38–41; nature of the
  act of 15–17, 20–2
evolution, different course of 27, 29
Ewing, A.C. 50
excellence, standards of, natural
  environment and 63–4, 67
experience machine example 87–92
external properties 13–15
extrinsic restoration 106–7, 111
extrinsic value, and intrinsic value 23–4
Exxon, and the Alaskan coastline 110

Fairweather, B. 59
faked experience, as being short-
  changed 87, 88–9
faked nature vii, 110, 143
fakes 83, 84; possibility of detecting
  96–7
faking: restoring, preserving and
  protecting 97–111; use of term
  97–9; see also token-faking; type-
  faking
faking art, analogy with faking nature
  93–7

faking nature 74–115; analogy with
  faking art 72, 93–7; use of phrase 132
false beliefs 34–5
fear of otherness 60, 61
Feinberg, J. 71
footprints, only our 119–21
forest, regenerated versus replanted
  130–1
forgery, use of term 98
Fox, W. 4
Fraser Island, sand-mining on vii–viii
  75, 76, 78
full value, and equal value 80–1, 146,
  148

Gaus, G.F. 49
generic valuing 17
genesis see origin
genotypes 155, 156
global warming 126; deliberately
  manipulated scenario 127, 139
Glover, J. 49
Godlovitch, Stan 2, 59, 69, 70, 71
'good in itself' 12
Goodin, R. x
Goodman, N. 83
Gorchov, D. x
Great Barrier Reef, crown-of-thorns
  starfish 134, 136
greed 115
Green, K. 12, 23, 24, 56
greenhouse gases, deliberate increase by
  nation-state for its own ends 127,
  139
Grey, William 135–7
Gunn, Alastair S. 97, 108, 112, 124,
  128, 130–1, 155

Hare, R.M. 2
Hargrove, Eugene 157
harmony with nature, living in 117–21
Higgs, E. 106
Hill, Thomas 53–4, 55–8
human action, claim it should not
  always be seen as unnatural 146,
  148–9
human influences on nature: claim that
  they are not always bad 146, 147–8;
  minimal 118–20

human intervention *see* intervention
humanization of the natural, increasing 138

ice-age 121
ignorance as deception, as being short-changed 88
impermissibility claim viii, 51, 114–15, 153
improving consequentialism 46–7, 49, 143
indexical elements of judgements 18–19
indexical theory of intrinsic value xi, 5, 9, 15–23; as a form of relativism 16–19, 32–41; as naturalist 16–17, 25–6; and normative debate 33–41; as subjectivist 16–17, 22–3, 23–32
indigenous peoples, impact on natural environment 123
information transmission, different in nature and in culture 128
ingratitude, and environmental degradation 58
instrumental value: and intrinsic value 6, 12, 132–3, 137; of works of art 68–9; *see also* constitutive value
intensifying properties *see* value-multiplying properties
intentionality: absence of in nature 59–60, 61, 68; of animal behaviour 122; of human actions, as non-natural 122, 123; and works of art 94
internal properties, as value-adding properties 13–15
intervention: diminishing value-subtracting force over time 111; and intrinsic value 109–11; and natural phenomena 134–7; in restoration 147–8; versus natural forces 90–1, 93
intrinsic disvalue 137
intrinsic property constraint 11–15
intrinsic restoration 106–7, 111, 125
intrinsic value 5–11; and aesthetic value 62–73, 63–73; axiological theory of 5–11; evidence for 8–9; and extrinsic value 23–4;

fragmentation of and moral phenomenology 32–5; and human intervention 109–11; impermissibility of destroying or degrading 114–15; Moore's theory of 5–9, 15–16; naturalness and restoration ecology 116–49; negative 132–3, 142; and obligations 1; relative to attitudinal framework of the speaker 19–20, 23; test for 14–15; truncated 23–6, 151; *see also* indexical theory of intrinsic value
intrinsic/extrinsic distinction 106–7, 108
introduced species analogy 122–3

Jordan, William x, 82, 118, 119, 124, 126, 143, 144, 145, 148, 158

Kane, G. 144
Katz, Eric ix, x, 26, 75, 108, 109–10, 112, 143, 157
knowledge, and evaluation 95–7
Korsgaard, C. 24

landscape, modifications to 121–2
last person examples: Benn's 63, 64, 66–7, 69; Routleys' 67, 69; Singer's 65–6, 67
laws of nature 117
Light, A. 106
location, as a relational property 102–3
Losin, Peter ix, 97, 143, 144, 146–9
Loucks, O. x
Lynch, T. 2, 69, 94

McCloskey, H.J. 3
McKibben, B. x, 144
Mackie, J.L. 7
maintaining consequentialism 48–9
manipulation of nature claim 143
Mannison, D. 3, 94
Maser, C. 75
Mathews, F. 160
maximizing consequentialism 5, 43–7
medical technology, and population 128
Meier, A. x
meta-ethical dependency thesis 4, 5

meta-ethical theories 14–15
meta-ethics: defining 2–3; and
    normative ethics 2–4, 17–18, 26,
    71–2
mining example 74–5, 76, 78
mixed ethic, of deontological and
    consequentialist components 52–3
mixed restoration 106
Moore, G.E. 13, 14; objective value 24,
    25–6, 34; theory of intrinsic value
    5–9, 15–16
moral beliefs, convergence of 36–41
moral categories, and aesthetic
    categories 4, 62–73
moral disagreement, and cognitive
    disagreement 33–41, 152
moral facts, mind-independent 36
moral phenomenology, and fragment-
    ation of intrinsic value 32–5
moral properties: denial of existence of
    non-natural 16–23; dependence on
    non-moral properties 9–10; and
    dependency relationship with
    natural properties 8; as non-natural
    properties 7–8; as relational
    properties 15
moral sentiments, about wild nature
    53–4
moral truth, motivation 38–41
Morrison, D. 143
Mosley, J.G. vii, 75, 78
motivation: and attitudes 20, 21–2,
    30–2; and disvalue 115; and
    evaluation 38–41; of future action,
    and judgements of intrinsic value 20,
    21–2; and replacement thesis 99
Mt St Helens' eruption 122; caused by
    human made explosion 137;
    possibility of human intervention
    135

Naess, A. 4
Nash, R. 124
national parks 124–5
natural: and the artificial 79–82, 115,
    123–30; coexistence with the
    artificial 126–30; defining 82; and
    non-natural 62, 116–23, 148; and
    non-natural continuum 82;

ubiquitousness of the 142; and the
    valuable 132–42; as a value
    differentiator 119–20; what is
    117–30
natural design, restoration and 131–2,
    149
natural forces: and modifications to
    landscape 121–3; shaping
    ecosystems 120; versus human
    intervention 90–1, 93
natural phenomena: and human
    intervention 134–7; as natural
    though not good 133–4
natural properties, compared with non-
    natural properties 7–8
natural value: determinants of 109;
    naturalness and other bases of
    58–62; the nature of 1–41;
    normative theory of xi, 41, 121
natural values: classification of modes
    of mucking with nature 110–11; and
    economic values 75; failure to restore
    77; as instrumental values 44; as
    intrinsic values 43–4; and
    perfectionist values 57; possibility of
    fully restoring 76, 78–9, 143; reality
    of restoring 76–7; and synthetic
    replication as an act of disrespect 89;
    time lapse between despoliation and
    restoration 77
naturalism: objective 9; subjective xi
naturally evolved, property of being
    viii, 12, 13–14, 15, 68, 79–80, 81,
    86, 144–5
naturalness 59, 72, 109; as basis of
    nature's intrinsic value 116; claim
    that it is not in itself value-adding
    143; degrees of 124, 126, 129, 131;
    and ranking of value 140–1;
    intrinsic value and restoration
    ecology 116–49; and intrinsic value
    of wild nature 121, 145–6; Losin's
    claims concerning 146–9; and other
    bases of natural value 58–62;
    possibility of disvalue 136–7;
    quantity of 140–1; as a source of
    intrinsic moral value 142; and value
    130–42; as a value-adding property
    viii, ix, 129–30, 132–3

nature: autonomy of 68, 153; and
culture 116, 123–30; claim of no
significant normative or
metaphysical distinction between
143; as dynamic against the idea of
preservation 125–6; end of terrestrial
144, 158; as nonmoral 69–70;
organizational complexity 61
nature's otherness 59–62
nature's response, to non-natural
stimuli 126–7
New Zealand islands, restored
ecosystem with human intervention
131
non-humans: as valuers 16–17, 30; *see
also* animals; plants
non-natural: and natural continuum
82; the natural and the 62, 116–23;
vs. the natural 148
non-natural properties, compared with
natural properties 7–8
non-naturalistic theory 7–8
normative debate, and the indexical
theory 33–41
normative environmentalism, tension
with subjectivism 27–30
normative ethics: defined 3; and meta-
ethics 2–4, 17–18, 26, 71–2

objective values, as person-specific 36,
152
objectivism 3; non-natural or natural 9
objectivist theory 6–7, 9
objectivity, and relativism 22–3
obligation: principles of 113–14; to
restore viii, 76, 111–15, 120–1; and
value 2, 42–73; *see also*
environmental obligation
obligations: indirect 1; and intrinsic
value 1
O'Neill, J. 24, 44
origin: antiquity of 140; as element of
value 79–80; naturalness of viii,
136–8; the normative significance of
83–97
original nature, vs. faked nature vii,
140
originality 104, 109, 111
otherness of nature 59–62

Partridge, E. 3
Passmore, John 53, 54
Pence, G. 53
perfectionist values, and natural values
57
Pettit, P. 52
philistinism 54, 55
photochemical smog 118
Pigden, C. 9
plants, shaping ecosystems 119–20
pleasure, intrinsic value 6–7, 13
Plumwood, V. 158
policies: mutually inconsistent 38–41;
and quality of human life 118; *see
also* preservationist policy;
restorationist policy
pollutants 124
population, and medical technology
128
'positive aesthetics' 61, 132
possible worlds 18–19; evaluation and
29–30
preference consequentialism 17
preference utilitarianism 2
preferences 2, 16–17
preservation: of dynamic nature,
incoherence of idea 125–6; links
with restoration and protection
107–11; via human influence 147;
see also token-preservation; type-
preservation
preservationist perspective, and
restoration ecology 144–9
preservationist policy: on a
deontological view 51; and
improving consequentialism 46–7;
and maintaining consequentialism
48–9; pre-emptive 125
protection 107–8; links with
restoration and preservation 107–11
psychocentrism, normative 26
psychological states: dependence of
judgements on 7; of non-human
animals 54–5; *see also* attitudinal
frameworks
puritanism 120

Radford, C. 83
rarity 12, 46; degree of 110; as value-

adding or value-intensifying 141, 142
rational capacities, involvement of 122–3, 158
rational discussion, of attributions of intrinsic value, possibility of 33, 35–41
realist theory 6, 9
recolonizing by nature 126–7, 139–40, 144, 145
reflection, and judgements of intrinsic value 20–1, 22
Regan, D.H. 130
regeneration: of devastated land reclaimed by nature 88, 91–3; value trade-offs in 92–3; versus replanting of forest 130–1
rehabilitation, degrees of 105
relational properties: internal 13–14; and intrinsic value 12, 13; newly dicovered re origin 86; second-order 16; and type-restoration 102–3; as value-adding properties 80
relativism 19; and the indexical theory 16–19, 23–41
relevant information, and judgements of intrinsic value 20, 21, 22
replacement thesis: defined 76; examination of 79–80; and motivation 99; rejection of 115; and the restoration proposal 74–6; and type-restoration 103
replicas: and token-faking 100; of works of art 84–5
respect for nature 39–40, 54, 121
responses to nature, compared with aesthetic evaluation 94–7
restitution: duty of 112–15; no justification for despoliation viii–ix, 114–15; positive value of 113; and value of restored environment 114–15
restoration: and anti-replacement thesis 108–11; assumptions of defence of vii; as compensation 75; defined 101; degrees of 105–11; links with preservation and protection 107–11; and natural design 131–2, 149; role of natural processes and design in 109–10; time factor of lost value 91, 92; the value of 111–15; *see also* token-restoring; type-restoring
Restoration & Management Notes ix–x
restoration ecology ix–x; claims of 143, 146–7, 149; naturalness and intrinsic value 116–49; philosophy of ix–x, 143–9; role for 145
restoration proposal 115; defined 76; and replacement thesis 74–6;
restorationist policy 125; on a deontological view 51–2; and improving consequentialism 46–7; and maintaining consequentialism 48–9
restored environment, value compared with original environment 145–9
right-making properties 51
Risser, P. 143
Rodman, J. 124
Rolston Holmes 3, 9, 13, 17, 55, 61, 96, 128, 130, 147; anthropogenic and anthropocentric value 24, 27
Ross, David 13, 14, 150
Rothenberg, D. 4
Routley, Richard 67, 69
Routley, Val 13, 61, 67, 69, 95, 96

sacred 121
sadism 89
Sagoff, M. 54
Sayen, J. 144
Sayre-McCord, G. 6
Schiffer, S. 6
sculpture, example of fragile 84
simulated wilderness, as being short-changed 87, 89
Singer, Peter 1, 65–7
Smith, P. 124
Sober, E. 128
species: point in time of endangerment 73; recovery and reintroduction of an endangered 149
species diversity 142
species extinction, due to climate change 130
subjectivism: and the indexical theory 16–17, 22–23, 23–41; and normative environmentalism 27–30;

subjectivism – *contd*
and objectivism, pragmatic
differentiation 32–41
subjectivist theory xi, 6–7, 9, 15
substantive theories of environmental
value, and relational properties 12
Sylvan, Richard ix, x, 44, 46, 51, 52,
55, 90, 91, 97, 108, 112, 147;
'Mucking with Nature' viii, 110

Taylor, P. 112, 153
technology: freedom from impact of
human 12; intervention in
ecosystems 128; and nature 123–30;
see also culture and technology
theism 153
Thompson, J. 44, 142
time: judgements indexical to 18, 19;
larger perspective on 135–7; net loss
of value over 145; value and element
of 91, 92, 111; works of art and
alteration over 101
token-faking 100, 104; and type-
restoration 105–6, 110
token-preservation 107
token-restoration 101–11; and
continuity 110–11; types of
106–7
transcendence by humans of the
natural 123, 128, 148
transformation, cooperative between
humans and nature 148–9
trilobites 27, 28, 151
Turner, F. 143, 144, 145
type-faking 100–1, 104
type-preservation 107
type-restoration 102–3, 108–9, 110;
not totally artificial 109–10; and
token-faking 105–6, 110
type/token distinctions 100–11

US, Wilderness Act (1964) 119
utilitarianism 2, 5, 43, 152

valuable, and the natural 132–42
value: and naturalness 130–42; and
obligation 2, 42–73; quantitative
across time as well as at a particular
time 91, 92, 111; and virtue, and

environmental obligation 53–8; *see
also* instrumental value; intrinsic
value
value conflicts 32–41
value difference, between preventing
damage and repairing it once done
125
value facts, Rolston's 9
value overall, and human destruction of
natural value 138–42
value trade-offs: in consequentialism
44–6; in regeneration 92–3
value transformations 11, 148–9
value-adding properties: essential or
non-essential 11–12; intrinsic
property constraint 11–15; and
intrinsic value 10–11; relative to a
context 10–11; and nature of the act
of evaluation 15–17; as non-moral
properties 10–11
value-blindness 55–8
value-in-isolation 14–15
value-inversion 11, 87–9
value-multiplying properties 81–2,
141, 142
value-neutrality 10
value-ranking, of restored vs untouched
nature 140–1
value-subtracting properties 87–9, 142
vandalism, environmental degradation
as 53–5, 57–8
virtue theory 5, 53–8, 153

Watson, R. 124
well-being, human impact on nature
and human 118
Wenz, P. 112
Weston, A. 4
wild nature: causal continuity with the
past 125; depletion and loss-
entailing phenomenon 73; intrinsic
value of vii, 1, 41, 46, 76, 114–15;
rawness of 59–60; relation to 58
wilderness, being turned into an
artefact 124–5
Wilderness Act, US (1964) 119
Williams, Bernard 59–60, 124, 152
Williams, M. 123
Wong, D. 151

works of art: analogy 68–9, 72; Benn's
    analogy 62–6; as intentional 94;
    provenance of 84–5, 93, 140; and
    replicas 84–5; Singer's view of
    interests and 65–7
wrong-making properties 50–1